ALBERT SPEER & PARTNER

A MANIFESTO FOR
SUSTAINABLE CITIES

ALBERT SPEER & PARTNER

A MANIFESTO FOR SUSTAINABLE CITIES

THINK LOCAL, ACT GLOBAL

Jeremy Gaines & Stefan Jäger

PRESTEL

MUNICH BERLIN LONDON NEW YORK

THE SUSTAINABLE CITY

Over the last two decades, few concepts can have gone through such an unarrested development as that of sustainability. The notion first caught the public eye in 1987 when it took pride of place in the report by the World Commission on Environment and Development on "Our Common World." The lengthy study came up with the first broad definition of sustainable development. In fact, it would be safe to say in this context that the term "sustainable" itself demonstrates how an idea can be used to such an inflationary extent that it becomes bereft of any meaning. Most major corporations today do not miss an opportunity in ads or annual reports to describe their work as being "sustainable," as if mere mention of the word issued them with a certificate of good conduct. Just about anything, it would seem, if it is only slightly "green," warrants being labeled sustainable: products, jobs, systems. Sustainable now seems simply to signify "eco-friendly" and "likely to last a while." Indeed, the term "sustainable development" has become so ubiquitous that if quantity counts, the concept is recognized worldwide to be of great importance, picking up about 24 million hits on Google (only half that for the World Cup), while "sustainable" outstrips the soccer event by a large margin.

However, inflation would seem to have led to obfuscation. If we bear in mind that as of 2008 more than half the world's population lived in cities, and this ratio will by all accounts continue to rise, then it would seem logical to expect a search for "sustainable cities" to land an equally massive trawl of results. It does not. The World Wide Web has only one hundredth of the hits to offer for that concept. It is as if the notion of the sustainable city got left by the wayside when concentrating on "development," and yet where will that "development" have to happen if not in cities.

A classic example of how abstruse the debate on sustainability has become is offered in the most modern of media: the Web. Inhabitat.com, which declares itself to be "a weblog devoted to the future of design, tracking the innovations in technology, practices, and materials that are pushing architecture and home design towards a smarter and more sustainable future," proudly reported the following in February 2008:

MASDAR CITY is poised to become world's most sustainable, zero-waste, car-free, carbon-neutral city. The model for the city was formally unveiled on January 21 at the WORLD FUTURE ENERGY SUMMIT in Abu Dhabi.... The city, to be built on an area of six square kilometers on the outskirts of Abu Dhabi, would be walled on all sides, and house 50,000 people and 1,500 businesses. The electricity for the entire city would be generated by solar energy. As for site planning, the city would be oriented north-east to south-west to ensure optimum balance of sunlight and shade. There would be no cars zooming around the city, with residents getting to and fro via trains and automated transport pods. The public transportation has been so planned that none of the city's inhabitants will be more than 200 meters from the nearest public transportation link. Systems would encourage reuse and minimal resources, with 99 per cent of the waste generated in the city getting reused, or composted, and all wastewater would be reused as well, with solar energy desalination systems.

Masdar will be a walled city in the traditional Arab style. And this is where one might ask whether the term "sustainable" has any meaning whatsoever in such a context. The traditional Arab city was, in fact, never so small, and the relatively small number of inhabitants contrasts with the major cost of realizing the plan. Masdar comes with an estimated price tag of USD 22 billion, which means USD 400,000 per inhabitant. "Sustainable" the town may in itself be, but hardly applicable at such a price to the rest of the world, where the overall population is scheduled to soar to 8.2 billion by the year 2030. Were the planners to use the above approach to cater for the approximately 1.5 billion people expected to join humanity over the next decade or so, then the cost of such sustainability would be USD 600 trillion – quite hefty if compared with world GDP in 2007 of about USD 65.6 trillion. In other words, over the next 20 years we would have to spend about half of world GDP (assuming it remains constant) to accommodate those newcomers to the world in a manner that was "sustainable" – leaving little financing for the present population.

The absurdity of such uses of the term "sustainability" can perhaps best be seen when one considers the following quote from inhabitat.com on the latest addition to the Masdar planning: "Not settling for mere zero-energy, ADRIAN SMITH + GORDON GILL'S MASDAR HEADQUARTERS are setting new design standards for green building, with their scheme that generates more energy than it consumes." Paraphrasing the architects' press release on the building outside of Abu Dhabi, inhabitat.com lauds it for being:

"… the first building in history to generate power for its own assembly, using a solar roof pier that will be built first to power the rest of the construction. The building's sustainability gave it the edge to beat 159 others in the international design competition. The $300-million, 1.4-million-square-foot headquarters will serve as the stunning centerpiece of the super-green, car-free MASDAR CITY. The building's aggressive approach to sustainability enables it to offer the lowest energy consumption per square meter for its class, one of the world's largest integrated photovoltaic systems, and the world's largest solar thermal-driven cooling and dehumidification system. The complex will utilize sustainable materials and feature integrated wind turbines, outdoor air-quality monitors."

Why, one might ask, do the architects believe glass and steel need to be described as "sustainable materials"? Common sense would surely suggest that perhaps a little less of the same in the middle of the desert would have enabled them to rely less on the ingenuity of wind turbines to drive the cooling system. However, common sense is, sadly, a quality sorely lacking when it comes to "descriptions of the 'sustainable city.'" We deliberately do not write "the debate on the sustainable city" because precisely that is most evidently lacking.

To be fair, all the hype on eco-cities should not be taken overly seriously, as the example of Donghan outside Shanghai shows, which inhabitat.com suggests is the "world's first sustainable city":

"The NEW CITY, which will be three quarters the size of Manhattan, will be built on the eastern end of Chongming, a large island that sits in the mouth of the Yangtze river delta a few miles northeast of the city center, close to Shanghai's new airport."

The city, we should add, will be a demonstration project, aiming, according to the Arup Web site, to be home to 10,000 people in three villages, with two thirds of the footprint devoted to agriculture. The planners' Web site goes on to boast: "It will be a vibrant city with green 'corridors' of public space ensuring a high quality of life for residents." Quite how three interlinked villages qualify as a "vibrant city" is perhaps something we should leave to the marketing experts to explain.

In its favor, the eco-city will deploy a comprehensive energy strategy "incorporating large-scale renewable energy technologies, which will reduce damaging emissions, and bring the city as close to being carbon neutral as possible. Other environmentally sensitive aspects include the development of a process to capture and purify water in the landscape to support life in the city. Community waste-management recycling will generate clean energy from organic waste, reducing landfills that damage the environment." In line with its pilot-project properties, the first phase will be completed by 2010, just in time for Shanghai's hosting of the World Expo. Again, this version does not seem to fit the bill for the "sustainable city" for our children and our children's children, as it is hopelessly under-dimensioned.

The latest addition to the hype on the eco/sustainable city is that surrounding RAK, or Ras al-Khaimah, an "emerging emirate," which opted to advertise itself in a 10-page "sponsored section" in the July 2008 edition of FOREIGN AFFAIRS.

Intended to be entirely sustainable and cater to residents' every conceivable whim within its four walls, the new RAS AL-KHAIMAH ECO-CITY DEVELOPMENT in the United Arab Emirates, is often likened to that of the zero-carbon, zero-waste MASDAR. Cutting-edge solar technology will power the 1.2-million-square-meter city, built using locally sourced Arabian materials and aesthetic styles to support the city's overall ethos of sustainability. Cunning planning means that the least amount of direct sunlight will strike the city's buildings during the warmest times of day. Lots of narrow streets and open green spaces have also been incorporated to increase natural lighting, shading, and resident happiness.... The development will consist of five phases, extending over 400 million square feet. Phase 1 will consist of an integrated city to service, support, and supplement the capital city of RAS AL-KHAIMAII. The estimated time for completion has been set at 2012.

One might be forgiven for thinking that if famous architectural offices are behind such projects then they must be sustainable. But if one reads between the lines of the above quote all one finds again is that traditional Arab town planning has been applied, coupled with the latest solar technology. It is a moot point whether that is enough to guarantee the project's "sustainability." Not to mention that it is highly debatable whether it makes sense to build cities in the desert, bereft of a hinterland to support them, let alone whether it is meaningful to build cities in which a large part of the population cannot afford to live.

One might equally be forgiven for thinking that the notion of the "sustainable city" is new. It is not. Since the mid-1980s, following publication of "Our Common World," often referred to as the "Brundtland Report," after the Norwegian premier who chaired the WCED's work, one man and one company have stood out for their singular commitment to the "sustainable city." And like the original meaning of the term itself, he and they (we will henceforth refer to them collectively as Albert Speer & Partners, or AS&P) have gone largely unnoticed, even within specialist architectural and urban planning circles. One reason might perhaps be that Albert Speer, like many another leading minds, did not proclaim his ideas as truths carved in stone or concrete, but preferred instead simply to put them into practice.[1] However, if the notion of the "sustainable city" is to be accorded the place it must have if people two generations down the line are to enjoy any urban quality of life, then it is high time for an exhaustive account of those ideas. And what better way than by describing the projects in which those ideas have come to fruition, from the smallest possible architectural unit, the single-family dwelling, to the largest, entire cities and regions. We therefore decided to find out for ourselves exactly how AS&P has gone about defining the "sustainable city," how they link this back to a notion of democracy, and what potential the definition has to foster a meaningful debate on what the city of tomorrow must look like if there is to be a tomorrow in a few decades' time.

AS&P first dedicated themselves to the task of designing an ecological model town at the end of the 1990s. The location was in China, back then already an emerging titan of the world economy. To be precise, the project in question was part of "planning" the expansion of Shanghai on behalf of the Lord Mayor of Shanghai, if it makes sense at all to write of "expanding" such an expanse. AS&P set out, typically with the support of an interdisciplinary team, to develop a town that would have an identity of its own (despite being essentially low-tech), be home to about 280,000 persons – and also be their place of work. For one of the obvious insights AS&P brought to bear was that if people live near their workplace then the planners do not have to pull ecological transportation systems out of the hat. And by skilful combination of technologies and traditional Chinese urban patterns, the final draft hinged on a solution that slashed CO_2 emissions by more than two thirds, reduced drinking water requirements by half, and boosted energy efficiency by a factor of two.

The project prompted Albert Speer to write: "Urban development is faced by enormous problems when controlling the development of a region, especially under the conditions of rapid economic and population growth. A region with 20 million inhabitants cannot be planned right through. However, development can be implemented if there is the right basic concept." The basic concept devised for the ecological model town hinged on the insight that an urban area "begins as a small cluster of modules and then develops into larger spatial structures." Common sense, Albert Speer proposed, would therefore suggest that if you can get the modules right, the chances are the larger spatial structures will function – and ensure that the additive expansion is managed and controlled. To plan and build big, you have to start small. And it was from the small unit – the mix of residential, work, and green areas that had characterized ancient Chinese cities for many centuries – that AS&P developed their blueprint for the future, blending a knowledge of East and West, or, as Fritjof Capra termed it, yin and yang. The manifesto for sustainable cities is intended as a turning point in architecture and urban planning, as an attempt to show why the high-tech, high-gloss and high-end projects mentioned earlier are not sustainable, do not deserve to be described as such, and, while being nice experiments in the Gulf lab, do not offer a model for the cities our great-grandchildren will inhabit.

Over the next few chapters we shall endeavor to give the concept of the "sustainable city" a sustainable basis, both theoretically and practically, by following progress on a few select AS&P projects. For we firmly believe that if we give the term precision as a concept it may indeed serve as the springboard from which we can move forward in a world shaped by debates on climate change, and the ever greater impact of such change. We will do so in manifesto form, by describing ten key pillars for sustainability. Each chapter will address one of those pillars, and since each pillar can stand on its own, so, too, can each chapter be read independently of the others.

1   Who today, when using the term "synergy," for example, remembers that it
    was given to us by Buckminster Fuller in his 1969 book Operating Manual
    for Spaceship Earth?

I

COMBINE THEORY
AND COMMON SENSE

"One in four of the world's urban population is living below the poverty line. In many cities, confronted with rapid growth, environmental problems, and the slow pace of economic development, it has not been possible to meet the challenges of generating sufficient employment, providing adequate housing, and meeting the basic needs of citizens." **UN Habitat**[1]

While there is forever talk of sustainability, there have been few attempts to define exactly what the term means. This difficulty of definition is reflected by the fact that over the last decade and a half, various attempts have been made to compile lists of key performance indicators with which to measure "sustainable" projects, but the notion itself has not gained greater precision, remaining instead blurred at the edges. While the term "sustainability" first became used on a broader scale in forestry to designate an approach whereby, roughly speaking, a balance was struck between the number of trees felled and the biodiversity and ongoing growth of the forests, since then, the term has become so widely used that we cannot see the wood for the trees. It is now often simply assumed to signify "that which does not prejudice the opportunity of future generations." This is, after all, the essence of Principle 3 in the famed Rio Declaration on Environment and Development of 1992: "The right to development must be fulfilled so as to equitably meet developmental and environmental needs of present and future generations."

Clearly the term also has implications for the point where the realms of the local and the global interact, for to "act locally" in a sustainable manner implies definitely thinking "globally," since sustainability is meant to apply to the entire planet. In other words, if I try to provide a solution for urban planning in North China, it must be devised in light of what is both to the benefit of the particular city's inhabitants and reflects global insights into how we should treat the environment, resources, etc. That is to say, if we speak of planning "sustainable cities," we refer not only to urban planning proper, but also to how it dovetails with overriding concerns, such as climate change (e.g., reducing a city's CO_2 emissions), squandering resources (e.g., food), the provision of clean water, and so forth. And to be realistic, there can be no talking sustainability without talking urban planning. As the world of the future will primarily exist in cities – and it is the cities that will be the primary consumers of energy, food, etc., be they new cities in Africa or China, or adapted cities in India – we must stop applying the old Olympic adage of "faster, higher, further" to economic and urban development, and return it to the domain of sport.

This was the insight promulgated in 2007 by the EU Ministers of Urban Development when they drew up the Leipzig Charter on Sustainable European Cities. It contains this key sentence: "In the long run, cities cannot fulfil their function as engines of social progress and economic growth [...] unless we succeed in maintaining the social balance within and among them, ensuring their cultural diversity and establishing high quality in the fields of urban design, architecture and environment."

The challenge to be faced as regards cities and CO_2 emissions is in itself immense. Sir Nicholas Stern calculates that CO_2 emissions worldwide need to be halved from their pres-

---

THE RIO AGENDA 21: PREAMBLE   **1.1** Humanity stands at a defining moment in history. We areconfronted with a perpetuation of disparities between and within nations, a worsening of poverty, hunger, ill health and illiteracy, and the continuing deterioration of the ecosystems on which we depend for our well-being. However, integration of environment and development concerns and greater attention to them will lead to the fulfilment of basic needs, improved living standards for all, better protected and managed ecosystems and a safer, more prosperous future. No nation can achieve this on its own; but together we can – in a global partnership for sustainable development.

1.2 This global partnership must build on the premises of General Assembly resolution 44/228 of 22 December 1989, which was adopted when the nations of the world called for the United Nations Conference on Environment and Development, and on the acceptance of the need to take a balanced and integrated approach to environment and development questions.

1.3 Agenda 21 addresses the pressing problems of today and also aims at preparing the world for the challenges of the next century. It reflects a global consensus and political commitment at the highest level on development and environment cooperation. Its successful implementation is first and foremost the responsibility of Governments. National strategies, plans, policies, and processes are crucial in achieving this. International cooperation should support and supplement such national efforts. In this context, the United Nations system has a key role to play. Other international, regional, and subregional organizations are also called upon to contribute to this effort. The broadest public participation and the active involvement of non-governmental organizations and other groups should also be encouraged.

1.4 The developmental and environmental objectives of Agenda 21 will require a substantial flow of new and additional financial resources to developing countries, in order to cover the incremental costs for the actions they have to undertake to deal with global environmental problems and to accelerate sustainable development. Financial resources are also required for strengthening the capacity of international institutions for the implementation of Agenda 21. An indicative order-of-magnitude assessment of costs is included in each of the programm areas. This assessment will need to be examined and refined by the relevant implementing agencies and organizations.[2]

ent level by 2050 if we are to bring a halt to climate change. In this context, we must distinguish between the situation in Europe, on the one hand, which is characterized by stagnation in the form of dwindling urban populations, the developed infrastructure of intact cities, and no major new wave of urbanization, and, on the other hand, trends in Asia, Africa, India, and South America. In the latter three, urbanization is in part only just getting under way and that world is changing far faster than the societies of the West. Since the two sets of conditions are so different, Stern calls for an 80 per cent reduction in Europe, an astronomical and ambitious figure that we will reach only with maximum effort. And where do we emit the most CO_2 after the inevitable massive amount produced by burning fossil fuels in power stations? – in buildings, where power is consumed for heating and cooling and to drive the internal appliances, and on transport between homes and workplaces.

URBAN PLANNING If we look at sustainable cities from the viewpoint only of cutting CO_2 emissions on a large scale, then the target is feasible in Europe if responsibility is duly shouldered by each of the individual countries and if they act together in a concerted coordinated manner – the local and the global interlock. And as has been shown by the varying responses to the "global financial crisis," when things get tough, governments are prepared to source treble-digit billions to save their systems. Things are very different in the Third World and in threshold countries such as India or China. With the exception, that is, of Brazil with its extensive alcohol-for-petrol program that has already cut CO_2 car emissions by more than a quarter. Small wonder that TIME magazine speaks of "Brazil's New Way" and that its sugar-cane industry is now worth $ 25 billion a year. Otherwise a massive leap forwards in technology is necessary if any real progress is to be made (in India, more than 40 per cent of the the country's inhabitants still do not have access to electricity, and the generating medium of choice is, naturally, coal, which is in abundant supply locally). Quite simply, the Third World will not succeed in making the required reductions if they have to rely only on their own resources and local technologies. And it is in the Third World that the urbanization of tomorrow will take place. In other words, any discussion of how to create sustainable cities must take place against the backdrop of the cooperation in the course of future "urbanization planning" between European countries, and the knowledge base they possess, and the countries that are bearing, or will bear, the brunt of urbanization. In this regard, Europe can function as the lab testing the long-term sustainable concepts and then transferring these incisively to other countries. This means that new forms of cooperation, support, and public private partnerships for the Third World must be forthcoming. Evidently, politics, science, and industry must interact meaningfully here, and Europe's urban planners have a shared responsibility, and shared duties, in these fields. At the same time, everyone involved must carefully rethink the balance of and interaction between urban to non-urban space in that future world.

THEORIZING SUSTAINABILITY

This is the "practical" side to applying the notion of sustainability to the cities of tomorrow. The theoretical side hinges on the transcultural aspects of the term, that is to say, the fact that the future of any location relies on the future of the rest of the world, whereby it is the issue of "climate change" more than any other that has made this fact unmistakably clear to everybody in the first decade of the 21st century. Sustainability entails a generally valid "common good" and implies norms and rights in a world of cultural plurality and heterogeneity. It is evident here that a mutual understanding and recognition of the need for "sustainable cities" must be the basis for human coexistence in a globalized and "glocalized" world. Put differently, the concept of sustainability may well be the universal "glue" the binds the world together – and it must be applied locally as required, for, as was observed a quarter of a century ago, "the challenge for human settlements policy is not to replicate the rich country patterns in today's poor countries. The challenge is to design and manage human settlements in such a way that the world's people may live at a decent standard based on sustainable principles."[3]

"Sustainability" aspires essentially to be an international law concept. It does not lay claim to the same status as the rights outlined in the Declaration of Human Rights, but in terms of its significance, it is equally fundamental. After all, if development were not to be sustainable, then before long humanity would manage to have eradicated the basis for its own survival. Critics of "sustainability" turn this state of affairs on its head when they claim that the concept and its protagonists are innately conservative and prevent entrepreneurial development by potentially curbing the use of (polluting) technologies. In doing so, they exploit this idealist or open-ended thrust of the term, by virtue of which there is such difficulty in defining it more closely. After all, the notion of sustainability hinges on the notion of doing something today that we will potentially not live to see bear fruit. There is thus an overt idealist thrust to it. Yet, since it cuts to the very core of anthropological endeavor, namely, to that instinct to ensure our continued existence, it also entails a very rational level. In everything we do, we must think of ourselves as historical, transient beings. There can only be "paradise on earth" of any sort for future generations if we act in a sustainable manner and bequeath to future generations a world that actually has a future.

It follows from the above that a sustainably planned and built environment is a "must be" and not a "nice to have." Nevertheless, to date, the term has neither been brought to bear in international treaties nor accorded the mandatory status innate in it. The international community has not mutually committed to acting only sustainably. This may be as much a reflection of the political will to think long term as it is of the difficulties inherent in defining the concept. Sustainability centers on the insight that our anthropological lineage will most probably continue only if we start to place sustainability at the heart of our achievements.

Urban planning is, by definition, an open-ended process that binds the past and present with possible futures. Just as architecture is, for the built city is again a mixture of past and forever new presents, and each building has a long-lasting impact on both its immediate environment and the environment in general. Here, we must distinguish carefully between sustainability with regard to existing cities, and sustainability as a yardstick when building new cities. While in the latter we can seek to avoid the pitfalls of their established counterparts, in the former we should emphasize a combination of rational insights and pragmatic solutions. Grand designs can perhaps be applied to a greenfield, but rarely help with a brownfield. There, quite manifestly, a sense of history informs any sense of future. This insight holds for existing cities at two levels: firstly, we must start to think of them more in terms of their evolution; secondly, we should take the built history within them as part of their fabric. A city can, like the proverbial cat, have many different lives, as the example of Cairo today shows (see Chap. 9), and cities are thus the built testimony to the dissynchronic nature of the lives that have been lived in them through the centuries. One of the key avenues in planning for existing cities must therefore be to find ways of meaningfully combining that history with the present, pragmatically connecting the past with rational insights for the future.

Speer's original balsa model of the Side, Turkey, plan. The creation of a new town around the ancient ruins is clearly visible.

Side today: the Greek theater is a stand-alone not incorporated meaningfully into the new urban fabric.

COMMON SENSE: THE EXAMPLE OF SIDE, TURKEY

It is perhaps no coincidence that one of the very first plans proposed by Albert Speer in the early days of the company concentrated precisely on such a marriage of past and future in finding a new identity for a city. In the mid-1960s, after Albert Speer, who had spent some time as a student in Turkey, quite literally scootered round Anatolia, the office developed a submission for the competition for the future expansion of the town of Side on Turkey's Mediterranean coast and now its Riviera. The concept put forward by AS&P was a far cry from the stringent one-size-fits-all approach taken by the mainstream urban planners of the day, such as Constantinos Doxiadis, the star town planner of the 1960s, who advocated a stringent functionalist approach. Instead of strict functional segregation, the suggestion was to integrate the town's archaeological sites, where excavation and restoration work was still ongoing, into the very fabric of a modern town center. Side, then as now, was one of the very best examples of how past and present could coexist and foster a new identity. With excavations being conducted in its very center, the town was lived history. Its position atop a peninsula was a reflection of the climatic knowledge possessed by the Ancient Greeks, for the houses here were cooled by the evening wind and avoided the marshlands, which were home to disease and mosquitos. (Archaeologists today suggest the demise of the city of Ephesus can be attributed to its marshland position and thus to malaria.) The town had been targeted for expansion, the suggestion being that tourist resorts be strung out on either side of it and the peninsula be abandoned to the archaeologists. AS&P relied instead on what common sense had told the Greeks and proposed that the original location be retained.

The archaeologists running the excavations had said they would need some 20 seasons to complete their work; after consultations with them, AS&P suggested that there was no rational reason why the season (usually four weeks in the summer) could not be extended, as climatic conditions permitted this, and while this might be unusual for the archaeologists it meant the work could be compressed into two single, lengthier periods. After all, the financing was available, and in this way the historical sites as excavated (the total acreage is not great) would be ready for display to the public after only two years and would not pose a logistical hurdle to a new, modern town – which could then be built around a large attractive ancient theater, the expansive Greek gymnasium, adjacent to the ancient aqueduct and accessed via a town gate dating back to the second century BC.

The AS&P entry in the pan-European competition in 1965–6 used the peninsula as the main location for the town as resort, a step that, if common now, was quite pioneering in its day, and possibly so unusual, theoretically speaking, that it was rejected: the town as archaeological park. Complete with the old avenues flanked by their pillared arcades that bissected the peninsula and parts of various larger temples – all of them components of a new town that was a radical departure from the competition brief, but which certainly made sense. On the one side of the peninsula, a new, 5-star hotel, at its tip a voguish yacht marina; and down the other side a thoroughbred corniche with jetties, viewing points, restaurants; and in between the two as the heart of the new urban settlement, something for tourists and locals alike, a mixture of Turkish covered bazaar, offices, and shops. And all the archaeological finds preserved in situ, covered by glass where necessary, and illuminated by night. The inhabitants and the tourists would thus quite literally live in history, without the need for massive change. It is something that today is one of the attractions of the boutique hotels on the peninsula of Alanya slightly further down the coast. But at the time it all added up to one thing, and one thing only: AS&P losing the competition.

Albert Speer comments that "if I look back on the plans today, they are really modern, with the little harbor and the pedestrian walkway right round the peninsula. I still find the solution we came up with as elegant now as I felt it was then. If you approach a site in terms of the overarching theory, and do not allow yourself to get bogged down in the brief or the specifics experts so love to champion, and apply a little common sense, then the new can usually be wedded to the old in a meaningful way and synergies exploited. That is sustainability. It is based on a reality check that brings to bear a combination of intuition and rational insight."

The AS&P entry for the Side competition shows that holistic planning may necessitate abandoning any attempt to create a city "from a single mold," as Speer likes to call it. "Because that mold rarely fits all. After all, in Side history offered us various aspects that with a little ingenuity could be given a new lease of life." The old outer town walls are a case in point. In the AS&P proposal they function as a sight-screen, shielding the "preserved" ancient town from the main road that runs along the coast. This was not something that could be readily demonstrated by submitting renderings or photos as called for by the competition rules. So Albert Speer and his colleagues again had to flaunt authority. They sat down and Exacto-knived a balsa wood model of the town and then had a photographer who sub-let one of the huge rooms in their office take an "aerial" shot of it for them. The photos that have survived show the peninsula as they imagined it. A mixture of commercial and residential settlements form the dense core surrounding the archaeological sites, thus supporting the town's transformation into a tourist destination. Additional hotels were placed outside the "new" old town along the main road to either side and further residential settlements were planned for the flanks of the mountains that form the immediate hinterland of the coast, to house those who worked on the peninsula.

There were good, rational reasons for planning completely new edifices, just as common sense said that to remove the town center from the ancient town would be to sever its original lifeline and to ignore the reason why Side, founded more than 2,400 years ago, stood where it was. Essentially, AS&P had departed on a path antagonistic to much city planning of the day and insisted on "sustainability" before the term itself was used. In doing so, they subverted the notion underlying the Le Corbusier-inspired 1933 Charter of Athens, with its insistence that "the keys to urban planning lie in the following four functions: living, working, relaxing (leisure time), moving, and plans will determine the structure of each of the quarters allocated to the four key functions and will establish the relevant location within the whole." The AS&P proposal insisted instead on mixed usage and yet upheld the call for strict boundaries between private and public space. At the same time, the entry envisaged bringing green into the city in the form of the small parks formed by the larger archaeological sites. First and foremost, however, AS&P had eschewed the Charter's wish to "service traffic's needs," something they banished to the main road – or to the sea, where it got in no one's way. As can be seen from the photograph of the balsa-wood model on the previous page, the main thoroughfares keep traffic out of the heart of the city.

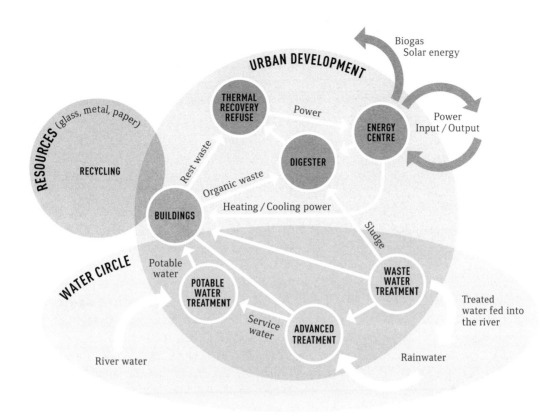

Biogas
Solar energy

URBAN DEVELOPMENT

THERMAL RECOVERY REFUSE

Power

ENERGY CENTRE

Power Input / Output

RESOURCES (glass, metal, paper)

RECYCLING

Rest waste

DIGESTER

Organic waste

Heating / Cooling power

BUILDINGS

Sludge

WATER CIRCLE

Potable water

POTABLE WATER TREATMENT

WASTE WATER TREATMENT

Treated water fed into the river

Service water

ADVANCED TREATMENT

River water

Rainwater

The chart shows how, if planning is right, recycling can be used to minimize the resource inputs.

THEORY: CITIES AND CYCLES IN CHINA

What the Side proposal did only indirectly was to consider the city as a system of cycles that need to be combined rationally if they are to function without the one straining the other. A classical case of such cycles is waste management, and here again stringent logic and common sense have to meld. Only if the city is considered holistically can the issue of waste creation and waste management be handled satisfactorily. Michael Denkel, one of the AS&P board members, comments that today "we produce far more waste than can be rationally justified. Just take the example of food." And Albert Speer adds: "It's a problem with which we are all familiar from our homes. If you go food shopping, unless you happen to have a good market at hand, you already become embroiled in an irrational cycle of waste production. Most things have at least one layer of packaging, if not two or three. Now this may make food more durable and more visually appealing, but it is the basic level at which the problem starts. There's no sustainability here without breaking habits."

AS&P has recently attempted, drawing on the assistance of outside expert engineers in the process, to devise an overarching holistic system for use in future urban planning in China. The theory being that any overarching system, covering supply through to disposal, covering water through to power, can best be improved by optimizing not the individual subsystems, but the way they all interact. Thus, if one devises the system from the outset and not for an existing town, such as Side, one part of the waste can be used to produce heat or generate electricity, another part can then be recycled, the material thus reclaimed for future utilization, and existing fuel sources supplemented by biogas and biomass, etc. This ensures the system remains open-ended and allows for future expansion of renewables as fossil fuels become too expensive. It is a policy already practiced by the major German energy utilities active in Great Britain (although surprisingly they do not yet pursue the same policy in Germany itself). This is the point where theory has to persuade policy-makers to likewise think holistically, because such national differences invariably tend to be the result of different tax regimes, whereby in one country a utility is encouraged by possible amortization or subsidies to think in cycles, while in another it is deterred from so doing. Again, international coordination is of the essence, as such disparities within so small a community as the "older core" of the European Union are neither rational nor common sense. Instead, the EU as a whole needs to be persuaded by voters and planners alike of the need for the sustainability playing field to be equally advantageous in all the member states rather than allow money to have primacy over theory. CHPPs are a similar case in point. While all member states preach such combined heat and power production via smaller plants, only a very few of them have implemented the theory, and then only at the local level. "Perhaps," Albert Speer moots, "the issues have become weighed down with ideology and this has obscured their universal meaningfulness and necessity."

In this context, Speer loves to cite the case of the four different trash bins that traditionally now stand outside each German home: one for paper, one for organic waste, one for plastic and packaging waste, and the fourth for everything else. He quips: "Whether theory and common sense really meld here to foster the waste cycle I really do not know. After all, the underlying issue is waste. Evidently, within the EU there is simply not a large enough incentive to think about what waste costs before you produce it, to consider what that waste really implies, how it impacts on the environment. I discern a similar mindset as regards cars. We do not find many people addressing the fundamental issue of whether modern society needs cars. Instead, the debate has been sidetracked into whether we can switch all the cars over from fossil fuels to electricity, and the real race is not Formula One but which car maker comes up with an effective battery first. Now that is all well and good. The vehicle makes zero emissions. But where does the electricity come from? Will we see a future where every home has to cover its roof with solar panels simply to make transportation qua mobility possible. That is a hefty cost for society to pay. And is it really the province of government to ordain from on high that each roof be so equipped if people are to be able to get to work?" In other words, the historic problem of transport growth concomitant with economic growth now has a new side to it: climate change. Given such structures, it is important that people themselves recognize that it makes sense to act differently, be it to avoid waste or even to be aware of what waste production involves. After all, people are not likely to consider cars a disadvantage or as waste as long as they offer them advantages. Declaiming the opposite will then simply fall on deaf ears. Instead, politicians and planners must seek to convince people to rethink their everyday habits; to consider a world in which cars are hydrogen-driven and used only for short-distant purposes, for example, an approach already being cultivated in Shanghai and Los Angeles.

AS&P has focused its planning efforts in China on according pride of place to energy as an issue. In its plans for Anting New Town in Shanghai's Jarding district (one of the "Nine Towns One City" project) it designed an overall system to be fed by gas. While electricity currently tends to be produced by coal-fired power stations, the planners insisted on a concept that involved gas supply as the energy source after five years and far lower inputs of coal, thus lowering emissions and attempting to save other costs. The difficulty here is to control who it is who saves the costs. After all, the homes in Anting have lower running costs, which raises the value of the domiciles, but it is not clear whether the purchase price is adjusted to reflect this. However, the example set by the Anting concept did lead to the notion of energy saving being incorporated into local bylaws.

This is quite a novelty in that the notion of energy saving as introduced into China from Germany is not as readily accepted in the country of origin, preventing East-West insight transfer. In Germany, given the link between insulation and heating costs, owners of apartment blocks seek to lower their operating costs by retrofitting insulation. Indeed, the government actively seeks to encourage modernization of existing buildings, as there is substantial room for improved energy efficiency. However, a German high court has ruled that tenants can rightly refuse to permit their accommodation to be upgraded in this manner in order to save energy unless their landlords accept that they will not pass on the costs incurred by raising rents. In light of such rulings, urban planners must inevitably and ironically focus on the specialist aspects of the "big" picture and leave the details of energy efficiency, combined heat and power production advocacy, etc., to the politicians, who, while elected to act in terms of the "big" picture, are the agents whose planning brief is shortest – generally through to the next election.

In this regard, urban planning as understood by AS&P is not an isolated discipline. Rather, as is evident from the issue of waste management in the cities of tomorrow, urban planning locks into any number of other "big" issues of today, such as how to educate society or how to feed the world. Why education? Because if people today were better educated, irrespective of the hemisphere they live in, then they would approach the environment and their environment differently, forever aware that it is a finite resource. That is common sense. Take the example of fishermen on an island who burn the bushes and mangroves along the riverbanks in order to be better able to catch the fish there. The fish, however, lay their eggs precisely in the areas protected by the bushes and man-

groves, so that in order to fish, the fishermen actually destroy the basis of their own livelihood. To paraphrase the Bible, they do so because they do not know better. Were they to know of the cycle in which they intervene they would no doubt act differently and seek an alternative solution. When applied to the cities of tomorrow, it is clear that the focus must always be on finding such new solutions, irrespective of whether the urban planning is for Africa, Asia or South America. The planners must factor into their own work questions such as continual access to fresh water for a new city in China or the poverty trap that urbanization brings with it in Africa. Only then can urban planning be "the generator" that Le Corbusier insisted it must be some 80 years ago. He went on to say that "without a plan, there is disorder, arbitrariness … The great problems of tomorrow, dictated by collective needs, pose the question of the plan anew. Modern life demands, awaits a new plan for the house and for the city."[4] It would seem that little has changed in those 80 years.

Two examples of AS&P's work in China show how common sense can fail completely when faced with institutions designed for a different setting, and highlight the difficulties of finding appropriate local urban planning mechanisms if one relies only on global methods. The one example relates to waste management. In Shanghai, AS&P advocated a waste-management system that would result in less waste being introduced into the cycle, less landfill, and smaller mountains of waste. The upper echelons in the municipal authority found the idea compelling. The problem, however, was not the technology, but the organization, as in China all the various subsystems active in the municipal waste-management chain work independently of one another, whereby these independent utilities are adopted from the West. Whereas in a city such as Frankfurt, Germany, the municipality has a holding company that controls the various utilities, this is not the case in Shanghai. This means that each utility in the chain has its own tariffs, its own fee-collection systems, etc. Yet if a cycle is to be introduced as the meaningful way to tackle waste management, then invoicing should occur only once – be it for energy supply or for wastewater disposal. The proposed system failed precisely because it was simpler, and thus far more complex to implement. One could justifiable insist here that solutions must always be local.

Water itself is the other example. Whereas water is becoming increasingly scarce in London, for example, although not yet on a scale to cause real fear, in China, water is a resource that is readily wasted, for historical reasons. The country's water resources are not readily available where they are needed. It rains less in the North, and more in the South and the Southwest of China. Water, moreover, tends to get used both in agriculture and in the cities without any great care for its conservation, because, following Mao Tse-tung's wisdom, it is considered a common good and has therefore customarily been provided by the state free of charge. Today, water costs something, but still not enough to cause greater circumspection in its use. Policy-makers have tried to get round the problem of the political heritage by not raising the cost of water,

←

Models of Anting New Town, Jarding District, Shanghai. The use of courtyards and meaningful public spaces is clearly visible.

and instead pumping up the price of wastewater. In other words, the state has recognized the problem and is trying to get a handle on it by introducing different tariffs for agriculture, for industry, for residential premises, and for cities. In the process, it has to contend with the strong ideology that proclaims "water costs nothing" and thus flies in the face of any notion of sustainability. (As does rapid economic development, which brings with it rapid entrepreneurial development and thus a mindset that focuses on the short term rather than the long term.) That said, given the strong autonomous position of the provincial or city authorities, it is to be hoped that change can be forced through, as planning at the level of Shanghai is not really urban planning for a city, but for a state, something that logically involves long-term policy.

Johannes Dell, the AS&P board member responsible for business in China, comments in this context that one of the key challenges posed when bringing the concept of sustainability to bear in terms of the cities of tomorrow is that it "is becoming ever clearer that what an urban planner does networks with everything else. Yet this is not something that is commonplace among architects and engineers worldwide. In fact, the opposite is the case. They tend to think only in and of buildings. OK, some of them now consider the buildings' possible CO_2 emissions, that is a beginning. But they are not thinking through the macro-theory, namely, considering factors such as where the buildings will stand, how the city will be shaped, what consequences it will have to put a building here and not there, to change the countryside in this way and not that, how access and development costs will impact on the fabric of a future city, affecting distances to work, etc. They are simply not interested in the overarching theoretical questions, even though these issues are just as much a matter of common sense as anything else. It is as though the discipline as a whole were a rabbit caught in the headlights of a disastrous future. Frozen rigid. Thinking only of CO_2 emissions and, with a guilty conscience, forgetting the rest of the big picture."

HOLISTIC URBAN PLANNING: AS&P INTERNALLY

At AS&P, cultivating the big picture and marrying theory and common sense are a question of structure, and one of which the board members are constantly and acutely aware. In order for planning for a sustainable future to be possible, the planners on any given project must themselves be duly broad in composition, ranging from sociologists and philosophers to traffic planners – so that anyone working on a project can simply cross the corridor if he needs a very different "second" opinion on how to best solve a problem. This means insisting that projects be handled by non-hierarchical teams to ensure that holism remains part of the problem-solving process and that one aspect is not prioritized to the detriment of others. It also means fostering open minds down through the generations, promoting common sense not rocket science. Dell himself believes this is the key contribution made by the Grand Old Man of the office, Albert Speer. "He has always as a matter of principle given all of us the freedom to move in this direction, and as our mentor or

Nestor he has encouraged us to do so. In this sense the freedom he offers each discipline within the office is the yeast that causes the cake to rise, while Speer himself is the baking soda." In this regard, Speer has carefully reared his own team, composed as it is almost exclusively of several generations of his own students. This has enabled him to nurture within the company a culture of critical inquiry and a rejection of assumed givens.

Indeed, this cross-fertilization as internal structure is possibly what enabled the office to think out of the box as early as the entry for Side. It also ensures that what the office champions, the combination of theory and common sense, is also the covert organizational principle. The board membership thus reflects the different disciplines involved and is able to function smoothly thanks to regular retreats, where each of the members can bring a discipline-specific angle to bear in joint discussions. Dell suggests that the corporate structure resembles that of a fractal that constantly reproduces itself in identical form, whereby the macro- and the microstructures are identical. He believes the structure is so successful because the product sold is an insight, namely "that in urban planning, as with our company internally, the whole is always more than the sum of the parts. This makes us so appealing to clients who have noticed that to a great extent we not only practice but also live what we preach."[5]

PRIORITIZE HOLISM OVER SPECIALIZATION

Urban planning for a sustainable future will, so everyone at AS&P is convinced, depend on whether cities worldwide succeed in adopting a holistic approach. To do so they must overcome the vagaries of the academic system typical of today, in which architects, engineers, and planners all receive in-depth specialist training. In itself this may be all very good and necessary. However, none of the students is taught either to think out of the box, or that it is imperative to network with other fields, to take a holistic approach, to cooperate with their peers in an interdisciplinary manner. Yet from what has been described above, it is clear that thinking in complex, multidisciplinary cycles is imperative if we are to create sustainable cities.

As Fritjof Capra emphasizes in The Turning Point: "In contrast to the mechanistic Cartesian view of the world, the world view emerging from modern physics can be characterized by words like organic, holistic and ecological. It might also be called a systems view, in the sense of a general systems theory. The universe is no longer seen as a machine, made up of a multitude of objects, but has to be pictured as one indivisible, dynamic whole whose parts are essentially interrelated and can be understood only as patterns of a cosmic process."[6]

Urban planning for sustainability must therefore hinge on selling a holistic idea, the cosmic design, and backing it up with the specialists' facts and figures. A building or city, if considered as a product that can be bought, will have permanence in the sense of enduring quality, energy efficiency if it relies on an underlying idea and does not just seek to fulfil functions. The idea must be credible, and what better idea than that of an enduring return for all stakeholders – that is another definition of sustainability. This involves construing each city as a metabolism, whereby the word "denotes the sum of chemical changes occurring in living organisms, and in cells in particular, that are necessary to sustain life."[7]

To close with the words of Albert Speer: "What seems clear to me when thinking through the concept of the sustainable city is that the main point of emphasis must be to find an individual solution that fits the particular metabolism. And that is one of our strengths, so I believe. We do not go round saying: What was right in Beijing can now be transferred qua insight onto the situation in Abuja or onto some other city of a smaller scale. And we do not say that what is good for Cologne will necessarily be good for Frankfurt. The days when what was good for General Motors was good for the USA are long since over. People in each city are different, the local environment is different, the culture is different, the thinking is different. For all the impact of globalization, it is crucial, so I believe, that at the end of the day we seek individual, specific solutions that fit the particular case. And our immense advantage is that we can present ideas here that prove they are better, that show that thinking locally functions. Even if only 30 per cent of what we suggest then gets realized. That doesn't matter. What does matter is to combine theory and common sense at the beginning and establish it as the culture. Given that conditions always differ, from one city to the next, there can be no holistic planning or theory that does not think local on the back of common sense on the ground." And the one critical insight here is that sustainable planning knows it is never finished. So sustainable cities must always be cities that can evolve, evolve creatively.

1 *UNCHS:* Cities in a Globalizing World: Global Report on Human Settlements, *(OUP, New York, 2001), p. 232*

2 *www.org/esa/sustder/document/agenda21/english/agenda21toc.htm*

3 *R. Stren, R. White and J. Whitney (eds):* Sustainable Cities. Urbanization and the Environment in International Perspective, *(Westview Press, Boulder, 1992), p. 36*

4 *Le Corbusier:* Toward an Architecture, *trans. J. Goodman, (Frances Lincoln Publishers, London, 2008), p. 86*

5 *AS&P was awarded the contract to create a master plan for Changchun Automotive Industry Development Area precisely because of this holistic approach involving numerous different disciplines.*

6 *Fritjof Capra:* The Turning Point, *(Simon Schuster, New York, 1982) p. 66*

7 *Ibid., p. 103*

II

GO BROWNFIELD, NOT GREENFIELD

RECYCLING AND THE CITY – THE DEFINITIONS

Back in 2003, when presenting her commission's document "Towards a Thematic Strategy on the Prevention and Recycling of Waste," which focuses on taking the sustainable use of resources forward and on preventing and recycling waste, then EU Environment Commissioner Margot Wallström commented: "This Communication launches a broad consultation exercise on the EU's future policy in this area. It invites stakeholders to comment on the policy options set out in the Communication. These options include issues like: how to avoid generating waste, how to reduce the use of resources, and which wastes to recycle. When we throw a product away, it represents much more than just a piece of waste. It also embodies all the resources used to produce it. If you add them all in, the real weight of a toothbrush becomes 1.5 kg, and that of a mobile phone 75 kg! To save resources and avoid pollution, the Commission is determined to put new focus on waste prevention and recycling." The Waste Framework Directive defines waste as "products or materials that are discarded." In the light of its consultations, the Commission then concluded that "there is no need substantively to amend the definition of waste, but that it is necessary to clarify when waste ceases to be waste (and becomes a new or secondary raw material). Therefore, an amendment to the Directive is proposed which would establish waste-stream-based environmental criteria to determine when a waste ceases to be a waste. This could both improve the environmental performance of recycled products, by encouraging businesses to produce recycled products that conform to these environmental criteria, and reduce unnecessary burdens for low-risk recycling activities.... Within the review of this strategy in 2010, the Commission will assess the effectiveness of the guidelines."

For all the emphasis the EU Commission's massive Environment Directorate places on waste and on urban trends, nowhere does it talk about cities as themselves a product of, or object for, recycling. And yet it is cities that both produce the most waste and that are themselves often, at least in part, waste. Not that the Environment Directorate is alone, as any search on Google for "recycling cities" quickly shows. Possibly the reason for this absence is that the city itself is rarely construed as a product (of the past) and tends to be regarded as a living organism, and thus thought of only in terms of the present/future.

Perhaps this reflects the fact that completely recycling a city is "a project that will invariably run across several generations," as Friedbert Greif, one of AS&P's managing partners, puts it. Yet it is surprising if we bear in mind that European cities, at any rate, can look back on a long tradition of reinventing themselves.

RENAISSANCE OF THE EUROPEAN CITY

A comparison of maps of Europe in 1800, 1900, and 2000 swiftly shows how cities have come and gone, grown or shrunk. First of all, urbanization entered Europe as a consequence of industrialization, and with its end left cities behind that had to be reengineered to fit a new lease of life as financial or service centers. A second factor that triggered a series of incisive changes in the face of

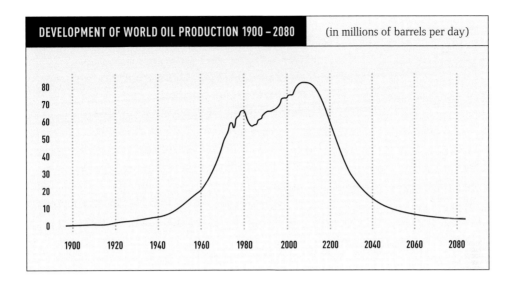

DEVELOPMENT OF WORLD OIL PRODUCTION 1900 – 2080 (in millions of barrels per day)

European cities was less pacific: the fact that the continent suffered the impact of two World Wars within the space of 30 years, the second of which, with the emergence of long-distance bombing technologies, significantly changed the face of many cities. And then, in 1989, the Wall came down, followed by a wave of infrastructure development that washed through East European cities like a flood. The key insight to be derived from these three phases is that today "new" cities are not needed, and existing cities, where they need to expand, must expand inwards not outwards. This is not just a coefficient of their footprints (see Chap. 6), but of their intrinsic sustainability in an epoch when forms of transportation are changing, and the function of the countryside with it.

In the 21st century, the European community has long ceased to outgrow its city boundaries, in part as a reflection of demographic changes and in part owing to the absence of new labor-intensive industries in the cities. The new "sustainability" epoch can be characterized as one in which it is high time to condense and compress cities, as if the urban trend should follow what is constantly happening in the world of data storage. And it is one in which European cities will experience a renaissance as the role model for urbanization. Indeed, it is fair to say that these cities are once again prioritizing the dense structures that originally characterized them, especially as resources dwindle.

European cities, Albert Speer emphasizes, must not use new land to expand – Europe's core metropolises already have sufficient land – it just needs to be rejuvenated. That is to say, sparing resources, and making greater use of what already exists and therefore avoiding resource wastage, specifically the most precious of resources: land. After all, the American example promulgated during the 1960s has led nowhere, with its functionalist separation of all zones of the city and the problematic strain on public infrastructure this entails. Only the "old" cities of New York and San Francisco avoid this conundrum, with Seattle possibly being the exception that proves the rule among the new cities.

This process calls for solutions in Europe different to those that need to be devised for the new emerging world of the BRIC states (Brazil, Russia, India, China) and the other non-Western members of the G20. And they will have nothing to do, say, with the strategic concept deployed by Chinese planners to meet the wave of urbanization there, namely, to plan and build new cities before the inhabitants arrive. Instead, the focus is on how to structure the future of European cities to heighten their sustainability. For European cities face a turning point of their own: they must go brownfield and cease to go greenfield, or they will not survive. And this will mean a rethink, certainly in Germany, of planning and zoning laws. These tend to be aligned to encourage expansion outwards. It is far easier to get building permission for greenfield housing estates than for reconstructing old harbor areas. The issues of inland waterway legislation, of toxic waste in the soil, of commercial zones, the rights of adjacent areas, etc., all have to be borne in mind. As Greif comments: "In Germany at any rate, all planning law has green fields in mind and that makes inner city planning for brownfield areas well nigh impossible. But that must change.

CHARTER OF MACHU PICCHU. 1977 It is now 45 years since CIAM elaborated a document on the theory and methodology of urban planning named the "Charter of Athens." Many new phenomena have emerged during that time that call for a revision of the Charter that will thus complement the original document, giving it the worldwide focus and an interdisciplinary analytical basis to foster an international discussion that will include intellectuals and professionals, research institutes, and universities in all countries.

There are some strong arguments for modernizing the Charter of Athens and this document is intended solely as the starting point for such an enterprise, as the first obligatory such effort, for while the Charter of Athens of 1933 is nevertheless a fundamental document for our own epoch, that, while it cannot be negated in its entirety, certainly needs to be updated, many of its 95 points are nevertheless valid and testimony to the vitality and community of the Modernist movement both in urban planning and in architecture. Athens 1933, Machu Picchu 1977

Places are significant, and Athens is known as the cradle of Western civilization, Machu Picchu symobolizes the independent cultural contribution by the rest of the world. Athens represents the form of rationality personified by Aristotle and Plato. Machu Picchu represents everything that is not part of that enlightened global mindset and everything that cannot be classified by its own logic.

The Charter's chapters are: City and region; Urban growth; Concept of sectors; Residential living; Transportation in cities; Availability of urban land; Natural resources and local ornamentation; Preservation and defence of cultural values and national heritage; Technology; Implementation; Urban design and architecture

Largest cities and urban areas in 2020 (in millions).

THE BIG PICTURE – CITIES AND COUNTRYSIDE

Thinking about sustainability in terms of going brownfield means constantly keeping the big picture in mind, namely, the best possible survival for humanity as a whole. This can hardly be the province of the urban planner or the architect, as Albert Speer constantly emphasizes, but as we have mentioned, their joint thinking cuts into the shapes that survival can and will take. If we assume that the trend of rapid urbanization will persist in the foreseeable future, with the current 50–50 urban/rural ratio moving ever more in the direction of the figure typical for the developed world, then the issue of sustainable cities becomes all the more acute.

One thinker who has related theorizing the survival of the planet to cities is James Lovelock in his elaboration of his concept of Gaia. He writes: "We have … defined Gaia as a complex entity involving the Earth's biosphere, atmosphere, oceans, and soil; the totality constitutes a feedback or cybernetic system which seeks an optimal physical and chemical environment for life on this planet. The maintenance of relatively constant conditions by active control may be conveniently described by the term 'homoeostasis'."[1] It may be difficult to construe human development against the backdrop of this notion of

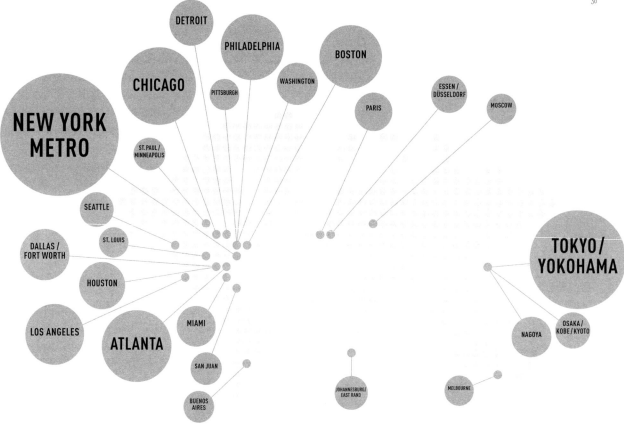

Largest cities in the world today ranked by land area (in km²).

stasis, especially as regards how human beings try to solve the "crisis of diminishing re-sources."[2] However, James Lovelock insightfully suggests that a prime cause of the prob-lem in getting humans to grasp how their actions impact on the Earth is that through ur-banization "the proportion of information flowing from the biosphere to the pool of knowledge which constitutes the wisdom of the city has decreased. … At the same time, the complex interactions within the city produced new problems requiring attention." Put differently, the cities forget that they exist as part of a larger whole and simply continue to eat into the latter's greenfields. Yet, paradoxically, the urban areas are those that man-ifestly most affect life on our planet. The urban areas are now the place where the large majority of humans live and work, and are the source of what Lovelock discerns as hu-mans' negative impact through pollution.

It would thus seem logical to try to find a way of recalibrating how human life in cities interacts with Gaia – and this will involve acting in line with two insights. First, that the current standard of living in the Western world cannot persist, as it rests on exploitation of other parts of the world. Secondly, that the development of the rest of the world may aspire to emulate that standard of living, but if we are to live sustainability, that aspiration must not be allowed to drive development. For while we seek ways of bringing renewable sources of energy to bear on a large scale, other resources, such as oil and precious and semiprecious metals, are indeed diminishing, and diminishing fast (see chart, p. 35). Human ingenuity has its work cut out to find ways of reinventing how we produce things over the next 30-odd years until oil becomes truly scarce. Yet this spells, or so Albert Speer suggests, a historical opportunity. He proposes that "the leading members of non-Western societies can now see how not to develop – just as they adopted mobile phones rather than build land lines, so they could try to avoid using old coal-fired power stations and rely instead on the latest technology available. New industrialization must not follow the patterns of the 19th century, just as homes today can get by with one TV set instead of five. The financial crisis of the first decade of the 21st century can serve to show the rest of the world what has become superfluous – for example, the family's second or third car, condemned to remain in a carport or get stuck in a gridlock going nowhere. And one such lesson is to expand inwards and upwards, not outwards." In other words, one key to planning in light of those two insights is to go brownfield.

FIRST TO GO BROWNFIELD – LUDWIGSHAFEN

Fittingly, the very first competition Albert Speer ever won a prize in was for a concept for the reutilization of a brownfield area – back in the early 1960s, when smaller cities in Germany either opted to create greenfield satellite towns (and thus tolerate the corresponding loss of tax revenues) or find new development zones within the ancient "city walls," as it were. The year was 1964 and it was a closed competition to which all the greats of German urban planning at the time, such as George Candilis and Friedrich Spengelin, had been invited. But there was a loophole: local architects were also permitted to submit entries.

The city fathers had decided, after the city's ruinous bombing during World War II, to relocate the central railway station, moving it away from a location on the banks of the Rhine and to the western edge of the new downtown area. As a consequence, the entire area covered by the former railway station was left free and needed to be developed. And it was ideas for the development of this area that they requested, as it offered completely new opportunities for restructuring the heart of the city and its transportation system.

Albert Speer recollects that although he was, at the time, employed as a young architect in the Frankfurt office of Apel, Beckert und Becker, the fact that he came from Heidelberg entitled him to enter the competition. So the spring of 1964 saw him spending his evenings working away at plans of his own in his attic apartment in Frankfurt's Westend, refining drawing after drawing. Yet he soon realized two things. Firstly, he would stand little chance of getting anywhere in such a prestigious competition if his presentation revealed that he was a one-man show. So, behind the veil of anonymity, he invested in having a model built, carefully created using colored foils that had just come on the market in the United States, and with all the texts prepared in capital letters using an IBM golfball typewriter borrowed from an ad agency. As a consequence, the finished product

looked as if it had been professionally prepared in a large office. Secondly, and more importantly, Speer did what he did in Side: he ignored the constraints of the competition brief wherever he felt they were inappropriate (see Chap. 1). The city fathers had elected to devastate Ludwighafen's new downtown by cutting it up with overpasses – highways on stilts that bisected the new inner city, channeling traffic in and out in keeping with the Charter of Athens, but destroying any potential quality of life, from the outset a key criterion for the city.

Speer felt that this would simply condemn the new to immediate death and in his proposal scaled the overpasses back to such an extent that they remained only as two flanks to the city, accessing the new railway station. He recalls that "when once I had the idea and realized that it was, to my mind, the only possibility, I suddenly became very unsure of myself. Dare I do it? In my uncertainty, I sought the counsel of my then superior at Apel and later partner, Diedrich Praekel, who had gained a wealth of experience in the United States, where he had worked for I.M. Pei and played a part in designing Philadelphia. He visited me one night in my loft and immediately said: 'Now Speer, that's very risky. But no risk, no gain.' So I hired a few helping hands to finish up the presentation and submitted it."

The result was, of course, typical of the competition world. At the end of June 1964 the jury awarded 1st Prize to Prof. Gerd Albers, the doyen of urban planning at Mu-

←

Aerial view of Speer project for a new residential district,
Pfingstweide, outside Ludwigshafen.

nich's Technical University, for his submission, which duly conformed to the brief. But the jury unanimously agreed to downgrade the prize money and allocate a far larger chunk to the winner of the 2nd Prize, none other than Albert Speer. By virtue of the fact that his proposal for the brownfield area flouted the brief, they were unable to declare it the winner, but by upgrading the prize money indirectly confirmed that it was the appropriate solution.

CREATIVITY IN BROWNFIELD PROJECTS

How? What he had done was to set out to expand the terms of reference for the competition: not only to cover the area being freed up with the exit of the old railway station, but to relate the zone to existing zones and attempt to find a new concept for the entire inner city, that gave it a "unique organic face and enabled the integration of new planning and the railway station into the existing business district," as the prize brochure reads. He placed the emphasis on integrating brownfield and existing structures. Speer stated there that: "The desired close linkage of inner city relationships is possible only if the new business district runs between the erstwhile core of the city, the cultural centers, and the new railway station. This will closely wed the new railway station to the inner city." Integration of brownfield and existing structures was meaningfully possible only by ignoring the competition brief. "Only if you are naïve enough," he suggests, "will you often be creative, because once you know too much about a project you tend to have scruples about really changing things. Later, once I was familiar with the ins and outs of juries and aware that the livelihoods of everyone in my office depended on our winning competitions, then I, on occasion, really got cold feet. But I am proud to say we have, nevertheless, over time, come up with some truly creative submissions – for example, here in Frankfurt. And have failed miserably in the respective competitions as a result. That I regard as a cachet of our success."

In other words, there is a subtext to developing brownfield, namely, that planning can be stimulated by deliberately thinking outside the box or grid. As we have seen, in China, AS&P has established a name for itself by championing a holistic approach that has otherwise got lost there. And at times it does so specifically by overriding the competition specifications. Evidently, this mindset pervades AS&P's work: Challenge yourself – set your own goalposts in addition to those set by the particular project competition or job description at hand.

Indeed, it has become almost second nature to the various project teams at AS&P, many of whom learned the approach as Albert Speer's graduate students at the University of Kaiserlautern. Speer insists that urban planners and architects alike must reject the constraints of so-called "hard facts," which say that capacities are not available or something is simply declared impossible or not appropriate. "The deeper you go into the background to a project and what it involves, the more you discover that the facts and figures given can be interpreted this way or that. In Ludwigshafen, the suggestion was that the empty strip that bisected downtown – a remnant from postwar reconstruction – should, by virtue of the fact that it ran north-south, automatically be used to create a road link over the Rhine, in addition to the two other overpasses proposed on either side: making a total of three overpasses. And that was nonsensical. Or so I felt. And I firmly believe that when you come across nonsense then you simply must look for alternatives that make sense. There simply has to be a different way to do things. I must at some level have connected to some pulse or other among the city fathers, as the overpasses were not built. After all, my proposal was simply one new axis for the inner city, a backbone from which all else developed in an integrated manner – as part of the city, not in opposition to it."

Simulation of proposed mixed usage on the Munich Laim brownfield development.

Overview of central idle railway sidings running into Munich showing possible usages and insertion into the urban fabric.

BROWNFIELD EUROPE – RESOURCE MANAGEMENT

Ever since the success in the Ludwigshafen competition, AS&P has sought, wherever possible, to apply a similar integrative methodology to brownfield areas and wastelands within existing cities. Over time it has become apparent that within German cities, for example, sites formerly occupied by facilities created for freight rail, tramcars or inland ports that have since fallen into disuse offer great potential – as did London's Docklands – not to mention industrial zones that today are still located within inner cities although the industry itself has moved on.

Two examples of this focus are Munich's Laim shunting yard station and Frankfurt's Holbeinviertel and Europaviertel, both hinging on the problem of reintegrating a derelict site into the urban fabric of the city. In the former case, the site was a container and switching yard positioned on the edge of Munich's urban core. In the latter, the respective sites were first, a freight rail yard (squeezed between an embankment and a 19th-century residential district) and secondly, a former main freight rail station (wedged between the back of the trade fair complex and a residential district that had seen better times in the early 20th century as a home to industry and that was undergoing redevelopment to enable mixed usage). Both projects thus intervene in the existing structure of the inner city and go beyond mere recycling of a brownfield area. They call for an integrative approach that not only gives them a new lease of life, but also ties them meaningfully into the city and accesses them accordingly.

MUNICH'S LAIM DISTRICT

The first step in the case of Munich was to devise a structured plan for urban development per se, as the foreseeable reuse of other derelict and unstructured sites along the same central rail axis running into the main train station highlighted the need for a comprehensive approach. The result was a

Nymphenburg-Süd / Laim

Birketweg

Post-Areal

Containerbahnhof / Mercedes-Areal
Milchladehof

Pasing

Paul-Gerhardt-Allee

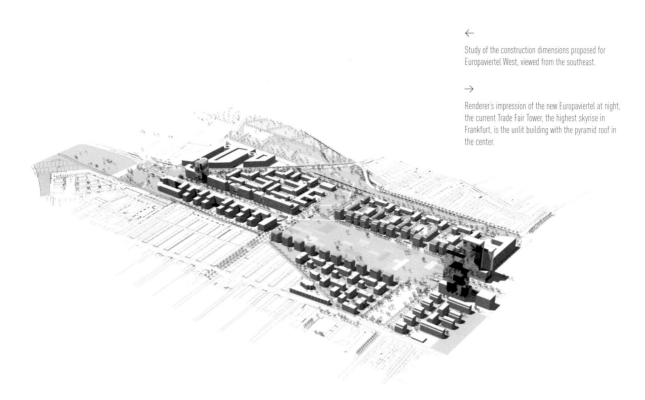

comprehensive master plan for brownfield usage that designed sustainable urban structures while integrating urban planning, transportation planning, ecological and design aspects. This involved acting as mediator, for the City of Munich and the owners of the properties (the German National Railway corporation) had conflicting goals. The result was a planning concept supported by all the fundamental participants that has since been adopted for urban development, so that the respective design competitions have taken place, and construction is now firmly underway.

The reason why new brownfield usage was possible is a typical example for a European city: the former shunting yard in Laim and other national railway, postal, and commercial facilities had become available for redevelopment in downtown Munich, laying the basis for an urban quarter for a residential population of 5,000 and the same number of new jobs in a district deliberately featuring mixed usage. Yet the area required "integration" at various levels, as initial plans for high-rises, for example, met with opposition from residents of adjacent properties and compromises had to be sought that avoided such conflicts. AS&P ended up proposing that the extended site, which will form Munich's future urban edge, emphasize precisely that boundary quality, with the high-rises positioned facing away from the city, while also accentuating the height of the area as a whole and blending with the historical aspects of the far older surrounding area, and interacting with the built structure and visual lines of downtown Munich.

FRANKFURT – HOLBEINVIERTEL AND EUROPAVIERTEL

The new "Holbeinviertel" district is a classic brownfield development. The quarter is being built on the wasteland where the former Southern Freight Railway Station once stood, located in Sachsenhausen, only a stone's throw from the city center, with its massive office infrastructure. The elongated site is located on the elevated area that was once the railway embankment and runs parallel to the tracks to the south of it. AS&P devised an urban plan that envisages pivotal buildings that grow in height from north to south in order to screen the residential properties from the noise of the high-speed passenger trains. The development is geared to the scale of local buildings in the vicinity while simultaneously remaining "airy" by providing an attractive view out over the city northwards. The plan seeks to integrate the new quarter into the existing urban fabric with a dense structure: In addition to residential properties, it features commercial sections and a childcare center. This brownfield development was also seen as an opportunity to ensure that planning also focus strongly on energy efficiency, whereby the entire district was configured to fit an overarching energy concept. Thus, efficient primary energy supplies, for example, via a combined heat/power plant, and apartments that comply with stringent energy-saving standards, guarantee affordable flats. The district features an above-average number of large apartments, with modern blocks angled around green courtyards, stand-alone buildings, and spacious loft buildings.

← ←
Impressions of the Europaviertel once finished,
highlighting the emphasis placed on preserving
"active" public spaces.

←
The residential blocks are designed to emulate the
proportions of the classical buildings in Frankfurt from
the turn of the 20th century.

The new Europaviertel is another instance of shunting-yard brownfield not only providing downtown space for mixed-usage development, but also raising issues on integration.
If the downtown area of just under 100 hectares was to be utilized meaningfully then it
needed to be tied into the existing district on one side and yet set off from the trade fair
complex on the other. AS&P resolved that the best way to achieve this was by giving the
new district a backbone of its own in the form of a central boulevard that, at one end,
offered a linkage to roads leading to the trade fair grounds and out of town while at the
other, locking the quarter into Frankfurt's central road network. The boulevard concept
likewise ensures that the district boasts the sort of open public areas that bring urban life
with them. Facing onto the wide boulevard are large, mixed-use buildings, while the side
streets at right angles again create public zones despite the high-density use of space. The
new district will also be accessed by public transport both overground and underground,
discouraging the use of cars and, for this reason, car parking, something that again means
the potential for open space is used optimally. Albert Speer views the thinking behind the
master plan as follows: "Cities must today guarantee mixed usages coupled with cutting
the distances that need to be traveled. The emerging reality we are seeing is one of urban
density, with areas being recycled once they have lost their function in the economic
cycle, such as industrial wastelands, old rail yards, military facilities, freight areas, ware-
houses, and depots. All European cities have great potential in this regard, and exploiting
such areas means intensifying densities further and moving down the path to a "sustainable" city. At the same time, it spares the surrounding countryside, which can then be
either parkland or farming land."

BROWNFIELD PAST AND PRESENT

Going brownfield offers European cities a twofold opportunity: it gives them a chance to fix planning of the past that went wrong or went bad, and it provides a basis for enhancing resource management. A good example of how this can function is the once infamous high-rise social housing estate in Birmingham's Castle Vale district, which decided to consider itself brownfield and to start again. Of the 34 multi-storey blocks only two have been left standing, giving way to new homes. The London Borough of Tower Hamlets, with its 11,000 inhabitants per square kilometer, saw something similar happen in the stretch of it that lies along the River Thames: with the evolution of London's Docklands, new, dense, mixed-usage properties integrated into the existing city by light railway and subway.

In Europe, considering residential estates from the 1960s as brownfield areas requiring redevelopment is, among other things, a financial issue, as often the municipal authorities are cash-strapped and need to interact with investors. Yet those very authorities often lack financial resources because they fail to recognize where their brownfield resources are assets with a greater value than assumed. A case in point is water. In London, for example, 30 per cent of the water produced is lost as seepage because the infrastructure is decrepit. Such wastage results from not thinking holistically and from not trying to change consumption habits. If water were to cost more, and people were to be persuaded to accept that this is necessary, then the authorities would earn greater revenue with it and have more financing available to repair that infrastructure. This is doubly astonishing if one considers that, owing to distribution patterns, water is a globally scarce resource that should not be squandered. Albert Speer insists that "if we in Europe were not to waste the brownfield resources we have – and we waste them simply because we have too much cash in our pockets – but managed them better, we would do many of the things differently. We would then think about them more beforehand and come up with more resource-sparing solutions. In the financial crisis billions were lost but the system did not collapse. However, an aging system needs to use its resources meaningfully."

REENERGIZING THE AGING – BAKU, THE TRANSITIONAL CITY

Baku is certainly neither a traditional European city of the West, nor a new city in an emerging market. Architecturally and culturally, it sits between East and West, and is a city with a sad history of abuse by oil pollution. Today, it is a city that seeks a new identity for itself. Ever since the world's first ever drilling for oil took place in Baku in 1848 the city's destiny has been closely bound up with oil. The "oil kings" of the day triggered a quite unprecedented architectural revival, hiring architects from Western Europe and Saint Petersburg to build palaces in the southern section of the city, buildings that emulate the turn-of-the-century blocks to be found in many German cities today. In Soviet days, planning often focused, among other things, on broad boulevards – such as the highly popular lakefront promenade in the South. It runs in front of Ichari Shahar, Baku's Old Town, and a UNESCO World Heritage Site since 2000, with its famous Kiz Kalasi, a

30-meter-high stone cylinder, whose exact origins remain unknown, and ornate sandstone facades. This is not a city that arose in a short period of time, but an organic entity that evolved over many years, yet one that was subjected to much abuse at the hands of socialist modernization plans. Nevertheless, in the elegant inner city today one can still feel the vibrancy of an old town such as would be encountered downtown in a European capital. Indeed, any visitor to the Old Town immediately notices that he is in a thriving city. People make great use of public space, and the corniche along the Caspian is frequented by thousands, as are the restaurants there in summer. Some 800,000 inhabitants live along the corniche and in the Old Town, where the bulk of the buildings arose between 1900 and 1920. That said, they are surrounded by the remnants of the on-shore oil fields, and the city is definitely hamstrung by a reputation stemming from a century of pollution accepted as the price for growth and development. The sad ring that surrounds the Old Town is a black ring of polluted soil.

Any brownfield development must concentrate on enhancing the overall quality of life, something already achieved by eliminating toxic waste. Thanks to its corniche, the city enjoys a marvelous location on the Caspian Sea that needs to be exploited to the full, and the basic preconditions for further growth along the waterfront are ideal given the constant wind. Moreover, the city possesses a Mediterranean climate that fosters nature and greenery, something the inhabitants with their traditional ties to the countryside and open space treasure. This contrasts sharply with the semicircle of oily wasteland that forms the hinterland. It thus seemed logical to AS&P to focus attention on augmenting the quality of the zone that comprises the corniche, and as a result not address the wasteland as a first priority. Friedbert Greif says that opting for such a focus would enhance the quality of life within the foreseeable future, while not forgetting that any seaside city has immense potential.

What to do to bring about such a change? Given the fact that perhaps as much as 60 per cent of the city requires modernization, and in the face of dire pollution and dereliction, should Baku perhaps be declared a "failed city" and be abandoned in favor of a new coastal strip? If not, what shape should any attempt be given that seeks to restore it to health? After all, under the socialist regime of the 1970s to 1990s the city was allowed to deteriorate into a catastrophic state. Pollution was simply taken as a given in the oil fields, and the oil and other more toxic waste have eaten their way into the substance of the land. Indeed, for more than 40 years there was no strategy at all for how the city should develop. Any development policies after the Wall came down simply followed what the particular mayor of the day desired and had little to do with coordinated and sustainable development. Trends were in part simply defined arbitrarily by an investor showing interest in a particular lot and then planting a high-rise on it. Greif reports that "those days are thankfully over and fortunately all that got really damaged was the semicircle surrounding the older town. And in the latter there is a lot of what one could term quality urban life. What is needed is a concerted effort to identify which brownfield areas can be

→

Old industrial wasteland in Baku today – testimony to an oil-producing era that has come and gone.

restored and then the political will to commence this gigantic task. Such an approach requires an initial spark, an event that will inspire leaders to push ahead with it, allocate the financing, and be daring."

Greif summarizes the situation when he says that "the old oilfields and brackish oil lakes really are a problem. I once stopped at one and threw in a stone, to be horrified when I saw that it as good as came to rest on the surface and then sank only very slowly. Wherever you go, you can smell the oil, meaning that there is a massive effort required to clean things up. I would say that at least 50 per cent of the total area of the city is brownfield – although perhaps it would be more appropriate to speak of blackfield. There are huge tracts of land in the city that are not used, and I consider that impermissible in a city such as Baku. Developers go greenfield outside the city because it is cheaper, but that will simply fragment the city in the long term. There is abundant brownfield there crying out to be restored and given a new lease of life – for all the constraints imposed by the city's topography. As along the corniche there are various derelict zones that could be chosen for development."

As the city continues to grow there has been considerable pressure on Baku to provide new residential properties and new office space. Yet the planning tends to have been arbitrary, with urban development following investor interests rather than an overall plan, irrespective of whether areas are polluted or not. In such a setting, Michael Denkel suggests, you need to "develop a conscious brownfield strategy, decide where to start with the detoxification and restoration measures, devise a phasing scheme for areas that can be restored faster and are most suitable for residential properties, and then set the priorities accordingly." The initial spark of which Greif spoke arose when Baku approached AS&P in the context of identifying potential areas for a possible Olympic Games complex and was busy doing its homework for a potential Olympic candidacy. AS&P discerned that along the northern edge of the city the pollution was such that it was best to leave the entire zone untouched and abandon it, despite the fact that it lay along the main traffic artery to the airport. Instead, AS&P proposed a clear brownfield focus on the lakeshore, where there are truly attractive locations that will require great effort to restore but the result will be new and interesting additions to the core city. (The fact that an Olympic candidacy served Baku as the spur to change based on brownfield redevelopment is not without precedent. Sydney's old industrial area gave way to the Olympic complex. An even older case in point is that of Munich. Sadly, other cities failed to put the Games to such fruitful use: neither Seoul nor Atlanta benefited as cities from the impetus the Games could have provided.)

↑
Plan of the lakeside corniche as planned by AS&P for Baku. Red marks the areas where new buildings would arise.

→
The corniche as it is today.
In the foreground: large disused areas on the shoreside.

AS&P set out to devise ways of reenergizing Baku as part of the Olympic Games scenario. The proposal they came up with was to bring the metropolis of Baku firmly back to the shore of the Caspian Sea by the modernization of a large polluted brownfield area on the shoreline; they subsequently developed a detailed design for the 83-hectare corniche area, creating a new district for the city. The area had remained neglected for many years and yet the 3.3-kilometer-long corniche zone and the lakefront boulevard behind it was deep enough to offer ideal opportunities for urban and traffic planning and laying the foundations for a modern leisure-time, residential, and business district. The interdisciplinary planning thus included not only new landscaping for the popular park close to the shore but also a series of different architectural projects, a restaurant pier, and the complete rejuvenation of the shorefront flood-protection wall. At the same time, in terms of urban planning, the concept covered the entire Baku Bay area and the immediate back-bay zone, hinging on mixed-usage redevelopment for the adjacent harbor and industrial zones that were in future to be relocated. The overall renewal program gave the historical lakefront promenade a brand new face and furnished Azerbaijan's capital with a new, modern district. In the final instance, the new master plan was not implemented, but it nevertheless highlighted the way such brownfield prioritization could create new space for the city and improve the quality of life.

From the experience gained on the project, Friedbert Greif concludes that "as brownfield restoration/usage, the Baku scenario differs from the Europaviertel only by degree, in this case the degree of pollution, which is far worse in Baku. In fact, it would probably be easier to implement such a project there as the political will is given. After all, the local system of government does not envisage civic participation in policy-making, which actually makes for streamlined processes once a decision has been taken. And where you have such immense brownfield chores to perform, that would be beneficial. But that is not to forget that in most European cities probably about 20 per cent of the total surface area is likewise brownfield."

There is a subtext to the Baku brownfield project. In many instances, investors and legislation get in the way of modernization and restoration. Investors invariably seek an easy return on their capital and are not necessarily interested in upgrading existing residences – and politicians tend to shy away from the billion-dollar commitments that would

Model of Baku corniche, with the city developed down
to the waterside, increasing the overall quality of life.

Simulation of how the city might look at night, with
the piers used, as in Britain, for entertainment.

often be necessary to reenergize brownfield areas or to modernize old buildings in European cities. Yet both activities would do much to reduce the eco-footprint each of those cities requires – and the specific use of brownfield zones to create the leisure-time facilities the cities still lack would again reduce the number of cars traveling out of cities at the weekend. It is a question of subsidies and financial prioritization. And that is the crunch issue to all talk of sustainable cities: sustainable development costs money. And subsidies tend to be the product not of coordinated master planning at an intergovernmental level but rather of piecemeal programs, often each with a different approach or intention. The same is true of various forms of tax relief intended to help the economy but which in their final effect curb sustainability. Albert Speer submits that in this regard the European Union is completely inconsistent. It still permits subsidies for motorized commuters on a scale that, in Germany, is equivalent to the costs of heating their homes instead of pushing through legislation designed to create more concentrated cities offering better facilities – by exploiting the brownfield potential.

HISTORY AND THE FUTURE

Directly after coming second in the competition for Ludwigshafen, Albert Speer was approached by the premier local industrial corporation to design a new district for its workers – a residential estate called the Pfingstweide that was tantamount to a satellite town. He could not initially decide how to achieve the required residential concentration in any meaningful way, and it was only after a visit to London and seeing multi-storey residential properties there that he came up with the idea of ignoring the brief as regards the number of buildings, but obeying it in terms of the number of residences. Unlike one of the other projects of the day, the Birkenheide satellite town outside Karlsruhe, Germany, the project was realized. Today, Speer is not convinced that such estates are a good thing, as greenfield satellite towns have no place in European urban planning today. In retrospect, what he considers the greatest benefit of the projects was that they showed that the planner's imagination can be inspired not by a piece of paper, but by what is to be seen elsewhere. "Going local requires time in this respect." And he adds with a chuckle: "I always told my students if they were not dreaming of the tasks I set them then they were not taking the work seriously enough."

"Planners must have an acute awareness of the place in history of what they do, as every choice they make is likely to impact much further down the line. Any European city planner who does not try to concentrate land use in inner cities by going brownfield will suffer 30 years down the road," suggests Michael Denkel. Because then there will have been sprawl instead and rising transportation costs will render travel between the outside and the inside improbable. After all, the age of the satellite towns is over, and should have been declared over after the end of the first oil crisis of the 1970s. "The satellite city was a response to a rising population, whereas planners today need to contend with the issues associated with an aging population!"

The line of European urban history runs from the satellite cities of the 1960s, when European populations were still growing, to the polycentric concentration of today and tomorrow, the integration of the erstwhile suburbs and satellites to form clusters. And this polycentric concentration, which will be the focus of Chapter X, is also an area in which brownfield restoration plays a crucial part – an interesting metropolis waiting for this to happen being, for example, Istanbul, a city that, like Baku, breasts two architectural cultures and a history spanning many centuries.

1   James Lovelock, Gaia. A New Look at Life on Earth, (OUP: Oxford, 1979),
    p. 10
2   Ibid., p. 130
3   In September 2006, the Ministry of Culture and Tourism commissioned an
    international design team consisting of AS&P in collaboration with Götte
    Landscape Architects, Dorsch Consult und Kardorff Ingenieure, to compile
    such the plan.

III

DECREASE ENERGY,
MINIMIZE TECHNOLOGY

"The most striking thing about modern industry is that it requires so much and accomplishes so little. Modern industry seems to be inefficient to a degree that surpasses one's ordinary powers of imagination. Its inefficiency therefore remains unnoticed." Ernst Schumacher [1]

Do we really need air-conditioning in a Central European city, even when it gets really hot? The board members gathered round the conference table at AS&P start debating the issue. Should we not simply open the windows and put up with a little sweat on our brows or stains on our shirts? How to convince a client of a low-tech solution if A/C is a status symbol? The background to the issue is, of course, how to find a meaningful energy balance in cities in emerging market economies or the Third World.

And in the industrialized world, in the West? Here, people clamor not only for more individual space but also for more heated space. The standard of comfort people expect has rocketed in recent years. Hardly surprisingly, for all the growth of the BRIC industries, it is the Western industrial nations that still consume by far the most energy and emit the most climate-killing CO_2. Sir Nicolas Stern calculated that worldwide CO_2 emissions would have to be halved by the year 2050 from their 2007 level in order to halt climate change. For Europe alone that would mean reducing levels by 80 per cent – an ambitious, not to say impossible, target and obviously one that will be reached only by massive and maximum effort by everyone. And what better way to proceed than to start where we blow the most CO_2 into the atmosphere, namely, buildings, and to scale back facilities technology, heating and cooling systems. The challenge is, of course, to do so without significantly impairing the quality of life.

The goal of really slashing CO_2 output is one Europeans will achieve only if the governments at both the national and supranational levels act in a concerted and interdisciplinary fashion. If things just get left to individual departments then the going will be tough indeed. After all, the financial crisis has shown that when it comes to allocating billions to save their financial systems, governments in democratic countries can act with the resolute determination falsely associated only with "strong men." One would think the same should be possible to save their environments.

The situation is very different in the Third World and in the BRIC countries. There, acute technological advances are necessary if they are to cope with the dual challenge of emission-reduction and ongoing growth. It is worth remembering here that more than 40 per cent of all Indians do not have electricity in their homes – and the energy source of choice to fuel new power stations is coal, which is readily available locally, but which, if fired in power stations without state-of-the-art combined cycle systems for combusting the flue gas, becomes the single largest CO_2 emitter imaginable – if we discount the holy cows, that is. Such countries will not, of their own volition and using only local technology, ever be able to meet the CO_2 goal.

There is agreement worldwide that we need to tread such a path into "green"-driven economies, as the threat of climate change and the ever-closing oil peak mean there is no alternative. And that action must be swift. In actual fact, planners and architects in the developed world can already deploy a veritable array of technical, energy-efficient solutions that would help here. Almost all the trades involved in construction already address the issues of energy efficiency and today the market offers the appropriate insulation materials, control systems, and energy alternatives required at ever falling costs. The goal here must be what Albert Speer as early as the 1980s called the "intelligent building," that is, a building that saves resources in all areas, a building that is economical and will stand

THE IMPERATIVE: CUT CO_2 EMISSIONS   The European Union has, in the run-up to the UN Climate Summit in Copenhagen in 2009, formulated the goal that needs to be met. To ensure that the temperature does not increase by more than 2°C global emissions must peak at the latest in 2020 and then be cut back by 2050 to a level that is at least 50 per cent below the figure for 1990. This calls for action in both the industrialized nations and in the developing countries.

The industrialized nations must blaze the trail and by 2020 must have throttled back their emissions to 30 per cent of the volume of 1990. The EU has set a good example by committing to reduce its emissions by 30 per cent if other industrialized nations sign up to follow suit. And it has already acted, initiating measures to reduce its emission levels by 20 per cent. The proposal hinges on special parameters designed to make certain that all countries have to meet goals that entail comparable effort and that no one country or set of countries is overly disadvantaged. All OECD countries, EU member countries, countries seeking accession to the EU, and potential future members are expected to set themselves emission goals.

With the exception of the very impoverished countries, the scheme envisages the developing countries cutting emissions by 2020 by 15–30 per cent of the volume that would be emitted if the efforts were not made, e.g., by swiftly acting to curb emissions caused by felling of the rain forest. The EU plan foresees these countries committing to put strategies in place by 2011 to foster low-CO_2 development in a manner that includes all the decisive sectors that impact on the climate. These strategies will then be assessed by a new international mechanism and the proposed measures then moved forward by suitable external support.

Independent estimates suggest that additional investments of some EUR 175 billion need to be committed worldwide each year through 2020 if emissions are to be effectively reduced. More than half of this sum will be required by and in the developing countries. (source: European Commission, January 29, 2009)

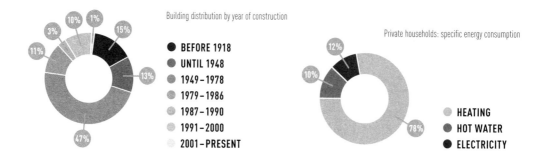

Building distribution by year of construction

- BEFORE 1918
- UNTIL 1948
- 1949 – 1978
- 1979 – 1986
- 1987 – 1990
- 1991 – 2000
- 2001 – PRESENT

Private households: specific energy consumption

- HEATING
- HOT WATER
- ELECTRICITY

the test of time, is flexible and eco-conscious as regards how it responds to the external climate, the weather, light seasons, changing user needs, media, and technologies.

Buildings, be they new or old, offer the West the greatest potential for saving energy inputs – and, for this reason, outputs, too. Far more so than car traffic. In Germany, for example, 80 per cent of residential dwellings were built before 1990 and are therefore not energy-efficient. On average, existing buildings require three times as much heating energy than do new dwellings,[2] and about ten times as much heating energy than energy-optimized buildings need. Not to mention that some 88 per cent of a dwelling's overall energy consumption goes into providing heating and warm water.

In total, buildings account for more than 30 per cent of energy consumption, for 33 per cent of emissions, and 40 per cent of the waste. It was only logical for the IPCC to state in its 2007 report that more efficient technologies could reduce CO_2 emissions from houses by up to 40 per cent by 2030. In fact, some quarters suggest that private dwellings could essentially become miniature decentral power plants that not only save energy, but on balance generate it.

So the crunch question is: When is a building sustainable? Without doubt, energy consumption is a decisive parameter when searching for an answer. In general, "green buildings," so the Organization for Economic Cooperation and Development suggests, impact only minimally on the buildings in their vicinity and on nature. The OECD's definition of sustainability does not limit itself to energy aspects.[3] Just as relevant are water consumption, waste production, air emissions, and land use, not to mention comfort and a mixture of social strata among the inhabitants.

In light of global warming, ever scarcer resources, and the increasing strain that exhausts and waste place on our environment, such an ambitious definition and, by extension, equally ambitious goals are absolutely imperative. In this context, the German Sustainable Building Council (DGNB) has issued a "Triple Zero" objective: "Zero Energy" means houses should not require more energy for their operation than they themselves generate through operation; "Zero Emissions" stipulates that houses should not produce toxic emissions of any kind; "Zero Waste" would make it possible to completely recycle the building without any residue requiring disposal. In recent years, various other certification systems have sprung up worldwide.

CERTIFICATION SYSTEMS Alongside support programs and subsidies, certification systems also provide an incentive to the extent that sustainability is an image booster and, as such, a quantifiable marketing factor and economic argument. Certification systems serve mainly as a way of evaluating and controlling sustainability as applied. Given that, in the case of buildings, sustainability can be quantified and thus tangibly measured, most of the evaluation systems focus on the built environment. The valuation systems that are brought to bear as regards urban planning tend, instead, to have only the status of underpinning recommendations or ascertaining whether sustainable concepts have been firmly taken into consideration and implemented at the level of local and municipal authorities. While adherence to generally applicable levels can be enforced with respect to buildings, the criteria in the field of urban design need to be adjusted regularly or repeatedly to the respective local situation. Alongside the independent certification systems for buildings (such as LEED) and for cities (such as EEA) there are rating systems devised specifically for and by the cities themselves (such as those deployed by Hafencity Hamburg or by Zurich).

Britain's Building Research Establishment Assessment Method (BREEAM) provides a certification system for evaluating buildings. As the name suggests, it was developed by the Building Research Establishment, a former government organization. The BREEAM methodology provides planning teams with a yardstick for their design and management processes. BREEAM defines and measures the building's sustainable performance in line with criteria relating to management, health and comfort, energy efficiency and eco-impact, as well as the resources the building consumes and the space it requires. To date, about 55,000 buildings worldwide have been awarded certification under the scheme.

CASBEE (Comprehensive Assessment System for Building Environmental Efficiency) is a self-assessment system that originated in Japan. It is awarded by JCBC and can be applied to any stage in a building's life cycle. The assessment is tailored to the particular project and focuses specifically on the environmental efficiency, meaning its energy efficiency, ecological quality, and overall ecological impact.

France's HQE methodology (Haute qualité environnementale) was developed by the association of the same name in 1997 and concentrates on all phases in a building's life – individually (initial contract, design, construction). The management system is evaluated during planning, as is the building's subsequent sustainable properties. Seven environmental and seven use-specific aspects are brought to bear, covering the overall ecology of the design, the structure's energy efficiency, and the degree to which user comfort is eco-friendly. To date, some 40 projects have been certified, the majority of them private rather than public buildings.

The LEED system (Leadership in Energy and Environmental Design) was launched back in 2000 by the US Green Building Council. The intention was to provide a rating system for the sustainability of buildings that took its cue from BREEAM. LEED is a voluntary national standard that obtains throughout the United States and has, since its inception, achieved international status, too. LEED functions as a design guideline for planners, as benchmarking, and as a certificate awarded, documenting and highlighting sustainability through each phase in a building's life cycle. The assessment system comprises nine minimum conditions over six different categories and is awarded in silver, gold, and platinum. As of early 2009, more than 1,400 projects have been registered as conforming to the LEED standard, and many of them make use of the certificate for image and marketing purposes.

In Germany, a relative newcomer to the rating systems is the one put forward by the DGNB, developed together with the German Federal Ministry for Transport, Building, and Urban Development. First inaugurated in 2009, the rating system is structured in line with building life-cycle criteria. The certificate is intended as a communications instrument for investors and property owners alike, documenting their commitment to sustainability. Alongside ecological criteria, the system attempts to place greater emphasis on economic and social factors. Moreover, technical criteria, the planning process, the building's use, and factors relating to its location are all assessed. These criteria are based on the

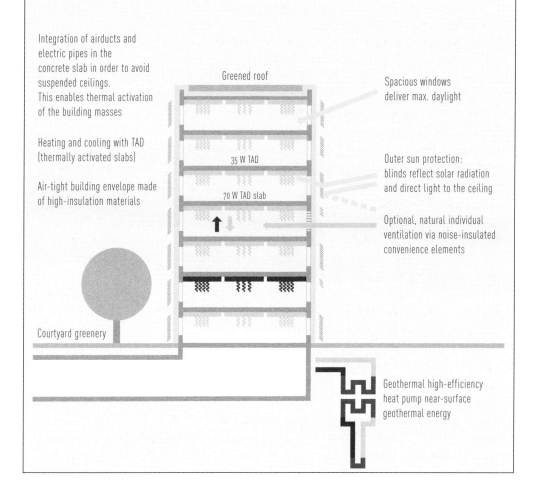

Integration of airducts and electric pipes in the concrete slab in order to avoid suspended ceilings. This enables thermal activation of the building masses

Heating and cooling with TAD (thermally activated slabs)

Air-tight building envelope made of high-insulation materials

Greened roof

35 W TAD

70 W TAD slab

Courtyard greenery

Spacious windows deliver max. daylight

Outer sun protection: blinds reflect solar radiation and direct light to the ceiling

Optional, natural individual ventilation via noise-insulated convenience elements

Geothermal high-efficiency heat pump near-surface geothermal energy

findings of a committee on sustainable construction initiated by the ministry to ensure in-depth thinking on the subject.

Moreover, the system is unique in that it takes into account current work to establish standards covering sustainability and quality certification for construction products as well as seals of approval for eco-friendly construction work based on the key international norm. The association is endeavoring to translate all the criteria into quantifiable requirements in order to provide a system that objectively represents building quality. The certifiers identify six areas of relevance to assessing a building's quality:

ECOLOGY: sparing resources and protecting the natural environment

ECONOMICS: life cycle costs (transparency and control)

SOCIO-CULTURAL AND FUNCTIONAL ASPECTS: user comfort, health, pleasant ambience, ventilation with fresh air, use of daylight, acoustic comfort

TECHNOLOGY: structural status (ease of cleaning, maintenance, and repair; outer skin's qualities in terms of building physics)

PROCESSES: concept and realization, integrated planning (inclusion of experts and the various authorities)

LOCATION: positive impacts on the environment and on society (e.g., by connecting to public transportation, recycling brownfield areas, etc.)

Today, most developers, investors, urban planners, and architects are convinced that it is imperative to bring intelligent methodologies and efficient technologies to bear in urban planning in order to save energy – and that the potential residents are just as important in the planning process. However, in certain cases, specifically if the financing is simply not available, more cost-effective alternatives need to be found. Here, we should remember that high-tech essentially entails high-energy inputs, for example, that required to manufacture insulating materials. After all, a solar cell still needs to run for several years to recoup the energy that was gobbled up making it – hardly a win-win equation. Only very few developers in the emerging markets of East Europe or the Third World can afford to invest in the relevant high-tech to create a superior energy-efficient structure. Urban theorist Mike Davis, for example, does not feel that the foundations for an eco-friendly city are necessarily a matter of especially ecological construction or innovative technologies. In fact, in a recent interview he even suggested that what really counts is "to accord general prosperity priority over personal wealth. In most cities, whether in rich or in poor countries, the potential eco-efficiency that arises from dense settlement tends to get completely ignored. Cities offer immense ecological potentials that have, to date, either not been noticed or left unused. Our planet would definitely able to provide a home for all its inhabitants if we were only prepared to structure society on a democratic notion of community and not around individual, private consumption. General prosperity – such as would be manifested by large city parks, museums with free entrance, libraries, and extensive opportunities for interpersonal interaction – now all of that is a real alternative to a high standard of living on the basis of a materialist, carnevalesque focus on entertainment. ... The egalitarian aspects of urban life provide the prime sociological and physical prerequisites to save resources and reduce CO_2 emissions."[4]

PASSIVHAUSSTANDARD – THE GERMAN STANDARD FOR LOW-ENERGY HOMES

In recent years, the so-called PASSIVHAUSSTANDARD has repeatedly been described as the measure of all things. The standard is not a registered trademark in any sense but does derive from certification that was first developed by Darmstadt-based physicist Wolfgang Feist. A "passive" or low-energy home reduces heating-energy inputs by more than 80 per cent compared with the standard stipulated by German law at present. Overall heating-energy requirements are less than 15 kWh/m²a (kilowatt hours per square meter and per annum), which means that an apartment of 100 square meters that conforms to the standard faces a heating bill of merely 10–20 Euro per month. This immense energy saving is achieved primarily by opting for especially energy-efficient structural components, good insulation, and ingenious ventilation systems. Fresh air flows in one channel while old air is extracted by another, whereby blinds separate the two channels and function as an energy exchanger – the blinds warm up when in contact with extracted air, and cool down when exposed to an inflow of air from outside – a time-tested principle. Like houses with thick clay walls and an indoor fountain in the hot regions of Syria, which cool the outside air "passively," a low-energy house that meets the PASSIVHAUSSTANDARD sources its heating needs "passively," drawing on the heat of the sun outside and the heat radiated by human bodies, household appliances, and lighting inside the house. AS&P is convinced that this standard sets the course for the future – such houses may not be completely sustainable in the sense that the materials from which they are built involve energy inputs, but they are low-energy consumers and thus semi-sustainable.

A variety of parameters need to be considered when designing such homes: good heat insulation and compactness, a north/south alignment, avoiding shadow and shade, windows with triple glazing and inert gas (argon or krypton) between the panes, an air-tight edifice, a structure that avoids heat bridges, mechanical ventilation using a waste-heat recovery system.

WHAT IS COMPACTNESS? Compactness is defined in terms of the A/V RATIO, whereby A = surface, V= volume. In other words, the ratio between the building's outer skin and the heated volume it embraces (compactness). A favorable A/V ratio (i.e., a compact structure) significantly reduces the overall heating-energy requirement and is thus a crucial factor architects should heed when designing buildings for cooler climatic zones.

These parameters must be adhered to almost fully if the final result is to be a low-energy house. Craftsmen, builders, and site managers need to be especially careful; an outside wall made of stone, for example, has to be vapor-proof, which means the plasterer must ensure that the coating of plaster runs all the way down to the floor of the building's carcass and does not, as in other dwellings, end where the finished floor will meet the wall. Only in this way will the building be air-tight and therefore perform adequately. The PASSIVHAUSSTANDARD sets very narrow limits of tolerance, otherwise the building will not meet the requisite norms. It is hard to offset the negative impact of construction or design errors, such as the wrong insulation under a floor slab, after the event. Here, retrofitting would actually involve rebuilding.

CAMPO – FRANKFURT / MAIN

Bornheim, one of Frankfurt's old inner city districts, features road after road of old tenement blocks dating back to about 1900. Until recently, a streetcar depot stood in the midst of one such cluster. Today, the area has been completely transformed, replaced by eleven buildings containing a total of 140 apartments, and the brick-and-iron hall now contains not trams but a supermarket (whose waste heat is used to warm the surrounding built environment). AS&P was commissioned by Frankfurter ABG Holding to handle the planning for the new sub-district, which was to be called CAMPO. All the apartment buildings were deliberately designed to meet the PASSIVHAUSSTANDARD. Sustainable architecture – but not such that this became obtrusive in the building's appearance. Indeed, looking at the buildings today, the uninitiated are unlikely to guess that these apartment blocks at the very center of the city have been built fully to the PASSIVHAUSSTANDARD. The entire complex has been designed to blend in with the lines of the surrounding century-old buildings and thus preserve the district's structure. There are new versions of the curb roofs so typical of the early 1920s, the structure of each edifice also takes its cue from the historical antecedents, and there is a clinker-brick base. "It is safe to say that in the form of this project," comments Martin Teigeler, one of the AS&P architects, "we have realized an energy-efficiency system that is about as complex as you can get today."

In order to make CAMPO conform to the PASSIVHAUSSTANDARD, the architects made use of timber frames as these have proven to be an especially sustainable structure. As a result, all the load-bearing structures are located on the inside, with the sole exception of the ends of the buildings. The buildings thus feature a cross-wall construction similar to that used for tankers, which means that large sections of the facade have no load-bearing role at all. Thus liberated, they can consist almost entirely of heat-insulation panels. Together, the timber frame structures and the compound heat-insulation system generate outstanding wall insulation in the case of the facades – despite the fact that they are comparatively slender, with thicknesses ranging from 35 to 45 cm.

Here, perfect insulation spells very thin walls, which in turn allows maximized living space and, by extension, cost-effective apartments – but extremely elaborate planning. After all, five or six-storey apartment blocks based on timber frames are not really per-

missible given the fire-protection regulations. And noise protection would actually call for higher-mass outer walls, which would impair their thermal conductivity. Not to mention that noise protection does not go hand in hand with highly energy-efficient windows since noise-proof windows come with hefty window panes, whereas the right windows from the energy-saving point of view are anything but bulky.

The architects who handled the planning were faced with many such conundrums. "At the beginning of the planning phase we found ourselves working with Swiss specialists, who were of the opinion a low-energy house could be built simply by using a standard blueprint," Gerhard Brand AS&P managing partner, recalls. "And the blueprint did not foresee any windows to the north, as low-energy dwellings purportedly open only to the south. I well remember the meeting where they took one look at the maps and ground plans and declared the entire zone unsuitable for low-energy building and concluded that the project was not feasible." But the CAMPO buildings today, with their large French windows opening to the north, are far from counterfactual, in fact they are very real.

Another headache for the planners was the east/west alignment of the CAMPO footprint, as it brought with it the danger of one building casting a shadow over its neighbor, which would allow neither the inhabitants to enjoy the sunlight, nor the buildings to profit from this natural heating source. Yet the solution found boasts balconies, not to mention loggias – something theorists suggest flies in the face of low-energy edifices. The solution found was to vary wall thicknesses as well as window and balcony dimensions depending on the exact position, and in this way the size compensated for the lack of direct light.

Needless to say, this flexibility spawns higher investment costs, something that will potentially deter developers or investors from going down the low-energy path, especially in times when credit lines are collapsing. That said, it is abundantly clear today

The dining room in an apartment in one of the new "passivhausstandard" Campo buildings

View from the street of a Campo building. The structure of the facade ensures it blends with older buildings.

that "if a developer opts for real estate that is not in an absolutely prime location, and simply does the minimum to meet low-energy norms, then, in Germany at least, he will find himself almost unable to market it," suggests Martin Teigeler of AS&P. This is where the desire for a "seal of approval for sustainability" on the part of prospective owners of homes is already widespread – and it is a perception that investors will have to square up to, particularly as markets tighten. While the falling price of oil has made renewables less of an economic proposition in the short term, the financial crisis forces property developers to go green. When commissioning CAMPO, ABG Holding evidently realized full well that if they were to be able to offer long-term occupancy with minimized energy consumption levels and a greater use of durable, high-grade materials, this would attract buyers. After all, owners occupying their own apartments or owners opting to rent out the property will both benefit from the fact that in a low-energy house the operating costs – that hidden rent on top of the actual rent – are far lower, a long-term benefit that far outweighs short-term gains.

CAMPO is a prime example of how a holistic approach bears fruit, especially if applied from the word go. There is no urban design that can be written in stone by an architect alone. What counts is an interdisciplinary methodology, precisely if the goal is energy efficiency, and that issue has to be factored into the equation from the outset, if possible, as in the case of CAMPO, before the first ground plans have even be drawn. And this way of planning naturally impacts on the design itself: gone are the days when a beautiful house was simply designed and the specialists for particular fields then did the detailed work. CAMPO shows how the urban planners, the architects, and the specialist engineers worked together to make certain the different disciplines interacted to create an energy-efficient "product." Seen in this light, there can be no sustainable city without sustainable buildings – and vice versa. The real art is to ensure that both are of a high standard and enhance the quality of life in the city. While the CAMPO buildings would probably look very similar even if they had not been designed to meet the PASSIVHAUSSTANDARD, they probably look even better if one remembers that they do conform to it. Indeed, they show that technology and aesthetics need not be mutually contradictory in a low- or even zero-energy future.

THE LIMITS   While the PASSIVHAUSSTANDARD may be meaningful in certain situations, it is by no means a one-size-fits-all solution. For larger housing projects it is often worth first studying the energy side to the real estate and establishing whether the standard is the most cost-effective tool that can be applied, or whether other norms may not be of greater validity. After all, as we have seen, there are numerous possible ways of gauging the energy- and the eco-impact of a given building. Moreover, there are at present so many technological advances being made in the field of energy provisioning that what may be a USP for a house today may be old hat the day after tomorrow.

The crucial thing, therefore, is to get the energy analysis right. Just as the layout of a city, for example, is critical for how efficiently it can be accessed, so, too, the first category to focus on is the building's physical shape: whether it is compact or a long block. It makes a great difference whether the structure is one deep volume or consists of several stand-alones, as the ratio of outer skin to built volume deteriorates dramatically in the latter. Shade is another category, as the alignment of buildings to one another and the presence of large trees all alter the parameters. Nature is pitiless in this regard: a building facing south quite simply forfeits its energy edge if it stands in the shade of another structure. And if it also has an underground car park that is not sealed thermally from the floors above, then the building really is disadvantaged. Technical solutions can be found to most structural difficulties other than location, but each answer comes with a price tag, and the more elaborate the answer, the higher the cost. No city is sustainable if the buildings that make it a city are too expensive for the average citizen to afford.

A key category that has to be decided is whether the building will be judged on its primary energy requirement or not. The PASSIVHAUSSTANDARD, for example, focuses exclusively on the energy requirement for heating, which is to ignore the primary energy inputs required for warm water and household electricity. There is some justification for this, as there is no readily apparent yardstick for the latter quantity, which will depend, for example, on usage in each apartment in a block. Obviously, legislators cannot stipulate how many PCs a household has – it is difficult enough to ensure that supermarket freezers be fitted with doors to counter the needless waste of energy that occurs by having to cool open freezers.

One way to get round the problem is to treat primary energy consumption in terms of a CO_2 equivalent – and then set an upper ceiling. This may seem great at the macro-level of what a society wishes as an overall emission target, but at the micro-level of the potential users of the dwelling it is less apposite. It simply does not tell them what the use of the house is going to cost them, which the *passivhausstandard* does, allowing the subsequent discussion of how the kilowatts get used, namely, by what heating medium. If the price per square meter is low enough, then there is little point in continuing to charge extra for heating in rented premises, and a simple utility flat rate can come into play – the costs of measuring what each radiator uses will fairly quickly exceed the actual cost of the energy input for the heating.

A streak of pragmatism is needed in all these computations. Careful calculations often show that the cost of upgrading a building to meet such a norm as the PASSIVHAUSSTANDARD can swiftly exceed the energy savings made:

AS&P explored an apartment block in Frankfurt with total living space of just short of 7,000 square meters. The heating-energy consumption was about 6 per cent above that set for a low-energy house, and trimming that value would be disproportionate to the savings achieved. The equation changes only if society decides that any excess energy is too much – and also takes the energy required for the conversion work into account. "If you want to get energy-consumption standards widely accepted," claims Martin Teigeler, "then you will need some leeway in the figures you chose, as there is no point in making people's houses impossibly expensive for them. Put differently, it is better if a lot of developers build houses that use 20 kwh/m²a of energy than a very few who opt for structures of only 15 kwh/m²a." Quite simply, what may be ideologically sound or politically correct at the general level may be completely impractical at the particular level. Take an expensive downtown location: the thick walls there, the result extra insulation, would simply reduce the gross floor area and spell a loss for investors – so here, too, society is challenged to strike the right balance.

APPLYING THE INSIGHTS – THE VICTORIA TOWER, MANNHEIM, GERMANY

The priority, therefore, if at all possible, is to harmonize different objectives. It was with this in mind that AS&P designed the office high-rise for the Victoria insurance company next to Mannheim's main railway station back in 2001. The tower unites two superlatives: first, at just short of 100 meters high, it is the tallest building in Mannheim and thus a landmark; and secondly, though not apparent to the eye, it was the fastest built skyscraper of its size. In March 1999, the developer started scouting for a suitable location, and only two years later the offices were occupied. The glass-covered tower with its diamond footprint rises up from the green of Mannheim's historical Schlossgarten and, depending on the angle, is either a broad block or a slender structure. The design reflects urban design criteria, as the unusual footprint responds to the axis of the railway station forecourt and the main road in the Lindenhof district. The plinth blends with the glazing of the projecting staircases in the two acutely-angled corners and on the top floor to form a single plane. The dual-skin glass facade hung in front of the tight office grid thus resembles one huge panel with a light frame that is illuminated by night.

↑
The Victoria high-rise in Mannheim – the stairwells
and double skin both clearly visible.

The Victoria Tower concept, developed by AS&P together with engineering experts from the University of Karlsruhe, delivers maximum energy efficiency. There was a clear reason for this. The Victoria company wished to catch the headlines with a reference high-rise offering prime office premises that were sustainable, and that meant, as Albert Speer recollects, "our making very sure the operating costs did not exceed 2.5 euros per square meter, half the customary figure. In designing it we inadvertently set ourselves a tough standard." Here, economic and ecological reasons melded, and the concept eschewed mechanical ventilation or air-conditioning. How? By deploying a dual facade with sun protection on the outside and natural ventilation on all floors – which not only provides noise protection but also prevents the building from cooling down too much at night.

ADVANCING THE CONCEPT –
FROM SHANGHAI TO FRANKFURT

In China, 8 is a lucky number, so 88 must be twice as lucky – and that is the height of the two office towers that went turnkey in Shanghai in 2004. Appropriately, since they set an example that all of China could follow, advancing the concept devised for the Victoria Tower. The Chinese developers visited Mannheim after the 2001 competition and were thoroughly convinced by just how much energy could be saved. They were also determined to demonstrate in the new district of Pudong that a high-rise could slash energy bills and avoid CO_2 emissions, a quite revolutionary approach for local Chinese society at the time. Chinese skyscrapers tended to be built the "classical" way – simple glazing, green or black toned glass, but definitely glass – and however hard the designers tried, what they built were kettles in which the temperature rose with the sun. "And not only do you then need a massive number of split air-conditioning units, you also need artificial light all the time, because the glass is so dark," Martin Teigeler reports. Both of which spell one thing: a hefty eco-footprint in the form of an electricity bill potential as high as the building.

The twin towers of the Administration Center developed for the Zhang Jian Hi-Tech Park mark a radical departure from all this. Following the Mannheim example, a dual-skin facade is deployed with solar protection on the outer skin, dispensing with the need for glass to be toned down dramatically and allowing sunlight to suffuse the rooms behind. Moreover – and this was absolutely trailblazing for China at the time – thanks to the second skin behind, the windows can simply be opened to ventilate the rooms and cool them naturally, something that can be done eight months out of every year in Shanghai.

For the Zhang Jian Hi-Tech Park, AS&P minimized the use of mechanical components while at the same time increasing the enclosed air space. "Normally, the Chinese build rooms that are 4.20 meters high," says Peter Kern at the company's Shanghai office, "and then insert a suspended ceiling to create a room height of 2.60 meters. The requisite technology is then inserted in-between." And a lot of space gets wasted. AS&P bundled the equipment and ducts in visible ring elements, and the rooms thus produced are 3.80 meters floor-to-ceiling, seem far more spacious than the usual rooms, and are filled with air and light.

There were many other ideas on how to trim energy-consumption levels, but the mood in Shanghai was quite simply not ready for those ideas back then. A classic example is thermally active ceilings that provide both heating and cooling – AS&P made use of the principle for the offices and apartments in the "Baseler Arkaden" high-rise at Baseler Platz in Frankfurt/Main. The water pipes are located in the ceilings so that the entire ceiling acts as a thermal sump that cools or heats the building as the case may be. The system resembles that of under-floor heating: the greater the surface area used for heating or cooling, the lower the energy inputs to increase or decrease the heat. With a conventional radiator on the wall, water is piped in at 70°C and it flows out again once it has cooled by 15 degrees. Under-floor heating for a large surface area requires water that is warmed to 40°C – which flows back into the heating system after it has dropped by ten degrees. The larger you make the surface area, the smaller the difference between input and output temperatures, and as it falls, so does the energy required.

The building at Baseler Platz relies on thermally active ceilings to cool the premises in summer and heat them in winter. In addition, a considerable portion of the energy requirement is sourced from groundwater by a geothermal pump: a borehole was drilled beneath the building to a depth of 80 meters. The groundwater there is already 17°C, and this water is pumped into the ceilings to provide heating and cooling.

Although the twin office towers in Shanghai feature neither a thermally active nor a geothermal system, they have still inspired the local population. Since going turnkey, they have been a constant magnet, attracting visitors from far and wide. The real kickoff back then was not the technology itself, but an image problem that worked in our favor," recollects Martin Teigeler. "There was an outbreak of SARS, or avian flu, and someone in the press started the rumor that it spread via the air-conditioning system. That was a real boon in disguise." Suddenly, people in Shanghai realized that there was a healthy low-tech alternative – and turned off their split units and opted for natural cross ventilation instead. Not only did the climate in the buildings benefit, but so did the world.

1   E.F. Schumacher, Small is Beautiful, (Vintage, London, 1993), p. 95
2   Assumption based on the German Federal Energy Saving Decree (EnEV),
     which is an integral part of construction law in Germany today. The ENEV
     sets down technical construction standards developers must meet in order
     to guarantee efficient operating energy-consumption levels by the parti-
     cular building or construction project. The decree applies to apartment and
     office blocks as well as to some commercial and industrial premises and
     sets an example other countries could follow.
3   "Environmentally sustainable buildings: Challenges and policies," OECD,
     2003
4   Quoted from Süddeutsche Zeitung (Dec. 20-1, 2009), "Wer baut uns jetzt
     die Arche?"

IV

KEEP SPACE OPEN

"In the freedom of nature we sometimes allow ourselves liberties we would shy away from in the confines of a city." Josef H. Reichholf[1]

Back in about 250 BC, a Chinese sage, a proto-urban planner, insisted that no city should be permitted in the nascent Empire that did not have sufficient land around it to ensure its inhabitants could be fed. Albert Speer comments that this Chinese predecessor's stipulation still applies if cities today are to be sustainable. In other words, there can be no sustainable city without an agricultural base. Just as there can be no sustainable urbanization without an effective agro-industry. Equally, a city can be sustainable only if it is sparing in its use of space. Not that this need automatically mean that the city misuses land, while the countryside uses it appropriately. In most cities in Germany, less than 50 per cent of the ground is paved or built over, while in the countryside more than 50 per cent of land is consumed for one use alone: agriculture. As a result, in many countries in Europe dense urban spaces are more of a diverse natural habitat than is the countryside.[2] And to keep things this way, urban planners must not only promulgate biodiversity but also prioritize a quality built/unbuilt environment. Put differently, they must try to offer a combination of improved air, sufficient space for recreation, leisure and sport, and a conscious focus on the environment. The sustainable city must therefore include large, coherent, open, unpaved spaces (such as areas of water to prevent heat islands) and interlink these, as they are imperative for our climate and foster biodiversity, while also providing attractive recreational spaces that help to reduce leisure-time mobility. All in all, sustainable planning must therefore always seek to bond the city and its surroundings, and link spaces within the city quarters and districts.

INCREASING DENSITY   How can an ever growing number of people live in due dignity in an area whose size remains constant? The megacities in the developing world are anything but magnetic if judged by Western standards, yet there remains a steady influx of those seeking their fortune in these cities, cities that are by no means only in China or India, but also in Latin America and Africa, where urbanization is just as massive a trend. This is not a problem as long as the cities themselves can expand in spatial terms. A good example is Abuja, the new capital of Nigeria, which has gone from zero to about 6 million in only 30 years, whereas the original plan for the city envisaged a maximum population of only half that number. Space is, however, increasingly becoming a serious problem. Take the example of India's capital, New Delhi. In the master plan devised by the Delhi Development Authority (NCTD) the scenario is described as follows:

Delhi, however, stands at the crossroads today. The choice is between either taking a road to indiscriminate, uncontrolled development and sliding towards chaos, or a move-

↑
Simulation of the Central Area of Abuja, Nigeria.
Originally designed by Kenzo Tange, AS&P has since introduced
a boulevard concept to breathe life into the zones.

ment towards making Delhi a world-class city, if handled with vision and care. From 1991
to 2001, the urban population of Delhi increased at 3.87 per cent annual growth rate.…
With the continuation of the present population trend, the total population NCTD by the
year 2011 and 2021 would be 182 lakhs and 225 lakhs respectively.[3]

That is as good as a population increase of 4 million within only 10 years! The answer to
this can only be greater density. After India's independence, large sections of the city, in
particular the civil servants' district, were built with very low densities. A conservative
estimate by the authors of the master plans is that the number of houses in New Delhi
will have to more than double. In order to provide affordable living quarters for all strata
of the population, the authorities currently vary the building types. One- to two-room
apartments for the poorer inhabitants are possible only in 3 to 4-storey buildings without
elevators. The affluent and burgeoning middle-class, by contrast, is expected to live in the
massive high-rise estates.[4]

Until very recently, the trend in the industrialized nations was precisely the opposite:
shrinking cities. This happened either because a lack of economic prospects led to cities
failing (as in East Germany), or (as in the stronger business centers) people continued to
dream of a house and garden of their own. Today, ever fewer people live in cities whose
size has remained the same, leading to lower densities. In many a once well-functioning
district the number of inhabitants has fallen so far that buses no longer have enough pas-

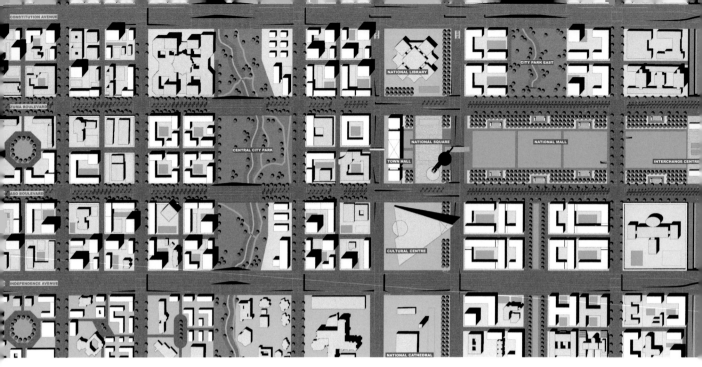

 Detailed structuring within the "super-blocks" in Abuja's Central Area.

 Physical model of downtown Shanghai, with clear "green zones" within the concentrated mixed-usage high-rises.

sengers to be economically viable. There is no sense in providing bus lines that run from one set of single-family houses to the next, and there is certainly no point in connecting them by mass transit rail links, because there is no mass to move. US suburbs are a classic example here: they function as a rule only if the inhabitants have cars. Even school buses are no longer a working prospect, as schools do not have enough pupils, while sewage systems collapse when insufficient water gets sluiced through them. There are now cities in Europe and the United States that have so emptied that drinking water has to be pumped through the sewage system to at least keep the medieval stench at bay. Indeed, the global financial crisis, coupled with a future rise in energy prices, may combine to make life in suburbia too expensive for many, and the green suburbs will then deteriorate, too. So-called silver-agers and singles are both groups that want much larger dwelling spaces – not because they are exceptionally rich, but simply out of a feeling of retentiveness. A single-person dwelling uses an inordinate amount of space. It is as if they were signing their own residential death warrant. For this trend means the entire technical and social infrastructure of such districts is ever harder to finance: the fewer people there are living in such district, the higher the costs for the technical and social infrastructure (sewage, schools, hospitals, etc.), leading eventually to the abandonment of entire sections of residential areas.[5] The result: a "perforated city," riddled with gaps. And once the holes prevent the remaining infrastructure system from functioning, the entire city is endangered. A green belt is pleasant now, but if the strips of green expand willy-nilly across the

entire settlement, the city collapses as an entity, quite simply because a certain bottom-line density is a must for a city to be sustainable.

Similar problems arose after the first round of city expansion in Riyadh. For years, one road after the next was simply built out into the desert, land accessed, and two-storey houses erected on the plots, as if realizing Frank Lloyd Wright's Broadacre City. Today, during rush hour even ten-lane highways can hardly cope with the traffic. After all, an overwhelming 87 per cent use private vehicles for transportation and a further 11 per cent rely on limousines. Riyadh now needs a mass transit metro system – it will be the first on the Arab Peninsula. Again, the metro is an economically meaningful prospect only if a certain population density exists to guarantee passenger levels. "However, the difficulty here is that it is hard to persuade planners in the Arab world that apartment blocks are the answer," explains Stefan Kornmann, urban planner and AS&P partner. "Traditional Arab housing always involves ensuring the privacy of the inhabitants, and that is clearly not possible if one block looks out over the next." AS&P has proposed seven-storey blocks to get density levels up to a meaningful level, but the idea was not exactly greeted with joy and the metro operators will face difficulties. In Hong Kong, by contrast, density is not a problem. On the contrary, those living on the top floors of the countless residential towers can often almost shake hands with neighbors in the next block.

The attitude toward sustainable densities is without doubt culturally specific. In Germany, the higher up the income ladder people climb, the more likely they are to want to demonstrate the fact by inhabiting greater space. However, since the planners realize the need to keep people in the city, the solution has to be more residential districts complete with green spaces close to city centers – by creating denser scenarios and building upwards, albeit not on the same scale as in Singapore, Hong Kong, or New Delhi. Most Eu-

ropean cities have potential for such denser structures. If cities were simply to return to the density levels of the turn of the 20th century in London, Paris, or Berlin, that would already be progress. After all, as the massive baby-boomer generation ages, its members will automatically start looking for places to live where they can reach the shops and the cultural facilities (and the doctor) on foot. Denser quarters are ideal for senior citizens, and offer more quality of life than suburbs or gated greenfield retirement homes outside towns, which is the common solution in Australia, for example. Keeping consumers in town also has obvious benefits for street life and retail outlets.

Residential estates composed of numerous high-rises now extend out around New Delhi, catering to the burgeoning middle classes.

Aerial view of the new quarter in Al Riyadh, Saudi Arabia.

Detailed view of new residential architecture created by AS&P and inspired by classic Arab insights in Al-Riyadh, Saudi Arabia.

What is required is a political push for greater densities. For today, as resources grow ever more scarce, the chances are that soon no one will be able to afford to live in suburbia and we will see an influx (back) into cities in the Western world. "In 15 years the suburbs and small satellite cities may have turned into ghost towns," suggests Axel Bienhaus, one of the AS&P partners, "even if we do nothing to influence the process. It is a fact that soon no one will be able to risk living in a village and catch pneumonia, because there will simply be no doctor near at hand." This may sound strange, given the still prevalent dream of a house and garden for the family out on the periphery, where there is ostensibly more flora and fauna than in the city. But it is a dream, rather than an option with long-term prospects. Gerhard Brand points out that while the choice may seem rational, it is not based on reflection but on preference. "For many years, everyone wanted to have an SUV or off-road vehicle, although these guzzled gas. The auto industry now offers the same vehicles – but with engines that consume 20 per cent less gas. So people say 'great, we've saved energy,' but fail to notice that they are still consuming far more energy than the world can afford. The same applies to housing, I'm afraid to say."

The architects face a dilemma. Professional ethics dictate that they design sustainable structures, where distances are short, for quarters where there is a mixture of social strata. But what to do if there is only a limited market for such high-quality density? Surely, the market will not change unless higher-density dwellings in the city become more attractive. But in Germany, for example, there are evidently hurdles to it really taking off because simply building upwards is not always a solution, as German legislation states that the higher the buildings, the further apart from one another they have to be. "Which is why we go for a dense pattern of quarters with blocks of, say, six storeys rather than high-rises," comments Martin Teigeler. Those marvelous apartment buildings from the late 19th century in Paris or Frankfurt would probably not get planning permission today. Lawmakers have insisted that the ratio of built space to the plot of land on which the floor space stands be lower than it was in the past, when the ratio of floor space to plot footprint reached as much as 3.0. The Charter of Athens called for a significant decrease in favor of "more light, air, and sun". In post-1945 Germany, the ratio accepted was about 1.0. While built density should not be too high, as this impinges on the quality of living in the city and the climate, the solution can range from a two-storey detached house to an eight-storey apartment block. After all, density is more than just built volume times the square meters of the site. But that is not felt density, and there is a difference if the plot is located next to a road that is 60 meters wide and not 20 meters wide, or on a riverbank, or next to a park. Some soft factors are evidently just as important as mathematics.

LIVING IN DENSER CITIES

The apartments must be easy to adapt given that changing demographic and social trends will require houssholds of different sizes at different times, as the baby boom generation will at some point have died out. The obvious path to take here is that of "universal design": In other words, we should not be designing residential districts specifically for families with small children or apartments for the elderly, but instead, adaptable flats and districts fit for everyone. An apartment that is easy for elderly or disabled persons to access also has its merits for families with children: there is little difference between the space required for a buggy and for a walking frame, and an elevator is not something that caters only to one generation. If universal design is taken to heart, then developers can be sure to get a long-term return on their investment irrespective of demographic patterns.

The apartment blocks built at the turn of the 20th century again provide the clue, as they contain rooms that were not configured to specific uses and were thus highly flexible. They are grouped round a hallway and the heights of the ceilings enable a "second level" to be introduced for kids. Gerhard Brand comments that all of this would be just as practical today, were it not for the mass of legal norms introduced by municipal authorities since then, specifying set sizes for children's rooms or living rooms. Needless to say, the market has since adjusted accordingly and common sense has got lost in a morass of regulations. This is surprising, as modern construction techniques allow for flexible footprints for homes: these can be larger or smaller units thanks to "switch-rooms" that can be "switched" to belong to either the one or the other apartment by including or excluding a wall. And they can be grouped as open-plan rooms around central cores that house the technical facilities such as the heating, hot water, etc. Here, planners can, at best, hope to persuade politicians and developers alike that this is the way forward. However, it would be wrong to expect more than persuasion, because, as Stefan Kornmann points out, "the prime task of urban design is to create quarters that enhance the quality of life, not impose ideas on people."

AN ALTERNATIVE: THE RESIDENTIAL HIGH-RISE?

A solution to the problem of space and density – albeit one that has not caught on in countries where there was no premium on land, such as Europe, the United States, and Australia – are residential high-rises. "They are the building of choice wherever there are land constraints, either because a location on a shoreline or plain is blocked on one side by mountainous hinterland or land is simply too expensive," explains Gerhard Brand. "Take Hong Kong, where, given the steep sides to the islands, land today is reclaimed by dredging up sand: all I can do in such a situation is build upwards. Contrast that with São Paulo, where downtown is a mixture of residential high-rises and two-storey dwellings with people living above their stores." Cities that are now facing a veritable wave of new inhabitants have almost no other choice than to go upwards, and this means in China, India, and, before long, Africa, too. "The less I waste my prime agricultural resource, land, the better. And if I opt for a dense web of six- or seven-storey apartment blocks I can achieve a lot. And possibly do without complex elevator or air-conditioning technology while supporting a large number of inhabitants within a small space," proposes Michael Denkel. As long as the infrastructure can cope. Not forgotten are the headlines from the hot summers in the early years of the 21st century, when in the larger cities in Italy, and even in Manhattan, power stations started to wilt under the strain of providing a higher peak load to drive all the air-conditioning that global warming was necessitating in buildings where windows could not be opened. There are manifest disadvantages in some countries, with some societies experiencing tower blocks as a loss of human scale and thus of social control. High-rises require elaborate and expensive facilities management, and in terms of energy they function like a cooling fin.

Albert Speer voiced a similar opinion as long ago as 1978: "Planning new residential districts must forthwith take into consideration the social, climatic, cultural, and landscaping factors, and not simply adopt high-rises, for example, with small balconies, that do not conform to what a culture needs or forget climatic conditions. While in Europe and the United States, residential tower blocks are felt to impact negatively on health and social cohesion, are not a good influence on the city's climate, and with a few exceptions no longer get built, Arab states are starting to consider such edifices as modern and desirable."[6]

To some degree, the differences in cultural outlook have historical roots. The aversion to residential tower blocks in Europe is related to the failure of social council housing schemes in the 1960s, with a similar mindset in the United States the product of the difficulties with "projects" there. The tower block as residence is associated with criminality and anonymity, suggests Gerhard Brand, while in the city-state of Singapore people are happy to live in the confines of agglomerations of high-rises. Indeed, most of them regard this form of living as real progress. Past experience has led Europe to forget that high-quality dwellings are, in fact, possible in skyscrapers, and so developers do not try to create examples that will change the prevailing mood. While a New Yorker is interested only in the view he gets, the location, and the size, an inhabitant of Cologne will not consider a building if it has more than ten different doorbells.

The engine that drives apartment blocks rather then detached homes will be energy costs, unless there is a quantum leap in solar-cell technology, for example. Many a European city is starting to devote brownfield areas to new apartment blocks, albeit rarely of more than seven storeys. Copenhagen and Rotterdam are two prime examples. There, developers have deliberately gone for the high end to persuade people that the higher up they live does not mean the lower down the social scale they have fallen. Yet it should not be forgotten that in Europe a maximum of seven storeys is the most cost-effective approach. After all, in terms of energy efficiency, skyscrapers are by no means an optimal solution. Numbers show that buildings with far fewer than 20 storeys provide an optimal ratio of site footprint to construction costs, operating costs, and energy prices. The gigantic and futuristic living machines envisaged by Le Corbusier or Colani may look impressive in glossy magazines but they will remain a thing of the future in terms of what they would cost to run.

→ An overview of green-belt planning for Frankfurt, Germany, ensuring that the outer green belt can be reached from downtown via green corridors.

EUROPAVIERTEL FRANKFURT/MAIN

Free space within a city is an invaluable asset, and it is always important to network the free spaces in terms of function and location. If they are greened, these building blocks for biotopes create opportunities for flora and fauna – and not least of all for people, who can use them as access to nature without having to cross town just to get beyond the city limits. Today, few developers in the West will repeat the nightmares of the past and reject green spaces in new urban quarters in favor of buildings, buildings, buildings. And this insight is fast spreading globally. The fact that our cities are getting hotter with climate change is further reason to make certain that sufficient fresh air blows through them, and that open spaces enable air to cool down. Using all the possible space in a city for residential and commercial properties simply prompts people to flee the city the minute they have an opportunity to do so, namely, at the weekend, with all the attendant problems this has as regards traffic and CO_2 emissions.

When designing the Europaviertel in Frankfurt/Main, AS&P had a chance to put into practice the theory that green space can boost the appeal of a dense urban quarter. Where once the main freight rail station stood, the master plan foresees a quarter with some 3,500 inhabitants and 5,000 jobs – the largest urban devel-

→

Plan of Cologne, Germany, showing the green belt around the inner city. The red areas designate new urban structures on the basis of the new master plan.

opment in Frankfurt since Ernst May's archetypal housing estates. A bird's-eye view shows clearly how the green belt running round the city center extends a finger into the new quarter, ensuring the requisite access. "We set ourselves the objective of extending the finger as deep into the city center as possible, that way linking up the next quarter, the Gallusviertel, to the greenery for the first time." Despite being a prime site for property speculation, 22 of the quarter's total of a good 90 hectares are destined for greening – a quite extraordinary achievement given the downtown location. However, and this is why the developers agreed, a service-based city such as Frankfurt, with its focus on competing globally for the best staff in the world, will increasingly need high-end, quality residential real estate. For if they are to live in pleasant homes, highly qualified staff can more readily be wooed by a pleasant ambience with plenty of green inside the city than by having to commute into town every day. In the knowledge society, it is this group of employees who will determine Frankfurt's economic prosperity. Not to mention that corporations now opt for a location if it offers the right human resources, and these resources tend to be all the better, the higher the quality of life a city offers.

A large amount of free space is not an absolute requirement, but culturally specific. In the emerging markets of Asia, cities tend not to boast as much greenery, possibly simply out of cultural habit. Cities in China often have lines of trees in the courtyards between the buildings, and that and only that is the green space. Yet there seems to be some sort of anthropological constant at work that says that people find green areas within the built environment pleasant. What would Manhattan be without Central Park, London without Hyde Park, or Abuja without its Millennium Park, which hosts thousands of picnickers each weekend? In megacities, green is also a way of structuring the built areas, and in Shanghai there are even attempts to encourage urban agriculture (allotments) within the "city walls," as it were – an economic necessity to ensure that fresh food is close at hand in the large urban agglomerations.[7] Green areas are a crucial component in any sustainable city, as is the design of the gardens.

Ever since cities have gone beyond the point where it takes 10 minutes' travel time to vacate them, and the city walls have become tourist attractions, they have boasted green spaces. Parks ceased to be the privilege of the aristocracy and, at the latest since the mid-19th century, have been generally popular.[8] Allotment gardens are a special expression of this need for green inside the city. Originally, they served to provide food for the poor that tilled them, and were donated to the poor by factory owners or the nobility, often as brownfield developments alongside railway embankments. Indeed, in post-1945 Europe, entire colonies of such allotments were entered on city maps to make certain the starving population had a chance to feed itself. The same policy still holds in many coun-

tries, such as Korea, where the ground between residential high-rises is interspersed with such gardens.

Then there is the question of garden design in densely structured quarters. Michael Denkel states unequivocal preferences: "The landscape planners must find solutions that say: 'Here is the center of the quarter' and in front of it there is enjoyable space. I am thinking of a modern, not quite so symmetrical Baroque garden, with French flair, ponds, islands of grass, promenades with trees, lawns you can lie on or play on. That is what a densely populated city quarter needs. That serves the office workers and kids at lunchtime and everyone else in the evening." Indeed, the gentle art of gardening and the use of free space strongly reflects the local culture. In Asia, the preference is for meditative artificial gardens, in Africa for large shady trees, lawns, and streams. But without gardens – and parks are just larger gardens – the quality of life in a city drops dramatically, as does its appeal. The battle by cities for new inhabitants will be won not on the playing fields outside the cities, but by the gardens and parks inside them. After all, it seems obvious that if people of different origins and backgrounds can all enjoy summer in a park, be it with a BBQ or playing a ball game, they will tend to identify with their city. And that is something the planners should bear in mind.

GREEN SPACES AND PUBLIC SPACES DOWNTOWN

Many a commentator has said that Frankfurt is a city with too few green areas, which goes to show how perception and reality often diverge. In percentage terms, the city has more green space within its limits than any other large city in Germany, much of it made up of the green belt – which is far larger than Manhattan's Central Park and no further from downtown than Central Park is from Wall Street. The crunch issue, therefore, is access: many people cannot readily access the green belt. A case in point for any sustainable city: the green belt must be accessible, inhabitants must be able to get to it without clambering through bramble bushes, as in the Lea Valley in London, or circumnavigating allotment garden fences, as in Frankfurt. "While the idea behind the allotment garden is great," Albert Speer comments, "the system has in many European cities been allowed to lead a life of its own, has become an outsized parallel world that does not relate to the whole."

Without open access, free urban spaces and green spaces have far less value for the quality of urban life.[9] They need to be accessible and subject to social control if people are to enjoy experiencing them. In Frankfurt, for example, the emphasis has been on making certain all small parks border on roads on all sides – as this makes certain they remain public. "It's not just a matter of safety, but also of appropriation," explains Michael Denkel. "If someone's back garden borders on a park then they must be tempted to tip their garden rubbish over the fence." Pushing a wheelbarrow piled high with garden clippings across a road works as a great deterrent.

A quarter requires well-proportioned spaces, with carefully designed limits and a diversity of functions, where social life can unfold subject to public control – as well as the infrastructure necessary to keep daily supplies rolling. A special exception are the shopping malls, which tend to be private property and thus elude public control. For that very reason, a city must be circumspect in choosing to approve them. The privatization of public space in this way, along with private security companies, etc., amounts to an incursion into valuable downtown areas that must be kept open to the public and subject to political control.

After all, gated communities are not an example that a sustainable city should follow. Unlike the United States, where as many as 10 million people now live behind such gates, cut off from public life, the idea has not caught on in Germany. But it is spreading fast in France, Spain, and England. And in East European metropolises such as Warsaw, Kiev, or Moscow, demand far outstrips supply. In all the major metropolises in developing countries, such communities promise security in worlds that possibly still lack the necessary degree of protection and thus have some justification, if only for a limited period. Yet gated communities are always an expression of segregation, rather than mixed use, of the fear the rich have of the poor. That flies in the face of the future championed by this book – in which the sustainable city stands out for the mixture of social strata in its residential and commercial quarters.

AESTHETIC QUALITY OF SPACE

Along with everything else, urban design must deliver aesthetic quality. That said, quality of that kind cannot be reduced to the outlines a new development offers if viewed from the satellite vantage of Google Earth, such as the lines of buildings in the Gulf of Arabia that form surahs from the Koran, since the prime aesthetic is that which is viewed by passersby on the ground. For all the technical difficulties, by contrast, the choice of palm-tree shapes or the like for new islands (as have been created from dredged sand in Dubai) may be quite functional: no tediously straight roads, a lot of beach front, a good deal of outside area in relation to the internal area, albeit at the cost of placing a considerable strain on the marine and local environment. Anyone who knows how to read a map can discern a carefully conceived spatial configuration. And if the map is a good one, then the layout will be experienced by those at ground level. The task of the planner must therefore be to create enduring lines of vision and expanses – to be visionary in the design given to the joints of the urban body, the intersections. Planners must therefore anticipate the effect the interfaces have, and must be able to imagine what it will be like to walk through the spaces and streets.

The planners designing Europaviertel therefore took great care to deliver something that is otherwise quite rare in Frankfurt: a boulevard with a long, straight line of vision. The aesthetic appeal here is that the city's high-rise skyline is emphasized from a completely new vantage point. Frankfurt did not originally possess any boulevards for parades, as did the European cities that were home to ducal or regal palaces. Nor did it have a Haussmann. In Europaviertel, a carefully staged vanishing point is now offered down the boulevard, with the scale of the buildings chosen accordingly. Smaller spaces are left around the high-rises that then open out, with street cafés providing seating space protected from the wind, as the houses around them are not so high as to funnel the wind in, and because only one side opens to the street. The idea: to use aesthetic criteria to functionally augment urban life.

In one section of Europaviertel, AS&P has opted for urban apartment blocks that border almost on the street, but which feature courtyards that are all open on one side in order to interface public and private space and attract life. It is a lesson the planners learned from work in China. There, quarters are regularly aligned north/south as apartments traditionally have to face the sun. While this may seem logical in terms of energy levels, it does not help to create urban spaces, as there are then no buildings running cross-wise – and the result looks like a suburb of long, parallel streets, the sole difference being that the basic units are not detached homes but apartment blocks. The interstices that then arise do not encourage anyone to use them. In the model city in Anting, AS&P therefore deliberately chose to break with tradition and insisted on courtyards with buildings on

THE BASELER PLATZ EXAMPLE Baseler Platz is of special importance to Frankfurt. Given its location between the Friedensbrücke and the main train station, it represents the southern entrance to the city center. In recent decades, however, the square has not really fulfilled its current function. Bereft of any interesting points of attraction and public facilities, it deteriorated in the course of time into a mere traffic intersection, leaving no meaningful pedestrian space, and confronting the residential buildings facing onto it with little quality of life. Architecturally, the first step towards enhancing the status of Baseler Platz was to restore urban quality: an ensemble of two prominent new buildings was developed, designed to link to the redevelopment efforts in Frankfurt's former West Port and to create new urban spaces between the predominant roads. Although formally dissimilar, together the two structures form an exciting architectural unit. The "Oval" at Baseler Platz and the "Baseler Arcades" bring urban life back to Baseler Platz, offering a diverse mixture of uses in the form of shops, restaurants, cafés, offices, and apartments. The resulting ensemble is marvelously rich in contrasts, giving the east side of the square a completely new face. The "Baseler Arcades" with its simultaneously strict and yet moderate style, forms the backdrop to the square, while the "Oval" is positioned as a self-confident stand-alone directly in the center of Baseler Platz.

three sides and squares with buildings on all sides. Initially, the developers claimed this would prevent anyone ever moving into the apartments. Today, there are plenty of grandmothers looking after children in the squares, and what was once impossible is gradually becoming accepted and, consequently, possible, namely, public spaces that act as kernels of urban life. Without them the city would be dead, and a dead city is hardly sustainable. Here, again, we see that urban design can involve conflicts between the protagonists as to the potential objectives. As in other walks of life, there is no black or white, no correct or incorrect urban design. The sustainable solution must find a way to consider culturally-specific criteria without bowing to dogma.

PLANNING CREATES SOCIAL SPACES

Given the scenarios of new and old phenomena of urban life, one of the questions that arises is whether spaces can be designed to be so open that they will not be the seedbed for social tension further down the line. Put differently, can we develop spaces that are more or less suited to ensure people feel good there and go there to meet others? Now planners can organize quarters in such a way that people meet coincidentally, but regularly – examples being market squares, central plazas, kindergartens, and stores. Not only are such spaces practical, they also generate what is generally considered the prime benefit of urban life – and what drove people to live in greater numbers in the first place. So what must the features of a public space, a plaza or square be if people are to feel good there? The crucial thing is for people to feel safe and at home, as Jane Jacobs argued back in the 1950s. An open area is not in itself a space, for a space has clear limits, even if it can be open on one side. Indeed, the rules that govern how squares and plazas function are probably as old as towns and cities themselves. For urban space first arises if the delimiting walls bear the right relation to the space they surround. There are narrow urban spaces and there are expansive spaces. The appropriate ratio is about 10-to-1 (distance to the buildings to the height of the buildings), and anything closer to 3-to-1 is experienced as crushingly confined. If the ratio is ignored, then the space no longer functions as an urban space, but is simply a gap in the built environment. Density is not necessarily relative, but must be seen in the built context. The closer I am to it, the stronger the effect of an open space. If I know that there is a park or square behind the next row of buildings then I am more likely to tolerate a higher density where I live, as I feel the park that I do not see.

Urban spaces (squares or plazas, covered or open) are certainly just as important as green spaces; they are the physical and communicative nodal points of city life. Not that plazas have to be large. Streets or pavements can have the same function as long as the proportions are right. "The latter are spaces, too," Michael Denkel comments, "and if dimensioned correctly will soon become a focus of urban life." Denser quarters also give rise to such plazas by attracting a sufficient number of potential users to ensure that the critical mass for urban life is reached. Creating vibrant squares in residential suburbs is almost impossible – whereas the same undertaking in a maze of six-storey buildings and five times as many people will soon be successful, be it in Frankfurt, Germany, or in Anting, Shanghai. The city simply requires a specific initial density. Without it you get a hodgepodge of residences and suburbia. The city grows functionally and spatially once enough people are there to use it. However, if the density is too great, then social tension sets it. After all, too many people crushed into too little space tend to respond by acting like rats in a cage.

1 Josef Reichholf, Stadtnatur, (Oekom Verlag: Munich, 2007), p. 124f

2 "Whatever the individual reasons are why so many people insist on living in dense spaces, this does not alter the fact that we are not alone in succumbing to the 'strange attraction' of the city. Many other creatures do so, too. Cities are so attractive that the diversity and frequency of bird species, for example, grows with the size of the city and not vice versa. Berlin is Germany's city richest in birds, with Hamburg following close behind.... About two thirds of all the bird species found within Berlin's borders are breeding species that can be found between the Baltic and the Alps throughout Germany. If we add the guests that drop by while migrating or come to Berlin for the winter, then the figure is about 2 to 3 birds per inhabitant. Similar levels are recorded for Munich and other major cities in Germany and elsewhere in Europe." Josef Reichholf, Stadtnatur, (Oekom Verlag: Munich, 2007) p. 17

3 Quoted from the Website of the Delhi Development Authority, http://www.dda.org.in/planning/draft_master_plans.htm, whereby a lakh = 100,000. The estimated population of urban Delhi in late 2007 was 15.9 million according to the United Nations.

4 For a satirical portrait of residential life in New Delhi see the novel that won the 2008 Booker Prize, White Tiger by Aravind Adiga. The novel suggests that the poor who move from the country into the city by no means find housing.

5 In her book The Shock Doctrine (Allen Lane: London, 2007, p. 415), Naomi Klein discusses how the privatization of infrastructure in the United States may have a similar result: "The American Society of Civil Engineers said in 2007 that the U.S. had fallen so far behind in maintaining its public infrastructure that it would require more than a trillion and half dollars over five years to bring it back up to standard. Instead, these types of public expenditures are being cut back.... It's easy to imagine a future in which growing numbers of cities have their frail and long-neglected infrastructures knocked out by disasters and then are left to rot, their core services never repaired or rehabilitated. The well-off, meanwhile, will withdraw into gated communities, their needs met by private providers."

6 ex: Deutsche Bauzeitung, 1978, no. 283

7 On urban farming see: Herbert Girardet, Cities People Planet. Urban Development and Climate Change, (John Wiley: England, 2008) pp. 236-53. In Germany, the allotment gardens that date back to the end of the 19th century are as good as sacrosanct and a "hands-off" for any planner.

8 See Peter Sloterdijk, Sphären, (Suhrkamp: Frankfurt, 2004) III, p. 338ff, for a discussion of the impact of Paxton's Crystal Palace on distinctions between outdoor and indoor parks.

9 Edinburgh would seem to be the exception that proves the rute, with its highly-subscribed private gardens.

V

CREATE A
CLEAR IDENTITY

"The sense of identity can make an important contribution to the strength and warmth of our relations with others, such as neighbors, or members of the same community, or fellow citizens, or followers of the same religion.

Our focus on particular identities can enrich our bonds and make us do many things for each other and can help to take us beyond our self-centered lives." **Amartya Sen** [1]

In an age of globalization, the sustainability of cities gains a new dimension. For a city surely does not bear sustaining if it does not have any inhabitants. So over and above its future in terms of energy consumption, land utilization, transportation system, etc., there is a fundamental requirement cities face: they need to retain their existing populace and potentially attract new inhabitants, for cities in the "globalized" world live in competition with other cities as regards both, that is to say, they compete for human resources. Bereft of a tax base, a city will gradually die out, for that tax base is generated by natural persons and corporations alike, by employers and employees. Given this global competition for resources, one level at which a city must act to ensure its continued survival, and thus its sustainability, is to create a clear identity for itself, and this goes beyond, but definitely includes, nurturing a brand image. In this regard, cities are no different from any other commodity in a market place. David Ogilvy, a branding guru, once said that "You have to decide what 'image' you want for your brand. Image means personality. Products, like people, have personalities, and they can make or break them in the market place." Assuming that cities are products "on sale" in the global market, then they, too, need to highlight their personalities and emphasize what makes them special, be they ancient cities, European cities, or new cities in the emerging markets.

CITY BRANDING In this context, most of the experts agree that the fundamental law of marketing is the law of leadership: it is better to be first, than to be better. A famous case in point is that of the PC: Microsoft launched in 1981 while Apple launched in 1984. Apple is better in hardware, software, and other areas but has only 3 per cent share while Microsoft has 94 per cent share. European cities often draw on the cachet of their medieval or Renaissance past to attract temporary residents, despite the fact that in terms of the efficiencies of life other cities on other continents are better positioned – one need think only of new cities such as Dubai. In the process, European cities need not focus their efforts on being better, but on being what they once were, i.e., on their current status as living museums. After all, if first is perceived to be best, and you can nurture the image of first, then automatically you continue to attract good people, good distributors, and so on. The crucial thing here is to nurture that perception of yourself worldwide, namely, that you were first and therefore by definition best.

It follows from this that much of the competition among cities is a competition about perception. The key lesson of marketing for cities is to make certain that they are perceived as being "best," offering the best "quality of life," the best "facilities" or "infrastructure." The nimbus attached to double-decker buses in London back in the days when they belched vast quantities of diesel particles into the air is a case in point. The "being first" can thus be a matter of the mind rather than of reality: Shanghai is the world's first city to have a superfast maglev system connecting its international airport to its subway system – but since the value of the "Transrapid" has been questioned, the city cannot anchor this mode of transport in outsiders' minds as being a "first" that makes the city an attraction.

The Ogilvy ad agency Web site claims that brands were never more valuable than today, yet suggest that never was it more difficult to adapt a brand to markets that are changing at an ever increasing speed. After all, if we assume that a city forges an identity for itself by giving itself or making of itself a brand, then it must adapt continually to massive change. In the Leipzig Charter on Sustainable European Cities, drafted in 2007, the EU Ministers responsible for Urban Development highlight the potential hurdles: "In the long run, cities cannot fulfil their function as engines of social progress and economic growth … unless we succeed in maintaining the social balance with and among them, ensuring their cultural diversity and establishing high quality in the fields of urban design, architecture and environment."

Any handbook on successfully positioning a brand (and let us assume it is a city) encourages an analysis of the brand environment, i.e., the consumer context, the business context, and the cultural context. The next step is to analyze the strengths, weaknesses, opportunities, and threats to the brand, and on the basis of all the insights devise a vision for the brand, thus defining the direction in which the brand is to go (e.g., Frankfurt 2030, see Chap. 10). This likewise provides knowledge about what challenges the brand will face and have to overcome if the vision underlying it is to be realized. Such an analysis will also include assessing what associations the brand should trigger among the target group. This means the target group(s) must be defined accurately (current consumers/inhabitants, future consumer/inhabitants, current/future businesses, etc.); this of course involves socio-demographic trend data, income forecasts. Starting from a broad swath of information, a core brand can be distilled that forms the unique footprint of the city in question. That core brand then has to be communicated to the target groups, who, so the theory, will be persuaded to remain in the city or to relocate to it if the brand has been formed appropriately.

ICONS AND IDIOSYNCRASIES

Albert Speer suggests in this context that while the focus on branding may be new, the underlying idea definitely is not, as it hinges on urban diversity: "The general principles behind the problem of urban rejuvenation and survival have remained essentially the same since the 1970s. The key issue is to 'preserve uniqueness', i.e., idiosyncrasies. In the past, each town or district had its own special character and was embedded in its own specific countryside and urban context. That is something we are in danger of losing if we continue down the road to bland, standardized high-rise conglomerations or suburbs. We must instead devise planning and architectural measures that emphasize precisely those local specifics, that special character." There are two aspects involved here. First, what status does an eye-catching "icon" have for the sustainability of a city? And secondly, is there such a thing as a failed city, one where, unlike a failed state, governance prevails but the city's administrators do not take the choices that allow the city a continued lifespan?

As regards the former, evidently it takes a global financial crisis on an unprecedented scale to persuade investors that perhaps there is more to life than simply reaching for ever greater heights. In fact, Albert Speer admonishes developers that high-rises reaching more than 300 meters into the sky are economically inefficient and technologically nonsensical. In his view, all recent attempts to top first 400 meters and then 500 meters have nothing in common with sustainable building. Architecture as an expression of business muscle is currently "out", at least in the industrialized nations of the West and for the time being, if only because the financing can no longer be arranged. Yet this is unlikely to stifle the temptation to rely on a single building as an attention-grabbing icon that does not primarily fulfill any functional requirements but feeds people's vanity instead. However, this is not necessarily at loggerheads with a focus on sustainability in buildings, as a series of new buildings worldwide show, starting with Norman Forster's prize-winning Hearst Tower, the new "LEEDS"-platinum high-rise on the edge of Central Park, Manhattan. It is "only" 182 meters tall, but is New York's first "green" skyscraper, with recycled material accounting for 90 per cent of the structural steel. Indeed, despite its outstanding aesthetics, the Hearst Tower blends in with its surroundings and its dimensions remain relatively modest by New York standards. "One should likewise mention Renzo Piano's New York Times building," suggests AS&P's Martin Teigeler, "as both buildings take the notion of sustainable architecture seriously, while aspiring to be icons. In fact, in most other cities, they would trulybe icons."

Bearing in mind Speer's statement that the problems of upholding the vitality of cities have not changed much over the last four decades, it is no great surprise that corporations and city councils choose to prioritize the construction of eye-catchers. In essence, this is but a current application of Aldo Rossi's famous insistence on "l'architettura della città," which hinged on the idea that the city as an arrangement of buildings generates the urban fabric, because those buildings forge a unique identity, and outstanding monuments then serve to characterize the identity and meaning, forging impressive places and narratives, that is to say, semantically-charged architecture.

↑

Beijing's National Stadium, known as the "Bird's Nest," certainly functioned as the
icon of the 2008 Olympic Games. Designed by Swiss architects Herzog and de
Meuron, the stadium was imbued with Chinese symbolism by artist Ai Weiwei. The
number of seats has been reduced from 91,000 to 80,000 since the Games.

Yet what is actually the substance behind all the talk of "iconic architectonic"? We should reflect that the term icon originally applied to a gilded picture of Christ, the Virgin Mary, or a saint, venerated in the Orthodox Christian Church and taken as the real representative of the revered person. The term was later taken to mean a person or thing regarded as a symbol of a belief or cultural movement. Most recently, specifically with the advent of Apple computers, the term has morphed, and has come to designate a picture on a computer screen representing the computer function that can be activated by moving the cursor over it. In other words, if the term is to have meaning in the urban planning and architectural context, then it can be understood only as signifying a building that stands pars pro toto for the city. In the case of New York, the Statue of Liberty, the Empire State Building, and, until their destruction, the Twin Towers were just such icons. Turning to Europe, the Eiffel Tower, London's Houses of Parliament, and Berlin's Brandenburg Gate could each be said to fulfill a similar function, although none of them is an especially modern structure.

Can new icons help a city to survive – possibly by forging a new urban identity? After all, there is no reason why the icon itself need necessarily entail a wasteful use of resources. Unfortunately, some architects, city councils, and developers evidently confuse "icon" with glitter, glamour, or expense, and design the buildings accordingly. Instead, an icon could even be modest and still fulfill an identity-forming function, offering people a point of identification with "their" city or with their future home.

To be fair, there are divergent positions on the status of icons. After all, as Gerhard Brand, board member and head architect at AS&P, says, "The talk of icons is often quite simply stupid. Just as their use is completely arbitrary. And as always, the exceptions prove the rule. Jorn Utzon's Sydney Opera House is a real icon located at precisely the right location. It is a landmark and has come to be understood as the city's hallmark, and has rightfully been included in UNESCO's list of World Heritage Sites. The same accolades apply to the Guggenheim in Bilbao. Both buildings make the city." However, he cautions, "if I try to build an eye-catcher a day then the time will soon come when no one looks their way. Regardless of whether the building was made by Zaha Hadid or not." Brand says that the emphasis on creating icons is often simply a matter of show and thus of show effect, and has long since parted company with any adherence to cost efficiency or operational profitability, let alone sustainability. "Often, the results are buildings that any architectural student can see do not 'work,' not even at the functional level. But the flavor of the month being what it is, all too often precisely these buildings win prizes." In other words, an icon that is both dysfunctional and fails to function as an icon in its context is itself not sustainable.

That said, the impact of icons has been widely recognized, and if a city can afford the building(s) in question then it is a worthwhile enterprise and can serve as a beacon for identification. A good example is Hamburg's new Elbe Philharmonic Hall, a lesson in how not to budget. Many an architectural company is evidently not accurate when it comes to quoting the costs of such fantastic designs. The developers behind the Elbe Philharmonic

Hall, and with them the countless Hamburg citizens who have made donations to enable the amazing edifice out in the old port to become a reality, have had to learn this the hard way. Indeed, the one or other star architect today seems to make a habit of taking the price and simply adding on a fifth or so to hedge his bets, in case the budget, if not the building, goes pear-shaped. In fact, it would seem that today developers feel that an iconic building can only be designed by a "star architect" – it is as if the celebrity-mania of the media has made inroads into building. This is to forget that the single most important aspect of iconic architecture is that it is the absolute exception – otherwise it does not stand out. If a city goes about building one icon after the other, then the impact of the first swiftly becomes diluted, and by the third there can no longer be any meaningful talk of icons – similarity rather than familiarity breeds visual contempt. Gerhard Brand severely condemns this trend: "I am against it as an urban planner and I am most certainly against it as an architect. After all, I must surely be obliged to create a design that still looks pleasing 20 years down the line. You can, of course, bring specific effects to bear and devise buildings that catch the eye, but if I want to transport some overarching message for the city as a whole, then that is something only one in a thousand buildings should do. Indeed, if you opt for a philharmonic hall, then you must be prepared to waste space in the process. That is in order. But if you decide that the icon is to be an office building, and as a consequence set about erecting an uneconomic and thus decidedly un-green skyscraper simply for the sake of the icon, then you are not fostering sustainability at the level of the architecture or the city. And that, quite simply, is where things have got out of hand."

URBAN ICONS   The classic urban icon of yore is the stadium; one need think only of Rome and the Colosseum, or, much later in human history, anyone saying Wembley meant London. Paul Henry, an architect at HOK Sports, recently commented as follows on the number of new stadiums springing up around the world: "What this is all about is designing a stadium with the maximum goosebump factor. Sporting venues, perhaps more than any other public building, resonate with the emotion of past and present glories."[2] Indeed, it is fair to say that the jaw-dropping sculptural stadiums of today are the 21st century's equivalent of medieval cathedrals.[3] Yet a swift glance around the world soon reveals that new stadiums have been reforging urban identities in many cities. There is Melbourne's eye-catching "Rectangular Stadium," the Nanjing Sports Park (the centerpiece of a new downtown precinct to the west of the ancient capital), Singapore's Sport's Hub, with its egg-shaped stadium (kick-off is in 2011), the new Wembley Stadium in London, Dublin's new Landsowne Road Stadium (scheduled to open in 2010) and, of course, the Munich Arena, the pride and joy of the World Cup 2006 organizers in Germany, a project organized and coordinated by AS&P from the first stages of location scouting onward. And there will be London's Olympic Stadium, in the Lower Lea Valley, specially designed for sustainability, as after the Games it will downsize from 80,000 to 25,000 as required to enable it to sit crowds on a smaller scale than those forecast to attend the Olympiad. It is fair to say that, in essence, stadiums are challenging the classical position of the skyscraper as the icon of urban modernity.

MEGA-EVENTS   This trend is closely bound up with a phenomenon that is as important as the icons themselves when it comes to "branding" a city and giving it a clear identity, namely, mega-events. It is a topic that is constantly being addressed anew at AS&P, as the belief there is that mega-events, and specifically sports-related events, offer cities a unique opportunity to reinvent themselves and thus create a new, sustainable identity.

Just how strongly a sports event can influence an identity is readily apparent if one imagines what a city such as Manchester would be if Manchester United or Manchester City ceased to exist as football clubs. Such a loss would invariably impact on urban developments in Manchester. Indeed, even cities that do not have a major sporting tradition can profit from seeking to host major sporting events, such as the Olympic Games or the World Cup. Friedbert Greif feels certain, for example, that Baku, which, as we saw in Chapter 2, was a candidate to host the Olympic Games and used the opportunity to commission new concepts for city development, would benefit from applying for other major events – as this would help move the city forwards. Although he quips that in any such instance the critical factor is "politicians who are proud of their city but not too proud to lose the race for an event."

In the case of the Olympic Games, however, the real issue is whether such an event can be organized functionally from the viewpoint of the athletes, the public, and the media, can impact beneficially on the city as its legacy both before and especially after the event, and can avoid going greenfield. Greif suggests that it is "becoming ever harder to meet all the different requirements, especially for the summer Games, as the number of media representatives, athletes, coaching staff is constantly increasing. But yet again, you can turn that round and say: Our city guarantees short distances for everyone involved. The city can profit from the planning, and so can the respective event." Indeed, AS&P, when preparing Munich's pitch for the Winter Olympics, came up with the claim, "Out of your bed and into your bobsleigh in 15 minutes flat." Yet Greif admits that it is a tall order to find the several hundred hectares of space needed to stage the Olympic Games and remain completely brownfield – after all, the average Olympic Village will house 20,000. Given such a scale, the important thing is to ensure the accommodation is functional and is used permanently after the event is over.

The Olympic Games in Beijing, Albert Speer submits, had the requisite aura to capture the hearts of an entire nation for change. And what was the message behind the Bird's Nest Stadium? "Power," Greif responds, "the power to make it happen. I am astonished by the extent of the fascination it exerted and just how many of us were skeptical beforehand, thinking it would not have such an effect. I remember standing in front of it during the construction phase, being interviewed and boldly saying what a complete excessive

London's Crystal Palace, designed by Joseph Paxton for the 1851 Great Exhibition. The building was some 560 m long, with an interior height of 33 m. Moved to a new site after the Expo, it was destroyed by a fire in 1936.

→→

Eiffel Tower, designed by engineer Gustave Eiffel and completed in 1889, was the then highest building in the world. Today, the icon is widely associated not just with Paris, but with France.

waste of materials it was and that it had nothing to do with sustainable architecture. Yet if you look at it in retrospect, then it could hardly have made a more permanent impact on society, and in this respect it was extremely contemporary. Its mere presence in the city attests to that ongoing spirit of can-do."

WORLD EXPOS

Ever since Hanover 2000, with its emphasis on "Nature, Technology and Us" (fittingly, it was AS&P who dreamed up the master plan for it), the world expositions have explicitly sought to emphasize sustainability. Yet in terms of branding and the iconography involved they often remain in the shadow of the FIFA World Cup or the Olympics. Essentially, the Expos suffer from possessing the image of often having gone wrong and of simply being overinflated market fairs. That said, "many cities simply fail to seize the opportunity that an expo can offer," claims Michael Denkel with a frown. "Expos, as we have seen from the work preparing plans for cities as diverse as Izmir and Shanghai, can really get a city moving." Yet two examples of World Expositions that changed their host cities and are separated by exactly 137 years show that Expos can hold there own. First, there was the Crystal Palace, built specially for the very first World Exposition, in London in 1851. It was an architecture that captured the hearts and minds of an entire generation. Then there was Brisbane in 1988, a notable exception in that it made superlative use of Expo 1988 to give itself far more than a facelift. In so doing, however, it eschewed the idea of "iconic" architecture. It seized the Expo opportunity to incorporate its riverbanks into the urban fabric, creating boardwalks and a mass of restaurants, cafes, and other outdoor meeting opportunities. Following suit, the city council introduced so-called City Cats, catamaran ferries that ply the river and offer a welcome alternative to road-bound transportation (albeit without covering as much of the river as would, given growth, today be appropriate: while linking the university, they shy away from the major industrial estates that border on the inner city). The riverbanks have since emerged as a

residential area, including large tracts of land hitherto ignored but located at the heart of the vast sprawl that is Brisbane today. There is also one piece of iconic architecture erected for a world exposition held between the London and Brisbane events that should be remembered for the way it inspired generations of architects and engineers alike: Gustave Eiffel's tower.

BRANDING VIA SUSTAINABLE MEGA-EVENTS

A city may need to weigh up the pros and cons in advance, but calculating the long-term value of mega-events such as the Olympics or a World Expo is difficult. If one of the planners in Munich back in 1972 had realized the Olympic grounds would now cost the city EUR 5 million a year in subsidies he would probably have counseled against holding the Olympics there. But the price tag is cheap. The public gets a huge recreational area, used intensively day in, day out, and the facilities are constantly utilized. "That is sustainable planning. If you look at it you feel '1972 is still alive.' Not to mention the fact that the city got a great subway network thrown in as part of the deal," Greif concludes.

There is another side to the sustainability of the Munich site. If the city's candidacy for the Winter Olympics is successful the complex will gain a new Olympic lease of life – a second life, and surprisingly enough the existing facilities can very readily be used for a new and highly appealing event. The infrastructure still exists, and the images are still in people's minds. This means it will be possible to turn summer into winter – and create a 70,000-strong backdrop for the Winter Games. A far cry from the nature reserves being felled outside Sochi in Russia as part of the effort to prepare for the 2014 Winter Olympics. "In fact," Greif says proudly, "we are really going the whole hog with recycling as there is even the idea of holding the curling competitions in the existing Olympic Swimming Center."

RECYCLING EVENTS FACILITIES

Friedbert Greif insists that "any city which is halfway serious and ethical about its application to host a sports or exposition event must ensure the sustainable use of the facilities. We must rely on temporary installations for anything that cannot be utilized after the event has gone. Then the facilities can claim to be sustainable while also helping to create the identity or brand the city requires. That is, incidentally, the principle behind the Munich application. After all, these days it is no big deal to erect a temporary, multipurpose hall to seat 15,000 and then take it down again afterwards. The added advantage here is that it enables organizers to take the sports facilities to the people – rather than expect them to do the traveling to get to the event. That is the insight behind the proposal to build the ice-skating rink on brownfield land inside Munich. Think of all the youngsters who will want to train there once they have seen their idols compete for medals on that very rink."

←

The EXPO 2000 grounds in Hanover – the brief: to create a sustainable setting and enduring mass transport links.

London, it should be remembered, won its bid for the Olympic Games by emphasizing, among other things, two aspects: the sustainable use to which the Games complex would be put and the fact that all the efforts would be brownfield, not greenfield. New Olympic facilities should likewise blend in well with existing installations; in a few decades' time, that is precisely what people will regard as the hallmark of the world's truly great architects – and not the fact that they created any number of "icons" in one and the same place. In the case of Munich, for example, anything and anyone attempting to top the beautiful curves of the stadium designed by Günter Behnisch and Frei Otto will fail, but the new structures that prevail will be those that draw on its strengths, recycling its image for new gains.

Sydney is a case of prime use of brownfield areas for the Olympic Games. The chosen location at Homebush Bay had previously been a disused, 750-hectare industrial site that included a dump for toxic waste. Sydney also opted to use solar energy wherever possible and designed the Olympic Village specifically with subsequent rental or sale of the small houses in mind. All of this was a success. When it comes to the sustainability of the sports facilities, however, the claim of being the "best Games ever" does not quite live up to expectations. Where that claim falls short is that, with the exception of the Swimming Center, the main Olympic complex itself is seldom used. This reflects the fact that the local rugby clubs prefer to be closer to downtown and their fans.

Friedbert Greif, the AS&P specialist for mega-events, suggests that while the Munich Games, like the Berlin Olympics, made an immense impact on German society – and thus, by extension, on him – the paramount example of how the Olympic Games can function both as an icon of identity and as a torch for city renewal is Barcelona. "That really showed me emphatically what you can transport with the Games. First of all, the Games joined the city with the sea for the first time – and in a manner so sustainable that it persists to this day. And then there's the Olympic stadium at Montjuic. Now to my mind they did quite an exemplary job of integrating it into the city, in fact, of integrating the Games into the city. And look at how the city has never looked back – and has scaled one height after the next ever since. The complex may not have the radiant architectural qualities of Munich, but did it need that exuberance? Did it need iconic buildings? No, because for Barcelona the icon was the event itself."

Elsewhere the iconic status of the event itself has helped, for example, to ensure the sustained existence of an Olympics complex. In Munich it is the iconic architecture that has protected the grounds from being bulldozed. After all, many years after the Games, the park was just parkland, in a prime location, and inevitably kindled desires among developers. Greif proposes that if Sydney had succeeded in giving its Olympic Park a clear architectural language, forging a shared identity among the structures, rather than simply opting for an aggregation of functionalist edifices, then the grounds themselves would today attract far more visitors and users than they in fact do. That, he feels, was a missed opportunity, but in juxtaposition to the Munich experience it is one that offers a lesson that future candidate cities can learn from.

THE BEIJING EXAMPLE

Johannes Dell, AS&P partner and MD of AS&P China, unwaveringly believes that the Beijing Olympics were an absolutely key event in the development of the city, both physically and mentally, i.e., both as icon and as sustainable facilities. They triggered a significant leap forward in the urban and transport infrastructure, stimulating developments far beyond the Games proper. "Just take the new public transportation that has been put in place, above all, the new subway lines – they make an incredible contribution to limiting the paralyzing gridlocks and pollution levels above the ground."

Dell goes on to say that the new, impressive airport, despite its gigantic dimensions, still manages to convey the impression that it is a building, and can, in fact, be experienced as a "continuous interior space. What more generous a welcoming gesture can there be for national and international travelers. I personally have noticed that I now check in a little earlier, because there is so much to see, and the hospitality outlets are such that you could almost come to the airport solely to eat a good meal. That changes the way a city is perceived."

Beijing has opted at the same time to go "iconic," commissioning various striking buildings, regarded by some as possessing great architectural quality and by others as all frills and no substance. In addition to the airport, there is the Rem Koolhaas and OMI CCTV Building on the 3rd Ring Road, not to mention the new opera, and a whole series of high-grade residential, administrative, and commercial properties that have mushroomed. And almost all of them are firm parts in a long-term urban plan that has been moved forward by the wish to get the Olympic facilities ready on time. The facilities for the Games posed logistical, technical, and economic challenges that all had to be mastered in a short span of time and more or less simultaneously. "That led to a kind of quantum leap in urban planning in Beijing," Dell recalls, "but it also meant the population's hearts had to be won over. After all, much patience was required of them, not to say a willingness to make daily sacrifices in the overarching interest of the Games while living for years on an ever larger construction site. But the fact is the Games were a success, so all those individuals feel that what they did was right and feel proud of their 'new' city and its elan."

For all the debates on Tibet and the Internet, for all the fiasco with the torch-bearing runs, and for all the awful coincidence of the May 12 Sichuan earthquake, during the Games themselves the inhabitants of Beijing formed a mass of relaxed and enthusiastic hosts and spectators. And since the Games, the city has definitely, so all visitors narrate, become more self-confident. It has stepped out of the international shadow of Shanghai. It has taken its rightful place on the world stage of major capitals, and the inhabitants have laid claim to that status with pride and dignity rather than with razzmatazz. Johannes Dell says that the litmus test of "ask the cabdriver" shows just how that confidence has grown. If we regard cabdrivers as seismographs for the collective self-assessment of the population of any given city, then "the fact that they responded with humor and a shot of self-irony to my observation that despite China's huge medals haul in the Games, if calculated on a per capita basis the country was actually quite a way down in the medals tables, proved to me just how they had benefited from hosting the Games." The Olympics had indeed given the city a new identity.

The statistics on visitor numbers during the so-called "Golden" October holiday week bear out Dell's assessment. For the first time in the 5,000-odd years that China claims for its history, it was not the Great Wall, an icon if there ever was one, or the Temple of Heaven that bagged the record for the largest number of visitors, but the Olympics complex: with more than 300,000 people – a day! And the city that only a year earlier was suffering awful pollution from traffic and factories, day in, day out, discovered that it could improve the quality of air, and thus of life itself, by telling its citizens to leave their cars at home. Some months after the Games, numerous civil groups in Beijing were insisting that they would welcome a continued ban on cars. In other words, restricting personal mobility with regard to cars has become something that can be discussed in public and partially implemented.

1 Identity & Violence, (Penguin: Harmondsworth, 2006), p. 2
2 ex: The Australian, Jan. 31, 2009, p. 23
3 Yet while Nobel Prize winner for literature William Golding devoted an entire novel to the building of such a cathedral (The Spire), it is hard to imagine the same happening about the construction of a stadium, for all the elegant and awe-inspiring names they now get given.

VI

THINK IN OVERALL CYCLES,
NOT IN SECTORS:
AVOID SHORT-TERM BENEFITS
FOR LONG-TERM GAINS

"An autopoietic machine is a machine organized (defined as a unity) as a network of processes of production (transformation and destruction) of components which: (1) through their interactions and transformations continuously regenerate and realize the network of processes (relations) that produced them; and (2) constitute it (the machine) as a concrete unity in space in which they (the components) exist by specifying the topological domain of its realization as such a network." **Humberto Maturana & Francisco Varela** [1]

PLANNING PLANNING – THE METHODOLOGY FOR LONG-TERM PLANNING

Developing sustainable cities is a never-ending process that must itself constantly be recalibrated to align with overarching strategies, new insights, and changes. The underlying methodology needs therefore to be open-ended and, as a consequence, geared to devising plans that are a series of staggered phases. Planning sustainable cities must in this regard rest on three pillars: an analysis of the respective situation, the achievement of relevant criteria and standards, and constant monitoring. As we have seen in the chapter on decreasing energy inputs, where we focused on the basic building blocks of any city (the individual house or home), sustainable planning starts by considering the overall life cycle of a project. Not only do countless different aspects need to be weighed up against one another, and if possible harmonized, by the interaction of short, medium, and long-term goals – they also need to be duly managed. This means ensuring that the various government, regional, state, and municipal planning levels are involved at the right time as required and that each of the subsidiary levels has the requisite degree of autonomy – a practice that has proved invaluable in developing resilient polycentric structures (see Chap. 9). It also means not forgetting that managing dynamic (planning) processes is a tall order as it requires constantly being prepared to question your own assumptions.

However, conceptually speaking, this is not rocket science, but commensurate with modern thought in physics, for example. We must construe any city as a complex system that is shaped by constant change and development and where factors such as energy, natural resources, transportation, and waste all come to bear, be it as input or as output. The acts of maintaining, restoring, stimulating, and closing cycles contribute to sustain-

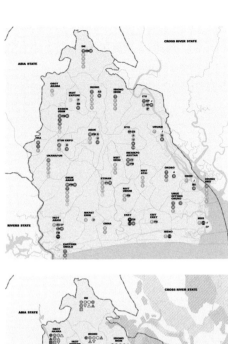

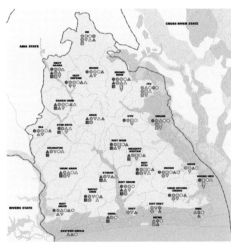

Different elements that go to make up the transportation
master plan for Akwa Ibom state, Nigeria. Rather than treat
transportation in isolation, AS&P first ascertained all the
different sectors that drive the development of the Akwa Ibom
economy, be they mineral deposits, existing industrial
plant, agriculture, or manufacturing. The planners then factored
this information into an equation that included conurbations
and existing transport routes in order to arrive at a holistically-
based proposal for a future transportation network.

able development. The methodological difficulty is in reliably defining system limits and time horizons (see Chap. 9 for a discussion of forecasting and futurology). Yet it is, of course, necessary to try to ascertain the environmental consequences, from start to finish, of a decision or action for the living organism, city, in order to evaluate different performances or compare options – even if this is not as straightforward as it might be when assessing the life cycle of a given product. To this end, AS&P has endeavored to devise a dynamic model for the city – and in true interdisciplinary spirit in this context drew on the assistance of specialist engineers and consultants. The variables thus included in the model of the city are the architecture and buildings, mobility and transportation, the environment (inside/outside), free space, parks, and agriculture – and as the input/output for these: energy, media, water, wastewater, and waste management. Needless to say, in keeping with the overall principle of "think local, act global," the variables have to be adapted on each occasion to the particular system. "It is like thinking in an almost endless series of interlocking cycles, a matrix in which each cell is imperative, but each cell can be optimized to the advantage of the entire system," suggests Michael Denkel. "Only if we think in this way can we start to save resources. And only if we save resources through well-considered urban planning do we have even a slight chance of starting to avoid the impact of entropy, as defined by the second law of thermodynamics, happening sooner rather than later on a global scale."[2]

GHA – ETHICS VS. SHORT-TERM BENEFITS

It is a race against time. After all, the globe is already fast advancing down that one-way path to the end of resources, as a glance at the ecological footprint of many of our cities shows only too clearly. The idea of an ecological footprint was first devised in 1994, and while it is not a certification system it does provide a fundamental yardstick for assessing urban sustainability with regards to the eco-quality of a city. It is also one of the tools AS&P brings to bear in the modeling. Thus, an account is totted up for a city's energy, emission and resource cycles (timber, food, etc.) and then divided by the number of inhabitants. The figure you arrive at is the "global hectare" (gha) or surface area you currently need to maintain your lifestyle per inhabitant (under current conditions). The results reveal that, above all, in Europe, the United States, and Asia a far higher figure is required than the 2.2 hectares cities can afford globally, according to the Global Footprint Network.[3] London requires 293 times its own size, or 6.63 gha per inhabitant – in other words, on average each Londoner is living exactly three times above the globe's means. Berliners on average need 4.4 gha – while inhabitants of the Third World consume, on a per capita basis, less than the possible 2.2 gha. Sustainable planning means seeking to create cities that do not live at the cost of others – a crucial goal in light of the fact that as a totality, the world's cities are already guzzling 80 per cent of the world's resources.

The agonizing fact is that ever since the mid-1980s humanity has, in ecological terms, been living on borrowed time. Which is to say it we have collectively been using more resources than the Earth can regenerate, whereby "we" refers primarily to the industrial-ized nations. World Overshoot Day offers a very graphic indicator of the extent of our ecological deficit: each year, it shows the day on which humanity begins to consume more resources than nature will produce that same year – a notion indebted to the concept of the ecological footprint. The first Overshoot Day, in 1987, was December 19, and the date has been creeping forward ever since. The Global Footprint Network calculated that in 2008 we overshot our ecological budget on September 23, putting us more than 30 per cent into the red – meaning that planet Earth would need at least fifteen months to re-generate what we consumed in only twelve.

So the crunch question here is: How can the ecological footprint be reduced to 2.2 gha by the means currently available to us? It is worth mentioning that about 50 per cent of the footprint stems from food production and transportation, and is thus a variable plan-ners can hardly influence. In light of the information available to them on the impact they are having on the world, its citizens must quite simply decide to change their habits. With regard to the remaining 50 per cent, it is the development, production, and operation of integrative infrastructure projects in particular, so-called "multi-utility concepts," that promise relief. It is here that the combined heat and power plants come into their own – potentially operated today by public private partnerships and therefore economically more feasible in countries where governments are cash-strapped and corporate gover-nance promises greater benefits than does government on its own. Relief can also come from waste management systems that help to prevent waste, separate the waste that is unavoidable, and use it to drive waste-to-power systems.

Just how necessary such careful forward planning is likely to be is more than evident if we bear in mind that in March 2008, that is, prior to the worldwide credit crunch, a McK-insey study concluded that by 2025 in China an additional 350 million people will have moved from the countryside into cities. A billion people will be living in cities and metro-politan regions. 40 billion square meters of space will be needed in some five million buildings, and 50,000 of those could be skyscrapers; about 170 commuter transportation systems will need to be put in place and operated to cope with the load. In fact, a total of 221 cities will then have more than one million inhabitants – compared with a "mere" 35 such cities in Europe today. Evidently, long-term planning is the only way out, specifi-cally with a view to keeping the gha to 2.2. And if we think of gha in terms of other big issues today, it is obviously a world problem. (Factor Africa into the equation, where ur-banization has just nipped past the 50:50 ratio, and where there is no notable agro-indus-try, and the globe does not face prime prospects at all.) Yet, as Michael Hebbert, Professor of Town Planning at of the University of Manchester, says: "Urban design is a set of very simple rules. Present the simple ideas to political decision-makers or the residents of the particular city as just that."

In China, the government is at least very conscious of the eco-strain that the modern-ization of its society entails. Back in 2006, Premier Wen Jiabao already insisted that eco-nomic development and the environment were equal state priorities, thus putting sus-

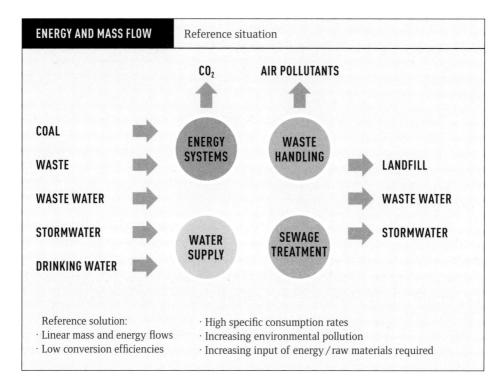

ENERGY AND MASS FLOW | Reference situation

CO$_2$ AIR POLLUTANTS

COAL → ENERGY SYSTEMS

WASTE →

WASTE WATER →   WASTE HANDLING → LANDFILL

STORMWATER →   → WASTE WATER

DRINKING WATER →   WATER SUPPLY   SEWAGE TREATMENT → STORMWATER

Reference solution:
· Linear mass and energy flows
· Low conversion efficiencies

· High specific consumption rates
· Increasing environmental pollution
· Increasing input of energy / raw materials required

tainability firmly on the Chinese agenda. The government identified 55 model cities to present methods of realizing ecological modernization and the path to sustainable development. And more than 70 new laws were enacted covering these areas. Examples like AS&P's new Jing Yue Ecological City project in Changchun – or the Anting New Town in Shanghai's Jarding district, which achieves energy reductions of more than 50 per cent – point the way forward. They also illustrate that China, with its culture of very long-term thinking, seeks support and technology from Europe when it comes to the modernization of its existing metropolises.

PLANNING CYCLES, NOT SECTORS

The planning process must be as far-sighted as possible, and to ensure that all aspects are taken into account in the planning itself the architects must design the building shells in such a way that they can have new skins draped over them without having to alter the core. After all, as Martin Teigeler explains, planning has to be both bottom-up and top-down, it has to be open-ended both at the macro and micro levels, and at the level in between. A prime example for the micro level is a focus on the life cycle of the smallest unit in a city, namely the dwelling or building. Creating each building's primary core structure, the carcass – the most expensive element in a building – entails the highest primary energy inputs. The carcass is also the most permanent part of the building. If it is not designed to take different outer skins (as changes in taste or function may require over time), then the entire building will have to be torn down each time a developer or owner wishes to change it, and its life cycle will, indeed, be a short one. If, however, it is designed to adapt to change, then its life cycle will be more enduring – in an optimal case, building physics suggests a well-built high-rise carcass can last a century. As for the use of steel, it should be reduced to the minimum required to guarantee future load-bearing, but not more than that, as steel is the greatest energy consumer in the building process.

The second level, where thinking in cycles applies in a different way, is the median level. This is where strategies to preserve clean air, water, and soil – and to make certain they are used judiciously – come to bear. It is also where they interact with a focus on a modern infrastructure and advanced technologies (enhanced water treatment, power plant performance, etc.), on reducing traffic, and on provisioning an extensive and adequately-scaled public transport system. The third and uppermost level of planning in terms of a large cycle of interacting elements is the functional level. Here, the master plan must determine the right balance between economic, cultural, traffic, and green-belt functions. The (politically-guided) decisions taken here feed back into the median level, of course.

Together with the engineers at Fichtner Consulting, and with a view to the massive urban projects on drawing boards in China, AS&P has set out to systematize the second and third levels in such a way that resource inputs are minimized and waste outputs are minimized. The critical areas identified are thermal refuse recovery, fossil fuel consumption levels, waste and potable water interaction. The sustainable concept developed on this basis hinges on an intrinsic urban cycle for energy/mass processes, maximized conversion efficiency, and ensuring responsible handling of economic reserves.

INTEGRATING CYCLES: POLICY-MAKING AND CHANGCHUN'S JING YUE ECOLOGICAL CITY

The 1st Law of Thermodynamics states that energy can be transformed, i.e., changed from one form to another, but it can neither be created nor destroyed. However, as we all know, the sad fact is that just because it is there does not mean it always gets used sensibly, and energy does not just get squandered as energy but also in all the different forms of matter that go toward making up a city. Changchun, the vibrant capital city of Jilin Province in North China, is a comparatively young city by Chinese standards, as it is a mere 200 years old. But it is already estimated to have a population of some 3.3 million, with another 7-plus million in the metropolitan region, a figure that is expected to swell by another 3 million by 2020. Given its growth and the fact that high-tech industries, such as the automotive industry, are relocating there, the city authorities decided to build an ecological city to show the way forward – with a footprint of a full 53 square kilometers and destined to house 400,000 inhabitants.

The master plan included all the requisite urban design and technical supply infrastructure, from a combined heat and power plant through to a light rail system, which is, after

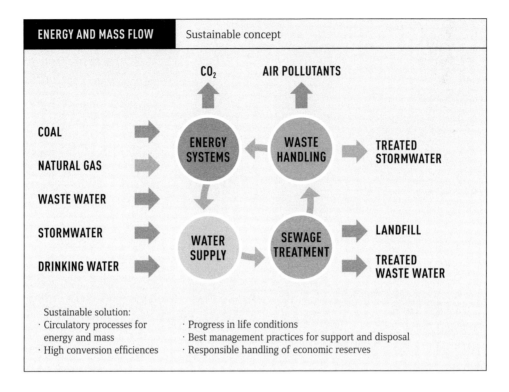

ENERGY AND MASS FLOW | Sustainable concept

CO₂ AIR POLLUTANTS

COAL → ENERGY SYSTEMS ← WASTE HANDLING → TREATED STORMWATER

NATURAL GAS →

WASTE WATER →

STORMWATER → WATER SUPPLY → SEWAGE TREATMENT → LANDFILL

DRINKING WATER → TREATED WASTE WATER

Sustainable solution:
· Circulatory processes for
  energy and mass
· High conversion efficiences
· Progress in life conditions
· Best management practices for support and disposal
· Responsible handling of economic reserves

all, cheaper to build than underground rail systems and should be preferred whenever space requirements permit. Yet it deliberately steered clear of trying to specify all the details. It organized and structured the space on a larger scale while leaving plenty of scope for detailed planning of strong-identity quarters and districts. The plan focused on ensuring that the various neighborhoods that came about would be recognizable as such, that the city was given well-defined entrances, boulevards, streets, and plazas, thus emphasizing public life, and that in all of this, the distances to be covered by the inhabitants would be kept to a minimum by prioritizing mixed uses. At the same time, equal emphasis was placed on making certain that the planning remained open-ended so that it would be able to adapt to long-term planning objectives, such as greater integration of the new high-tech clusters arising to the south, beyond the interstate ring road that acted as the city's boundary.

The key criterion the AS&P planners set out to fulfill was one they had already proposed ten years earlier for Shanghai's district of Yangpu Dinghai, namely, the very same set of interlocking cycles outlined in the charts above. Back then, Chinese society was evidently not ready for the idea, because while the proposals were praised, they were not realized, whereas Changchun has declared all systems "go." The master plan structures the city to match the old canals and rivers and to reinforce the existing green belts, subdividing the eco-city into six districts in line with the notion of a multitopia – each has its own center with all the functions described above as the third planning level:

dwellings, education, culture, leisure, business, and administration. At the same time, all service facilities and public transport stops are walkable, something that is both a novelty in China and a necessity if fuel prices rise. Moreover, the transportation feeds into the regional and urban road network – the north/south boulevard stipulated by Chinese tradition is adopted here to connect the city with recreation zones around the reservoir to the south. To underscore the significance of the boulevard, there are eight metro stations along it. In short, the crucial aspect here is that, thanks to dense dwelling structures and mixed usage, short distances reduce mobility from the outset. In this way, with the right initial decisions at the master-plan level, real savings can be made further down the road at no cost.

This integration emulates that proposed for the urban technologies the city will need. The pivotal idea underlying the master plan is its introduction of second-level planning into China: the dovetailing of transportation, goods, energy, and water cycles to spare resources. This is absolutely critical in light of what international advisers have recently stated in connection with growth in China.

This is then supplemented by a recommendation, with regard to building technologies, that the deliberate policy be to adopt low-energy solutions – in other words, to plan carefully at the first level. Peter Kern, who has been leading the planning team, comments: "Here in China the status of integrated systems is not yet as great as it could be, but the trend is positive. We expect that our Changchun proposal will be received favorably and therefore be realized, at least in part. Despite the fact that it does not promulgate one of the two typically Chinese solutions: an ornamental city layout or a highly technical solution that prioritizes uniformity and monotony for the sake of uniformity and to the detriment of livability. To this end, we are currently exploring deeper-level planning and working out details for the overall construction management, such as calibration of eco-impact and compensation."

Perhaps what is so unusual about the plans for Jing Yue is the way in which they interlock all three levels and seek to coordinate cycles that are otherwise disparate in most Chinese metropolises. The bane of much Chinese planning has been that, probably owing to the sheer size of the administrations, much of the work in the various departments has not been coordinated with the work done by fellow planners. AS&P insisted on taking a different approach when tackling the work for and in Changchun, and having championed an integrated, cycle-based planning methodology there for the last four years, is gradually encountering far greater acceptance. The focus in Jing Yue, therefore, was first on where the city was, what surrounded it, how it would interlink with this "hinterland" (that is to say, the north/south axis described above), and then on deciding how to meet the objectives. To this end, all the existing plans and information first had to be compiled, itself not a matter of course. After all, cities often do not know what data resources they have lying round in drawers in the different departments. Here, the master planners essentially act as mediators, bringing everyone together at the table, and when everyone is finally at the table, they are often surprised to learn what their peers are doing – giving a

new meaning to integrated planning. Michael Denkel recalls one such session, in this case relating to planning for Abuja West, in Nigeria, where the technocrats in question were horrified to find out what the various parties involved in the process were doing. "Since we were responsible for the master plan, one of the first things we did was to bring all the various agencies and consultants together. On closer inspection it transpired that the Chinese railway engineers had designed the run-in to the main railway station without noticing that they had a river underneath it. Sadly, such mistakes are not a rare occurrence. Often, one department does not know what another further down the same corridor has planned. We even had an instance in Cairo where the high-voltage pylons were suddenly positioned in the middle of a road. The crucial thing, of course, is to notice these things before they actually get built."

With this in mind, AS&P made it a priority in Changchun from the outset to find out what it was that connected the different districts, the waste cycle, and the water cycle, and to make very certain that decisions about specific functions were not made parallel to each other. After all, it is abundantly clear that any uncoordinated decision will prejudice the others and will eventually become a thorn in the side of the planner doing the detailed work or, even worse, in the sides of the future inhabitants. Indeed, the contract for Jing Yue explicitly directed AS&P to determine how – in the morass of already approved fragmented plans and ideas, of island solutions here and there – a structure could be created, and guidelines established for future, purposeful, streamlined, and focused development. Johannes Dell comments with a smile: "Coordination is imperative as if you want to build a city that will be driven by industry: plan a major chemicals plant on the drawing board, you must make certain the zone you go for is not beautiful countryside that is better suited for residential dwellings, by which time you have stuck the dwellings somewhere that is sub-optimal and far from its inhabitants' workplaces – and then it is all too late anyway as the bulldozers are already rolling. That situation would be very bitter for all concerned and would waste public funds and energy."

ENERGY PRODUCTIVITY   *"Energy demand is rising in China and worldwide at high speed. Oil and gas are getting scarce and expensive. Coal is available but causes big environmental problems locally and globally (global warming). Renewable sources of energy enjoy strong growth rates but will for a long time to come remain a limited option, chiefly for reasons of space and cost. Nuclear energy in relevant amounts will face serious problems of uranium scarcity (uranium prices have risen much faster than oil prices in recent years), not to mention the problems with radioactive waste, and the nuclear cycle's vulnerability to terrorism and wars. The core of the answer to the energy challenges may come not from modified energy supplies but from a systematic, long-term strategy of increasing energy productivity, which essentially means curbing energy demand while further increasing prosperity." Ernst Ulrich von Weizsäcker*[4]

The master plans for Jing Yue therefore set out to channel all efforts and ensure that the zoning and land-use plans always kept the overall structure or bigger picture in mind, taking their cue from the topography and geography. For example, if there is a reservoir, think of how it can be used to enhance the population's quality of life and do not put a detached commercial or industrial estate there, and in the catchment area, where there are canals or rivers, opt for "soft solutions", i.e. non-industrial structures. As we have seen, these very elementary considerations played a clear role in the master plan, although the planners no doubt trod on the feet of the various groups who had vested interests in the one or other solution. In any country worldwide, land-use rights always involve possible future value increases in the assets concerned. There are plenty of examples around the globe of cities which, mindful of the value of their land assets, have aligned the land-use rights to ensure maximum financial benefit for the municipal authorities. In days of cash-strapped municipalities they are essentially acting rationally in the interests of their shareholders, the inhabitants. Yet irrespective of whether the cash accrued is devoted to municipal services or not, that short-term benefit does not offset the potential long-term detriment to the city of land zoning, which makes no sense, even if it does make dollars. Here, again, we can discern the difficult tightrope that planners have to walk when advising politicians.

INTERACTING VARIABLES IN NIGERIA – PLANNING SUSTAINABILITY ONE LEVEL HIGHER

In 2000, the new, democratically-elected government of Nigeria came to realize that the situation in the entire Nigerian transport sector involved logjams in three crucial areas: between the critical demand if the country is to grow and the ability of the transport sector to meet this demand; between the resources required to maintain and renew the existing transportation infrastructure and the resources available; and between resources allocated to different transportation modes and their importance within an efficient transportation system. Given this state of affairs, a decision was made by the Federal Ministry of Transport to develop a "Master Plan for an Integrated Transportation Infrastructure in Nigeria" featuring an integrated approach. In a unique alliance, the Ministry of Transport teamed up with the planning experts at AS&P to compile that master plan. Little did anyone realize at the time where this undertaking would lead.

VISION 2020 FOR TRANSPORTATION

The scope of the plan hinged on an analysis of the status quo in the Nigerian transportation sector: the road and railway networks, seaport facilities, airports, inland waterways, and pipeline systems. And it did so in terms of the third level discussed above, for the basic presumption was that the "transport infrastructure must be seen as being more than an instrument towards the transportation of goods and people; rather, it forms an essential foundation for future economic and social development."[5] It followed that an analysis of the transportation infrastructure, while indicating what was possible, said nothing about how that infrastructure might need to be adapted to reflect spatial developments at the national level, be it urban, industrial or agricultural growth. In other words, it became clear to everyone involved that any transportation plan had to dovetail, on the one hand, with an overall national development plan and, on the other, with local detailed implementation. Here, again, the notion of thinking in cycles rather than specific sectors was imperative, for it was clear that what suited one sector (banking) would not necessarily help another, such as agriculture. The planners therefore first defined spatial development, namely, new economic zones which could be regionally developed, and derived from this proposals for the country's transportation sector.

As a first step, the planners set out to try to establish recommendations for an efficient transportation infrastructure – the yardstick being travel duration, travel speed, and distances; environmental protection; interconnectivity; logical hierarchies in prioritization – in light of the national planning goals as a whole. The latter focused on development of three economic sectors in particular, namely: a) agriculture, mining, and quarrying; b) industry and manufacturing; and c) services. Somehow, the transportation master plan would need to factor all three areas into its equations.

Consequently, the planners and strategists considered a wide range of variables, such as a projected population increase of approximately 50 per cent 20 years down the line. This was critical in the calculations, for if the population were to grow that fast it implied that the agricultural sector would have to be semi-industrialized in order to guarantee a sufficient food supply without importing food crops. It also implied that the food would have to move from the farms to the cities in time for it to be eaten – most Nigerian families do not have refrigerators, so food has to be bought fresh and eaten fresh because unrefrigerated food does not last long in Nigeria's hot, subtropical climate. Preliminary studies revealed that Nigeria's Middle Belt was the obvious prime base for agriculture and that the country was already experiencing difficulty in getting bulk agricultural goods into urban areas quickly enough.

The crunch question the plan therefore had to answer was: How must transportation evolve to enable it to handle the incredible tonnage of food that would be required in 20 years' time? The solution identified key road corridors, most of which already existed but were in need of maintenance. At the same time, priority was attached to the phased introduction of a railway network backbone based on standard-gauge tracks that ran centrally north/south and east/west to the south of the Middle Belt in a loop that connected the country's four major seaports. The plan put its case here in very unequivocal terms: "Lagos shall be connected to the southern urban agglomeration areas and to the farm areas along the River Niger and in the north to ensure a stable food supply in the future."[6] The planners went one step further and reintroduced a traditional form of national transport as a crucial contributor to future growth: the inland waterways. The planners pronounced: "The areas directly adjacent to the rivers are predominantly agricultural land

and are underdeveloped compared with other parts of Nigeria. Therefore, one objective should be to promote development in these areas by making the inland waterway mode of transport attractive."[7] The study likewise discerned that industrial locations needed to have better access to infrastructure, primarily railways and roads, in order to support economic development.

↑

A third of Nigeria lies in the tropics, where the rainy season is especially fierce and the torrential downpours often turn unpaved roads into small rivers within only a few hours.

The planners also concluded that by 2020, traffic volumes would have doubled, with the existing major transportation corridors carrying the majority of the transport volumes, leading to capacity problems and potential rapid deterioration of the road network. In the field of road transport they therefore set immediate priorities in the form of three road corridors. However, in doing so they realized that the volume of funding required would place an immense strain on the national budget – and they thus moved back from the mega level to the micro level, suggesting shorter toll roads that could be run as PPPs. As a result, the finished master plan includes a recommendation that systematic privatization be deployed to promote private-sector investment to the extent that it hinged on proposals for a prudent transportation infrastructure that integrated and interfaced the different transportation modes and defined priority projects.

This new integrated transportation network was designed to provide an optimal multi-mode transportation system within the major communication corridors to support economic and regional development through 2020. In the process, efficient, flexible, and integrated connections would be firmly established between the major cities, the capital Abuja, and major areas of economic activity, such as Kano in the north or Lagos in the southwest. The integrated transportation infrastructure proposals culminated in a suggested policy framework for the country going forwards. Put differently, what started out as a request for a study on transportation issues morphed into policy advice on how to enable the country's economic growth within 20 years.[8] In the process, the short-term benefits of the traditional, exclusive focus on roads were eschewed in favor of the long-term advantages of rail and inland waterways. To this end, discrete processes were networked, sectors interlinked, and the country as a whole taken seriously as a "concrete unity in space."

1   *Maturana, Humberto and Varela, Francisco ([1st edition 1973] 1980),* Auto-poiesis and Cognition: the Realization of the Living. *Robert S. Cohen and Marx W. Wartofsky (eds.), Boston Studies in the Philosophy of Science 42. Dordecht: D. Reidel Publishing Co., p. 78*

2   *Reichholf has written elsewhere that full sustainability is a contradictory concept if construed in terms of input/output: "... if there really were complete cycles or rather perfect recycling, then this would simply contradict the basic laws of nature, or to be more precise the second law of thermodynamics. Perfect sustainability would be a 'perpetuum mobile,' and is thus impossible." Reichholf, Josef H.,* Stabile Ungleichgewichte – Die Ökologie der Zukunft, *Suhrkamp Verlag Frankfurt/M., 2008), p. 117*

3   *http://www.footprintnetwork.org/en/index.php/GFN/; table with the eco-footprint of selected cities: ecological footprint atlas 2008 version 1.0, as a pdf*

4   *ex: Ernst Ulrich v. Weizsäcker Website*

5   *Master plan for an Integrated Transportation Infrastructure, Nigerian Institute of Transport Technology, February, 2002, p. 16*

6   *Ibid., p. 180*

7   *Ibid., p. 188*

8   *The detailed work in the study was enough to attract potential financial backers, such as the International Monetary Fund (IMF) and the World Bank at a later date.*

VII

DO NOT LET TRANSPORTATION MODES COMPETE FOR SPACE: PRESENT MOBILITY FOSTERS IMMOBILITY

"Bangkok and Dar es Salaam, for instance, have more cars per capita than Tokyo and Mumbai have. On the other hand, in Singapore, the number of private vehicles per 1,000 inhabitants is lower than that of many cities in the developing world – a result of the city-state's effective mobility policy." **UN Habitat**[1]

KEEP FUNCTIONS SEPARATE! was the battle cry of the Athens Charter, penned in 1933. Yet instead of bringing us more quality of life, what it resulted in was primarily one thing: distance. Namely, the distance between your home, your place of work, and the stores selling the goods you need to survive.

So how many kilometers does a yogurt travel until it reaches the cooled shelf in the supermarket? Estimates vary, but the distance is most definitely a few thousand kilometers. The reason: rationalization in the food industry has led to most regional yogurt suppliers going bankrupt. All that remain are central, large-scale dairy factories spread across Europe. Over the years, the path traveled by each individual item of food to get to the consumer has become longer and longer. In fact, today, identical products are increasingly often the subject of cross-border transactions. An example from Great Britain illustrates the point: in 2000, it exported some 213,000 tons of pork while at the same time importing 272,000 tons. "That tots up to 20,000 ecologically quite superfluous truck rides," gauges Alois Heißenhuber, Professor of Farming and Transportation in Bavaria. He calculates that a good 80 per cent of the contents of an average basket of food could be stocked with produce from the vicinity.[2] Not least the rising price of gasoline at the pump proved this approach nonsensical. In fact, do we find ourselves taking a detour on that brief shopping trip to town just to avoid a jam on a main road during rush hour?

It would seem obvious that we must quickly start looking for pragmatic ways of changing well-trodden mobility patterns. Primarily, this involves cutting back on personal means of transport in old and new cities alike. Crush-hours tend to be the product of commuting, such as in London, or of urban residents wanting a day in the country, as in Frankfurt. "We won't get a handle on the commuting problem by simply building more and more roads, or introducing tolls. Instead, we must start insisting that people live *and* work in the cities," Albert Speer says defiantly. And the gridlocks associated with people all heading for the countryside at the weekend could likewise be solved if a city offered its inhabitants a far greater range of green areas for leisure-time pursuits.

A glance at the immobility in threshold countries goes to show just how the current view of mobility has to be changed if it is not to morph completely into immobility. If we consider Abuja (Nigeria), Bangalore (India), or Caracas (Venezuela) as the ABC of the three fasting growing cities on the planet, and remember that each of them is plagued by a blanket gridlock every morning and every evening, then we soon realize that things cannot go on this way. The number of cars in each city has rocketed, while road construction has been left in the slow lane. Jams are the rule, not the exception, with the result that people forfeit quality time with their families, and blast massive amounts of CO_2 into the air at the same time in a vain attempt to move forwards – more so because these are also countries where air-conditioning in cars is the norm in summer. This is happening, of all places, in countries where skilled staff are desperately needed; those very employees spend an average of three hours, or almost half a working day, traveling to and from work. This resource madness is compounded by the fact that the cars they use guzzle far more gasoline and are subject to more wear and tear than the cars would if they were driven steadily over long distances.

This problem is unknown in Curitiba, Brazil, where the city council decided as long ago as the 1960s to establish an effective and cheap mass transport system and has even dedicated two lanes on dual carriageways to buses. Istanbul, Turkey, has been forced into action and is now finding out to its dismay a) how long road-building takes, b) what social tensions clearing a right of way can cause, and c) that building streetcar systems into existing road structures can be a planner's nightmare.

Traffic, as we know it today, is primarily the product of high speed. Practically speaking, this means that we take just as long as ever to get to work but think, because our cars are faster, that we travel longer distances in the process. Time spent in traffic has, so statistics reveal, increased only slightly in recent decades: each person spends an average of 1 to 1.5 hours on the road each weekday. In other words, the time that commuters spend in traffic, the travel-time budget, is not affected by the speed of the preferred type of transportation. Scholars are currently debating whether our travel-time budget as a constant of the age of (im)mobility is not perhaps a standard human physiobiological variable. This would at least explain why the number of paths a person takes each day likewise remains more or less unchanged: on average, each of us takes one of three paths: to work, to school, or to shop. Irrespective of where we live, each path takes an average of 20–30 minutes. Modern man as prehistoric wanderer?

SUSTAINABLE MOBILITY

The terms mobility and traffic are often used as synonyms. When, in fact, there is a crucial difference: "MOBILITY is what you need to cover distances in order to perform activities outside the house. TRAFFIC is the actual change of location of people or goods that depends on human actions and the environment involved."[3]

To put it in terms accessible to the non-expert: traffic always arises when people make factual use of their mobility and thus move from A to B. How can they do so in a sustainable manner? What can sustainability mean in the traffic context? Does more mobility automatically spell less sustainability?

Such definitions are a good starting point to show the three steps AS&P uses to define "sustainability." Thus, reducing traffic is the *ecological* side to sustainable mobility, as this impacts positively on energy, resource and land consumption. Moreover, when planning and building sustainable infrastructure, there must be an *economic* focus on cost efficiency, in particular if public financing is involved. Finally, sustainable mobility has a *social* component, as it involves participation in social life and the protection of the built environment.

Essentially, it remains hard to define sustainability with any precision, specifically as regards mobility, because competing areas interact or depend on one another (business, politics, social criteria, technology, leisure time), and the goals quite obviously often conflict. It may be sound environmentally logical to build roads to eliminate traffic bottlenecks, as this guarantees traffic flows, the eco-strain is reduced, and costs are lowered, yet by increasing the amount of traffic through a specific area we encourage an increase in traffic per se rather than mobility. This is not to say that planners and politicians should lose sight of the key goal: a sustainable city requires a concept of mobility anchored in the notion of sustainability.

THE FUNDAMENTALS OF A SUSTAINABLE CONCEPT OF MOBILITY

The results of a survey conducted in the summer of 2008 by the "meinestadt.de" urban portal show that, contrary to popular opinion, a reduction in mobility does not necessarily entail less quality of life for those affected.[4] The findings were that a good half of all Germans still live in or near their home town and that a good quarter of these non-movers still live in the parental home, which indicates that mobility needs to be defined more closely.

In general, the goals of a sustainable concept of mobility are: cuts in toxic and noise emissions, greater traffic safety, reduced consumption of resources, lower levels of land utilization, and enhanced accessibility. Many of the approaches that seek to achieve these goals focus on strengthening mass transport and prioritizing slower traffic. They position an expanded mass transport network as the spine of urban development. If the various modes of transport stop competing for space, and if mass transport and cycles are given their own dedicated lanes, then cycling becomes more appealing. Moreover, mass transport networks need to be fine-tuned to the specific structure of the respective districts. Put differently: stops must be located close to the highly frequented areas in a district and thus guarantee that only short distances need to be covered on foot.

An attractive network of pedestrian areas and cycle tracks (the latter supported by a variety of services) further detract from the need for cars. Only if networks are sufficiently close-meshed and the dimensions scaled appropriately will they be comfortable and easy to use. "There's nothing worse, as any car driver will tell you, than having to watch out for cyclists weaving in and out of traffic in front of you, popping out of concealed entranceways or intersections. There's nothing worse," claims Michael Denkel,

↑
An ideal combination: cycle racks outside the
access to the light rail system in Frankfurt.

↑
Frankfurt's park guidance system directs motorists straight to free spaces in car
parks and reduces the need to cruise on the lookout for a free parking slot.

"than worrying whether you are going to be run over by the car driver behind you who
is revving his engine and raring to overtake you, or whether he'll stick to the mandatory
two meters the law allows cyclists as a safety cushion."

Municipalities tend to rely on a variety of carrot-and-stick measures to reduce motorized traffic. The carrots include mobility centers (for example, car-sharing hubs) while the
sticks involve legal restrictions (such as eco-levies, limited-access car parking) or access
restrictions (car-free districts). In general, mixed usages (feeder roads or reduced speed
zones) and compact, densely built housing reduce travel distances – and make good carrots. Another measure that makes a good stick is to gradually force parked cars off the
street, for example, by providing mechanical parking systems and car parks (if necessary,
under public spaces, parks, and roads) that are always located at the same distance from
bus, streetcar, or subway stops. If they are specifically positioned on main trunk roads
and feeder roads then car-based traffic will be further reduced. The urban space that will
then be available is potentially immense.

Private and commercial goods transport into urban quarters can also be better coordinated or minimized: options here are goods-transport distribution hubs as well as waste

disposal systems that run regular routes, mobility counseling, freight exchanges, combined rail/road terminals, and assistance in loading. All of these would reduce traffic levels.

INTELLIGENT TRAFFIC MANAGEMENT

Given financial constraints, and urban planning and ecological goals, it is hardly likely that the transport infrastructure will be expanded in the foreseeable future to meet greater demand. However, a city will suffer if its traffic system is dysfunctional, as this will impair the city's appeal. One instrument that can alleviate things is intelligent traffic management. This begins with how existing infrastructure is used. An example: AS&P has suggested that on the interstate ring round Frankfurt the hard shoulder be opened to traffic at peak or stress-load times, thus eliminating the need to devote immense sums to building an extra lane.

Traffic flow in Frankfurt is controlled and managed from the city's traffic management center, whose functions were likewise defined in an AS&P study. One result has been a series of electronic panels on main trunk roads leading into town informing traffic participants which diversions they can take to avoid road construction sites or tailbacks. "By providing information at such an early point in the process," explains Michael Dinter, AS&P managing partner and traffic planner, "and thus motivating people to switch to mass transport or to drive a different route, I'm doing a lot to improve the quality of life in the city by slashing emissions, minimizing lost time, and making sure traffic does what it should do: keep flowing." This sounds easy, but involves complex theoretical plan scenarios that respond to specific traffic conditions: when Problem A arises, deploy strategy B.

Needless to say, such a communal system also comes up against (natural) constraints, because traffic does not just stop at the city limits. "That," Dinter says, "is the trickiest thing about traffic, as you must never analyze a problem in isolation but think of all the different aspects equally." Not even the best traffic control strategy will work if the next level up in the administration, or other mass transport operators, do not think and act the same way – one city on its own cannot act efficiently as regards traffic, since cars must obviously come from somewhere and go somewhere. Strategies thus need to be coordinated at the state level, and include interstate links and regional mass transport authorities. However, achieving such a level of cooperation and dovetailing is no mean task, as most traffic planners will tell you.

The idea behind the system in Frankfurt is the by-product of a feasibility study conducted in the late 1990s. The system was put in place in time for the 2006 World Cup, and soon proved its mettle. The highways round the stadium on the outskirts of Frankfurt are under the jurisdiction of the State of Hessen, while the roads connecting them to the car parks outside the stadium belong to the city. Precise plans were devised for filling and emptying the car parks before and after the soccer matches. One of the AS&P staffers involved recalls with a grin: "Suddenly everyone was working together – after all, no one wanted the embarrassment of a mess-up at the World Cup."

AS&P likewise planned the automatic status displays for Frankfurt's car parks. They provide "direct guidance," steering the flow of cars down streets that largely do not impact on the urban fabric. The primary objective was to stop cars circling the city in their hunt for parking spaces and keeping them on the roads on which they belong. This focuses traffic in spatial terms: for example, visitors entering downtown Frankfurt from outside do so via roads that access various car parks in order to ensure that they find spaces. And the success rate? Michael Dinter reports proudly that "our system has reduced by 20–30 per cent the number of cars hunting for parking space" – showing how IT can help to spare the (built) environment.

MASS TRANSPORT

Even the best traffic management system will fail from the outset if a functioning mass transport system for commuters does not at the same time take the edge off things. No larger city can afford to neglect mass transportation, unless it wishes to collapse into chaos, as happens in London, for example, when its subway trains fail to run. In the United States, the "European" cities of New York and San Francisco with their extensive mass transit networks seem to be best prepared for the tide of change in mobility. The worldwide renaissance of the streetcar, which started in the eco-aware Scandinavian countries, marks the start of this changed mindset. "I still remember well," Michael Dinter recounts, "how at the end of the 1980s the Frankfurt City authorities decided to abolish streetcars altogether. The slogan was the 'streetcar-free city center'." Yet relying only on streetcars is equally ill-advised. What counts is to get passengers from the surrounding region into town as quickly as possible. Once people reach downtown, then the two or three minutes' difference between taking a subway train, streetcar or bus is of little consequence. And the fact that subways are quickest is not really perceived as such. Not to mention that going underground means descending into long dark passageways that eat up the time potentially won – just as subway construction eats up treasury coffers fastest.

LIMITS TO PLANNING

Just knowing what is techn(olog)ically possible does not suffice. You have to start with the problem, not with possible theories or ideologies, as that way you soon find out what is feasible – and holistic pragmatism is as apposite here as it is in other aspects of the sustainable city. Traffic guidance systems, shifts in traffic flow, and avoiding traffic may all help to lessen the strain cars put on cities, but they will not change the fact that there are cars, as long as this form of mobility is attractive. The renaissance of the European city over the next few years[5] will help reduce traffic levels further, as urbanites will have to cover shorter distances between home and work. Yet traffic planners are now asking themselves new questions, such as how to serve the regions where population density is dropping dramatically – and where rail lines have already been abandoned as unprofitable. In some regions, all that remains are school

LAGOS LOST N120BN TO CONGESTION IN OSHODI
The Lagos State Governor, Mr. Babatunde Fashola, on Sunday said that government was forced to pull down illegal structures in Oshodi since it was losing N120bn annually. Fashola, who was fielding questions from an occasion organized to mark his first 600 days in office in Alausa, said that demolition of illegal structures in Oshodi was necessary to save the state N120bn being lost as a result of the heavy traffic jams in the area. According to the governor, most people resident in Lagos avoid the area and prefer to travel long distances to their destinations instead of using Agege Motor Road, which is shorter. He said, 'Though the demolition is painful, the interest of the few who have constituted a law unto themselves cannot override the general interest of the people of Lagos State.' Efforts are being made to ensure that those displaced are accommodated in markets being developed by the state government in various areas in Lagos State.[6]

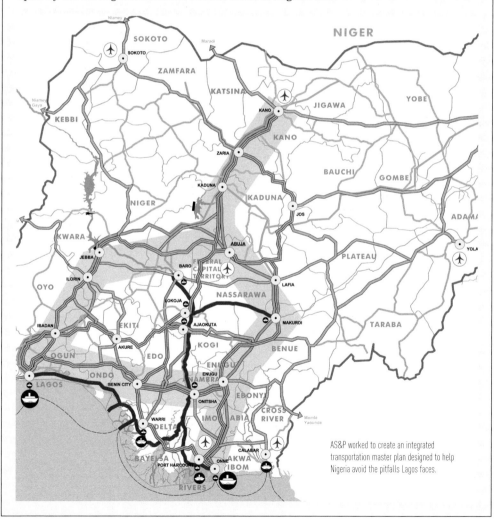

AS&P worked to create an integrated transportation master plan designed to help Nigeria avoid the pitfalls Lagos faces.

buses – or cars. Having studied Frankfurt in the course of his work, Albert Speer suggests that "we must not completely sever our ties to the countryside and simply focus on cities. But the issue of how rural areas will in future be accessed by public transport, and it will be necessary for the elderly in the population, has still to be confronted properly."

There is no silver bullet to ensure you choose the right traffic-planning instrument that gets you success in time. The road to progress is littered with examples of purported solutions that went wrong and with solutions that were wrong at the time but have since been proved right. Is Bangalore right to opt for complete pandemonium in its downtown for a number of years because the building sites are necessary to erect an overhead streetcar system – or should the city have tried to keep the cars out? Predicting the future is a complex matter, specifically for traffic planners, and sustainable urban planning must thus specify mass transport zones in the master plans long in advance of the need for them – or risk the ire of home owners when buildings have to be torn down later on to make way for tracks. It is a lesson that many a city worldwide has learned the hard way. Today, if planners seek to use such zones for a different purpose they find themselves hard pressed by colleagues and politicians alike to justify their proposals. Planning is, after all, itself a process in flux and has to be as open-ended as the sustainable city itself.

TRAFFIC EDUCATION

There is an ongoing debate at AS&P over the general level at which traffic and mobility can be managed in terms of sustainability. Michael Dinter is of the opinion that "we must not restrict mobility, but develop alternatives. The decisions are for society or the politicians, not for us." Michael Denkel contests this, claiming that there is too much mobility: "As an urban planner, I think people should move closer together, we must build denser structures. I would expect traffic planners to call strongly for a change in behavioral patterns. We once lived with far less mobility." (The big background issue, of course, is whether we can afford the same standard of living ad infinitum irrespective of the cost.)

What produces results? Compulsion or intelligent technology plus patience. The combustion engine, for example, is an outdated technology and is bound to become extinct in the not too distant future – if only because of its cost. Indeed, today, in the West at least, we are witnessing a nadir in the prestige associated with cars. Sales of new cars have sagged, and cars on the road are being kept on it far longer than once was the case in an industry that thrived on non-sustainable, built-in obsolescence. And only a very few (well-heeled) people expect to derive distinction from driving gas-guzzlers or Hummers, given the disastrous climate change hanging over our heads. Can it be coincidence that the new museums of the icons of the German auto industry (Mercedes, Porsche, and BMW) are running a retrospective on "automobility"?

So is there a future for cars in the sustainable city? "Well, you don't really need to own one," Michael Dinter cautions. "There's car-sharing instead – which means car numbers could be slashed dramatically – and would be used only for very specific purposes, such as buying furniture. Or at the weekend, or for vacationing. For which you could hire them, checking them out of the garage in your own district." Ironically, in Germany it's the railways that are blazing the trail – by running the largest car- and cycle-share pool.

Albert Speer points to the price of gasoline as a simple corrective here. Once it rises again, so the days of fossil-fuel-driven cars will be numbered, he suggests. After all, who will be able to afford a car that they use only twice a week? Traffic and mobility patterns would then change in line with the market. Is the debate one that will be resolved by time itself? And will we see continued asymmetries between the industrialized and the emerging markets in this respect?

Prompting a change in behavior by education is perhaps an even lengthier process. Experience shows that people do not change their travel habits simply because they often get caught in gridlocks. If that were the case, then Rio de Janeiro and São Paulo would long since be car-free in the morning and early evening. The success of voluntary acceptance of a traffic concept is the product of a good mass transit system. Put drastically: if the car driver sees the bus in the bus lane whiz past him every morning when he is stuck in a traffic jam, he may end up buying a bus ticket sooner rather than later. In megacities such as Cairo (see Chap. 11), buses are not about to change much, as there are no bus lanes. "What counts here is to make sure no two types of transport compete for space. That is the crux of the matter. And that will decide the future, of that I am sure," suggests Michael Dinter.

However, mass transit systems must be affordable. This is a matter of equitable policy-making. There are hundreds of millions today who cannot afford their own car. They take the bus or the streetcar anyway. The sole reward they could get for their exemplary behavior would be cheaper tickets.

Wherever appeals to common sense have not borne fruit and mobility patterns have remained unchanged in a big way, the only option has been prohibition and rules, or rather going for the motorist's jugular: his wallet. Traffic lights are a case in point: crossing them at red costs money in most countries. Parking fines are another. Money is a prime traffic-management instrument, as the example of London has shown conclusively. Lord Mayor Ken Livingston introduced a so-called Congestion Charge in 2003 – and despite being the butt of criticism then, he has since been proved right in terms of traffic management – even if one considers only the numbers of bicycles now apparent in the City. One month after the plan was launched a newspaper wrote:

"The London congestion charge has made less money than expected because thousands of motorists have stayed away from the centre of the capital. Fees paid by road users in the first month of the controversial project – the country's biggest experiment with congestion charging – have been estimated at £9m. A member of the board for Transport for London (TfL) said traffic in the eight square miles of the zone had fallen by 20 per cent, rather than the 15 per cent planners expected."[7]

The example of the London congestion charge has also convinced Michael Dinter, who now gladly recommends it as a traffic-planning tool all over Europe and Asia. A similar

CURITIBA BUS SYSTEM The bus system in Curitiba, Brazil, exemplifies a model Bus Rapid Transit (BRT) system, and plays a large part in making this a livable city. The buses run frequently – some as often as every 90 seconds – and reliably, and the stations are convenient, well-designed, comfortable, and attractive. Consequently, Curitiba has one of the most heavily used, yet low-cost, transit systems in the world. It offers many of the features of a subway system – vehicle movements unimpeded by traffic signals and congestion, fare collection prior to boarding, quick passenger loading and unloading – but it is above ground and visible. Around 70 per cent of Curitiba's commuters use the BRT to travel to work, resulting in congestion-free streets and pollution-free air for the 2.2 million inhabitants of greater Curitiba.[8]

instrument that works at a different level has recently been included in the array of planning tools used by German municipalities: eco- or fine-particle certification. Originally, the idea was to banish vehicles emitting soot particles in their exhausts from inner cities that were reeling under heavy concentrations of fine particles. "And that was just the beginning," Dinter claims, "as the idea of certification has given local authorities an instrument that in the long term will enable them to directly influence the scale of inner-city traffic."

VISION OF FRANKFURT IN 2030 – MOBILITY AS A CORE THEME

Frankfurt, where AS&P has its head office, is a classic city of commuters. During each working day, the population swells, doubling to a good 1.2 million. The figure itself indicates just what traffic strain the city has to endure compared with its size. It is, therefore, hardly surprising that mobility is one of the core themes that AS&P discusses in its study on "Frankfurt For Everyone"[9] – the primary goal being to secure sustainable mobility for the future and minimize its negative impact.

Before any new rail tracks get laid or zones are declared closed to traffic, political hurdles have to be overcome, as Frankfurt itself has only a limited influence on traffic flow. It needs to reach agreements and cooperate with other cities and towns in the vicinity if a new mobility concept is to be a success – especially given the exemplary polycentric structure of the Rhine-Main region. In such a setting, it is disastrous when a mayor in an outlying town decides to approve new housing estates located well away from rail connections, given that more than 70 per cent of commuters into the city still insist on traveling by car – despite the fact that when their opinion is polled, many go on record as saying that they could reach their destinations well or very easily using public transport. Not to forget the leisure-time traffic going in the opposite direction, as estimates indicate the volume will grow by one third by 2030.

All of this simply goes to show just what potential for mass transport slumbers in the Frankfurt-Rhine-Main region – be it by bus, rail, bicycle, or on foot. The fact that Frankfurt is already doing a good job in this regard, compared with other German cities and given the prime rail-based links in the region, shows just how much room for improvement there is. If a significant number of commuters were to decide overnight to switch to mass transport, the system would soon bottleneck during the rush hour; and in the absence of massive public investment in expanding the network, the number of passengers using it could be increased only if they change their travel habits and become more flexible. This is quite conceivable. School pupils flood the mass-transport systems in the early morning. Were schools to start an hour later and then to last an hour longer, this wave of users would not get in the way of their adult counterparts and vice versa.

In the long term, Frankfurt and the surrounding region will simply have to bite the bullet and expand their public transportation network, which is currently a radial system with all tracks leading to the city center. AS&P believes one obvious way to solve bottlenecks would be to build a streetcar line that runs a ring around the city.

→
The Bangkok overhead loop – like that in Chicago, the system makes certain cars and light rail do not compete – giving the latter a real time advantage.

What is crucial is to make motorized transport compatible with the city. The prime tool brought to bear to this end: a speed limit of 30 km/h. Today, many German cities already insist on such a speed limit in various commercial and residential streets, but do not apply it consistently to entire districts, which tend to get carved up by various streets where 50 km/h is the norm. Therefore in future, so AS&P proposes, the higher speed limit should be permitted only on a few select main thoroughfares. The lower speed limit would apply in the rest of the city, taking the interests of residents, pedestrians, and shop owners – traffic safety, safer sidewalks, enjoyment of street life, less noise – more strongly into account.

In the AS&P mindset, there is a clear no. 1 mobility option: the bicycle. Pedal power still tends to be the exception rather than the rule in Germany or Great Britain, in Manchester or Munich – whereas in Holland, folding bikes on local trains are a familiar sight at the end of the office day. Yet European cities with their compact layout and lack of real hills are ideal for cycling, so the proportion of bicycles in street life could easily rise once they stop having to compete with cars for every inch of space – and once there is a dedicated infrastructure for them. The latter would hinge on an attractive, express bike-lane grid that on a few key routes gave priority to bikes at the lights – like the lights that switch to green for the bus lanes whenever a bus drives up. Bicycles could have right of way on the express routes – and lights remain green for those cycling at a steady 20 km/h, saving wear on the brakes and excessive sweat. If each route were, in addition, highlighted by color-coded signage and marked on the road surface, awareness of it would increase. These low-cost measures could be enhanced by information signs and folding maps distributed by the municipality to improve orientation and acceptance of the express routes, getting cyclists swiftly and safely in and out of city centers. This would spell a change in how the "push-bikes" are seen: gone would be the days when they were used only for distances of up to five kilometers, and the customary range would no doubt quickly expand to as much as 15 km, heralding the potential mass breakthrough of bicycles as the preferred form of commuter transport.

A bicycle infrastructure must include bike stations offering the loan of a cycle free of charge. Citizens, commuters, and tourists could then simply hop on a bike whenever they wanted. A bike station at a central location, such as on the main shopping street in Sydney or Paris and one at the city's railway station, would already lay the foundations for more quality services for cyclists – as would mobile puncture-repair squads. Furthermore: if the stations also provided bike shelters and lockers for luggage and clothing, or even first aid, then their appeal would go up a gear. Not to mention possible additional services such as bike or component rental facilities, a bike store (selling bicycles, components, and spares), advice (tourist sights, events, repair courses), and a hose for cleaning the bikes. The list could go on, and indicates just how many jobs could be created with a means of transport as simple as a bike – an insight that those ardent champions of the automobile the world over should take to heart.

1   State of the World's Cities 2008 / 2009, *(United Nations Human Settlements Programme [UN-HABITAT], Nairobi, 2008), p.178*

2   Süddeutsche Zeitung, *(Sept. 8, 2005), p.22*

3   *Forschungs- und Entwicklungsvorhaben im Auftrag des Bundesministeriums für Verkehr, Bau- und Wohnungswesen, FOPS Project no. 73.314/2001,* Final Report, *(University of Dortmund, Department of Transportation and Traffic Planning, 2004), p.16,*

4   *As reported in the article "Heimat Existiert," in* Süddeutsche Zeitung, *July 19–20, 2008, p.6*

5   *Above all as a result of demographic change, as older people can remain mobile in a city longer than they can in the country.*

6   *ex:* The Punch, *a Nigerian daily newspaper, online version, January 19, 2009.*

7   *ex:* Independent, *online issue, March 18, 2003, one month after the launch.*

8   *ex:* Race, Poverty & the Environment, *(Winter 2005–6) Urban Habitat, Oakland; http://www.urbanhabitat.org/node/344*

9   *AS&P + Polytechnische Gesellschaft,* Frankfurt für Alle – Handlungsperspektiven für die internationale Bürgerstadt, *(Frankfurt, 2009), also available as a download from www.frankfurt-fuer-alle.de*

VIII

ENCOURAGE CIVIC PARTICIPATION

"A city-state is clearly not just living together in a shared territory for mutual defense and the exchange of goods. It is, rather, a partnership among households, clans, and villages for living "well," for the sake of a fully developed and self-sufficient life. Those who contribute most to a partnership of this sort have a greater part in the city than those who are equal or greater in freedom or family, but unequal in political excellence, or those who outdo them in wealth, but are outdone in excellence." **Aristotle** [1]

Crucial to a city's sustainability is that it continue to be a home to its populace. All too often, either the politicians, or the planners who act as their consultants, or both, overlook the fact that the inhabitants are one of the key stakeholders in each and every city, and need to be consulted just as closely as does the business community (as the providers of jobs and the potential source of tax revenue) or the city's public representatives. If a city fails to satisfy its population's needs not just today but in the future, then it will dwindle in significance as the number of persons willing to live there will drop – to the extent that there are other cities which are more attractive. Like happiness, here quality of life is not necessarily something that can be readily quantified or described in terms of key performance indicators, but it is something that people "feel" and can therefore articulate as needs. If a city is to be long-lived it needs to have a vision of itself not just for tomorrow but also in the more-distant future. And creating a vision of that future must logically include a consultative process designed to encourage civic participation.

At the same time, planners must seek to keep their plans open to suggestions from the public rather than rule them out in advance, like politicians who, in response to election cycles, are inevitably often tempted to restrict their thinking to the wishes of their immediate clientele in the electorate. "I recently met a young local politician," Albert Speer quips during a panel discussion on urban development in Frankfurt, "and he said to me that 'we are aware that all of this can be done, but we don't dare say it.'" In a society such as Germany, which is generally regarded as a democratic and free country, politicians evidently do not trust the population to be able to reach considered opinions, and therefore what is possible is not even debated, let alone put into practice. Were the German government, for example, simply to cancel all subsidies for commuters who use cars, then the level of protests would no doubt be lower than 20 years ago, when fewer had a clear idea that the planet's oil reserves really were running thin. AS&P regularly encounters politicians who are not prepared to think strategically enough out of a fear of losing electoral support and who are backed up by an "administration that is getting ever more unwieldy. In such a world we definitely need to find new ways to move planning forward," Albert Speer insists. "And that means consulting those affected by planning."

PUBLIC FORUMS Most people would no doubt agree that unless citizens assume a minimum of responsibility for the urban space that they inhabit then it is unlikely that planning will come up with sustainable solutions. Elections every four, five, or six years do not help sustainability. Yet planners the world over are fully aware of how widespread the distrust of planning is among inhabitants. "Whenever a planner takes to the lectern at a public meeting," Michael Denkel narrates, "most people do not look forward to hearing about improvements to the quality of their lives and instead fear that they will be deprived of something or that things will deteriorate. While this may be some psychological constant in us human beings, otherwise I do not think I would have seen it happen so often, it tends to block meaningful dialog. So we have to find a way of overcoming the fears." Especially in the case of decisions, which, as so often in politics, get taken behind closed doors.

Keeping traffic out of residential areas or instituting local underground car parks are not likely to really catch on if the local residents are not involved in the decision-making. And for this to succeed, a degree of transparency is necessary. Elements of participation foster transparency. Transparency is the best way forward, and if the stages in the planning process are presented openly, then citizens can learn what the decision-making involves, will be able to follow the reasoning, and reach a more informed opinion. The spin-off may even be regained trust in the political system. In other words, the key to sustainable solutions that reflect real life are grass-roots polling – forums where planners and citizens meet and interact – as long as such meetings are not just window dressing.

However, Michael Denkel cautions: "We should not delude ourselves into believing that citizens of all people will be able to assist us substantively as regards the thinking on highly complex issues." Instead, the focus must be on down-to-earth matters, such as building-approval plans or changed land-use plans for a neighborhood where the citizens in question live, because, as Friedbert Greif adds, "the contribution those citizens can make are always very, very useful, and as a planner in an office one invariably overlooks the one or other item." By contrast, if the debate centers on fundamental aspects of urban development, then private interests often mar public discussion, and overarching issues get dragged down to the level of people's front or back gardens. This is something one encounters the world over. Civil forums and discussions are all well and good, and give planners a good idea of whether emotions are running high or not, but only in exceptional cases will they deliver tangible results. This is not surprising, as there is a logical contradiction at work here: holistic planning, by definition, involves the big picture viewed at a distance by an expert, while citizens focus on the smaller frame. Given the dilemma of acceptance that can thus arise, it would seem to be more meaningful to simply poll the opinions of the key players and include them either in larger rounds of discussions or in one-on-one meetings.

All sorts of procedures tend to get used in this context. Moderators are hired, bits of paper stuck on walls, and pens passed round. Weekends get spent in retreat. "But all too often the result is a plan with a swimming pool here or a playground there, and lots of great detached homes – and sadly none of it is affordable, either for the city or the citizens. So everyone goes home disappointed," comments Albert Speer. The thinking underlying such civic participation is evidently muddled, because once again it overlooks just how complex planning issues can be. However, if the exercise succeeds in fostering a spirit of trust between residents and planners as regards urban development, then this will, in turn, foster sustainability.

The example of England shows just how much can be achieved in this regard. In the "Millennium" district of New Islington, in Manchester, the "Urban Splash" office run by Nick Johnson actually called on citizens to paint pictures of what they wanted to see. "We encouraged people to take part in developments and create the wildest streets in all of England." Admittedly, the information-gathering process was completely unprofessional and crazy, but "we fired their imaginations, challenged their ambition, and got their commitment." The inhabitants ended up choosing the architects who would design their streets. "And they now consider the district their own, as they participated in developing it."[2]

Michael Denkel has a similar tale to tell: "There are countless examples of projects we have tried to move forward and where we would have got nowhere without the strong commitment of the local population." This is especially true if ecological aspects are involved, or if the focus is on the choice of the right type of transportation. Here, people's habits and education play a strong part, meaning that the inhabitants first have to be persuaded to change their habits – and the best way to do that is to give them a sense of personal involvement, namely, by inclusion. No one can be forced by administrative fiat to ride a bus. No one can be forced to keep the windows closed in a self-ventilating, low-energy house. These are personal decisions, and will be taken depending on the knowledge at hand. Needless to say, the same applies to people's choices when it comes to where they live or where they work. Planners can simply try to make sure the two are not too far apart and thus help keep traffic-emission levels down.

The question that begs an answer here is why people should be persuaded to change their habits now if they will not see the effects of their actions until they are much, much older, if at all? Is the assumption that I am having a beneficial impact on the world of my grandchildren and can help to protect them from greater harm by climate change sufficient motivation here? Is the goal of a cross-generational pact generally accepted worldwide, culturally specific, and to be encountered more in Asian communities than in the fragmented societies of the West? Experience all too often shows that in the West, people tend to act only once they are up to their necks in a mire. The exception to the rule: the Netherlands, where systems are already being put in place to protect the land from the rising level of the sea.

Germany is gradually emerging as a world laboratory for experimenting with sustainable building, urban planning, and renewable energy (as we have seen in the case of solar photovoltaic systems, there are good reasons for this). Likewise, the civic participation processes currently being practiced and fine-tuned in Germany, Switzerland, and Scandinavia could serve as a model for other societies, as long as those societies have the relevant institutional and economic foundations, as civic participation is something a society has to be able to afford. In ancient Athens, it was the rich who were the citizens and could afford the then-equivalent of high-tech. Today, just as we require high-tech on our roofs or for our heating systems, so we also require highly complex and efficient decision-making processes in the differentiated civil societies we live in – from imaging facilities through to Internet polling.

MUNICH: THE ALLIANZ ARENA

A now classic example of such civic participation is Munich's Allianz Arena, located in the district of Fröttmaning. The old Olympic stadium in downtown Munich was no longer adequate and at the turn of the millennium a decision was taken to build a new stadium – with all eyes firmly fixed on the World Cup in 2006, and all decision-makers thus under considerable pressure to find quick fixes. Yet when the time came in the fall of 2001, with AS&P entrusted with handling a public hearing and a formal petition for a vote to determine the right location, almost 40 per cent of the Munich electorate took part – more than had ever before shown an interest in such a public petition. It was an object lesson in grass-roots democracy on a planning issue.

"When I first learned we were going to push for a public hearing followed by a vote on a civic petition," recalls Matthias Schöner at AS&P, "I immediately thought: Oh my God, just another piece of unwieldy organization, and one that is likely to be followed by massive planning hurdles." And things were not helped by Germany's most famous footballer, Franz Beckenbauer, scoffing that "the only things living in Fröttmaning are a few frogs," and being quite scathing about the petition, declaring, "I don't even know whether they are even authorized to hold one." "They" referred to the City of Munich – and the city was indeed authorized to do so; it also knew that there was a very high probability of citizen action groups opposing the choice of Fröttmaning as home for the new stadium, to be named the Allianz Arena. AS&P had carefully studied a total of 25 possible locations and ascertained that only Fröttmaning was suitable. Nevertheless, it was clear that there would be protest from various quarters – ranging from inhabitants fearing for their peace and quiet to citizens who as a matter of principle did not want the infrastructure for professional soccer clubs to be financed from public coffers (the Alianz Arena cost EUR 200 million of taxpayers' money). The City of Munich elected to take the sting out of the issue

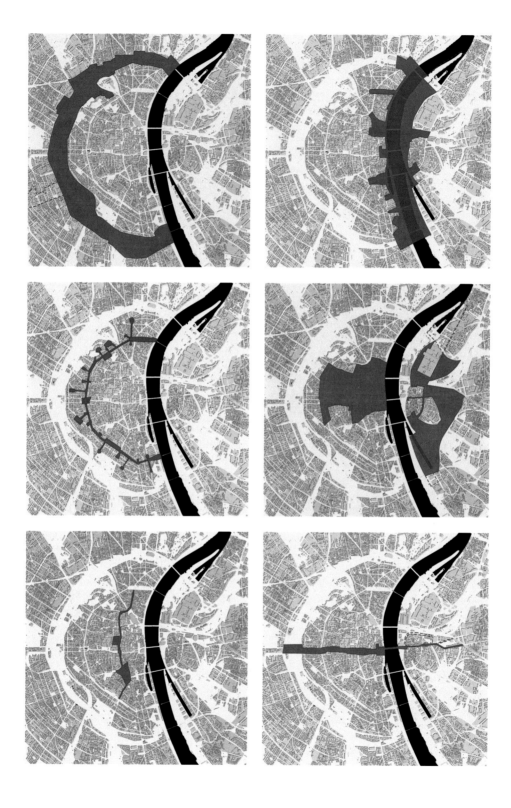

Excerpts from the Cologne master plan
(From top to bottom, left to right)
Inner green belt
Concentrated Rhine-side urban space
Existing inner ring road
Core urban zone
North-south axis
East-west axis

by giving everyone a chance to vote on it at as early a stage as possible. "I really had to be persuasive to get the city fathers to agree to the petition," recalls Munich's Mayor Christian Ude. "Some of my political opponents thought I was supporting the petition only because I secretly hoped it would be the kiss of death for the project." Nothing could have been further from the truth – Munich's mayor was simply convinced that the public's voice was mission-critical if a result was to hold water. Switzerland is a prime example of the cathartic effect that public votes on petitions can have, healing wounds and moving processes forwards.

Ude's instinct for grass-roots involvement proved right, and Franz Beckenbauer's angry claim that his soccer club need not appeal to the public wrong. "After the public hearings, he got his stadium – and all it cost him was a few angry words aimed in his direction at the beginning of the hearing, which was a pretty good price," remembers Friedbert Greif. What the public hearing achieved was to smooth the path for the swift construction of a now famous stadium. With a massive majority of 65.8 per cent of the votes cast, all the objections the opponents had raised were brushed aside, once and for all. "It was as if the project had been approved by vote," suggests Matthias Schöner. As a consequence, no one could subsequently say that they had not been consulted.

MASTER PLAN FOR COLOGNE SCALE 1:1000

The new master plan for Cologne is another prime example. Civic hearings can also constitute an important way of fostering participation in the creation of a master plan, albeit not the decisive one. The idea of commissioning a new master plan came from citizens of the city, not the city itself, and it was also Cologne citizens who actually commissioned the plan. "The master plan was completely financed by a Cologne business association," explains Albert Speer. More than 30 companies of vastly differing sizes from various sectors joined forces to form a nonprofit association, Unternehmer für die Region Köln e.V. (Entrepreneurs for the Cologne Region), and put up a good EUR 500,000 to fund the project. "Business does not need to hide and can take a political stance, but not a party-political stance," suggests Paul Bauwens-Adenauer, President of the association and also of the Cologne Chamber of Commerce and Industry. Bauwens-Adenauer is the grandson of Germany's first chancellor, Konrad Adenauer, and, as such, grew up in a home culture infused with a blend of business and politics. "I think it is great that the politicians accept our business initiative here, as it was by no means a matter of course that they would," Adenauer continues.

Ulrich Soénius, Deputy President of the association, reports that the general public concerned itself closely with the master-plan process and says that from the point of view of the association this was "definitely desired but definitely not very typical." After all, citizens tend to raise their voices if planning schemes potentially affect their immediate neighborhoods, and do not frequently participate in the evolution of overarching issues, such as those addressed by a master plan. Yet before long the master plan had quite literally become the talk of the town and the citizens realized that it did not simply focus on one particular district, but the entire downtown area.

→

Albert Speer at a public forum discussing the structure of Cologne's inner city.

Politicians may be the civic decision-makers, but they are so only insofar as the citizens elect them to that function. All the more reason to establish a loop that feeds back to the citizens and ensures their involvement at an early stage. And this was precisely the approach taken with the master plan. Fritz Schramma, the Mayor of Cologne, learned invaluable lessons from the master-plan process: "We now know how best to go about including citizens in advance when it comes to planning issues. If you wait till afterwards, all you get is anger and upset. Citizens know best what things should look like in their own immediate vicinity. Of course, not all citizens are experts, but they, too, will learn during the planning process. Which means that by the time the experts and citizens have sat down together and thought hard, and the experts have gone away, reached their conclusions, and written up their findings, the politicians can then choose what their priorities will be – and feed that back into the consultative process, namely, into public debate. That is the basis of true civic democracy."

STRUCTURE CIVIC CONSULTATION

For more than a year, ten AS&P staff members conducted an intensive process of dialog with all the relevant stakeholders in Cologne: politicians, the local authority, businesspeople, trade unions, the churches, citizens action groups, and members of the cultural scene. This interaction with the public offered AS&P regular opportunities to test the durability of its own concepts. Albert Speer declares that "there are very few instances in the past where, from the very word go, a holistic planning system was deployed involving all the various experts, the architects, the urban planners, the traffic planners, and the green-belt planners – and that reflects the fact that we were responding constantly to what we heard from stakeholders." AS&P also acted as the regular interface to the local authorities to try to achieve a consensus on all issues, despite the fact that the brief for the master plan was a private contract, and by a company from the outside at that. This may have been a blessing in disguise as it meant AS&P was able to act neutrally and objectively.

"At the beginning we spent a lot of time walking round town and analyzed everything we saw," Albert Speer recalls, "leaving us with a huge mountain of suggestions, ideas, and data." The subsequent work ensued in three phases: initial investigation, in-depth studies, and the preparation of conclusions and findings. Dialog with the relevant stakeholders took the shape of six so-called "workshop discussions," spread across the year. "In our workshop discussions," Michael Denkel says with a smile, "we found ourselves meeting some three or four hundred people, which is a huge number for such a process – but they were the people who provided the real, substantive input. I would hardly call such discussions sustainable in the long term."

The general public was kept abreast of the AS&P work through four "inner-city forums" that served to provide information more than to procure key insights. Denkel continues: "While some of the ideas we took up originated there, that was not the primary purpose of the forums, as they were simply to ensure that citizens were always involved and aware of what we were doing." Then there was a working party, including all the relevant local authorities, which convened six times during the period. After all, in Germany it is the local authorities that have the final word, so, irrespective of who paid for the master-plan, if the relevant technocrats do not agree with it, it will simply not fly. Only if the local authority approves a plan will it be enacted and have a legal status, and the working party was therefore just as critical a factor as the other meetings. Given the legal status the final product was to have, the City of Cologne insisted that a very structured process accompany the work on the master-plan and contracted a company of architects to handle this on the city's behalf.

When drawing up a sustainable master plan, and this was not secondary to the civic participation process, AS&P tackled the core questions: What scope and potential does the Cologne inner city posses for developing its urban area over the next 15 years, and what would be the central tasks in this context? Albert Speer calls the urban-planning master plan that evolved "a screenplay for future decision-making." It provides Cologne's politicians with an instrument that explores the city's opportunities at the level of urban design, traffic planning, and creating leisure-time space. The master plan concentrates throughout on the issue of "rejuvenation from within." In other words, it is a description of the status quo, a test instrument, and an interpretation rolled into one. It not only identifies the opportunities but also sets the time frame for key future events and projects.

Achieving the above was a tall order as Cologne's downtown is one of the most vibrant urban spaces in Germany. Some 130,000 people are packed into the 1,600 or so hectares, and 180,000 people work in the same zone. The greater the diversity and density, the harder the tasks facing the urban design. Yet what worked in the planners' favor was that the unmistakable matrix of ringroads, axes, and historical urban fabric with a variety of different social milieus strongly approximates the ideal European city. In future, gradual and careful expansion within these spaces and the sustainability of modernized infrastructures must, so the master plan detailed, be dovetailed far more closely. Only integration will ensure a sensitive treatment of the marvelous old town in the most diverse of projects. The master plan consequently defines seven "intervention spaces" that go to make up Cologne's underlying urban fabric. And these intervention spaces were specifically fueled by the feedback from the workshop discussions, the inner city forums, and the working-party meetings, as the insights gained there provided clarity about how to proceed. The result, as presented to the City of Cologne in November 2008, is an outline for a sustainable, modern, yet historical inner city intended to last well into the century. The city has undertaken to keep its citizens informed of the practical work that will now be done to realize the various projects now on the table.

COLOGNE AS AN EXAMPLE   Can we transfer the example of Cologne onto other municipalities in Germany and abroad? "Everyone here welcomed us with open arms," recalls Albert Speer, only to qualify things by saying, "which would not be the case in every city, as outsiders who come along and weigh up whether past decisions or current planning are correct are not greeted everywhere, are not necessarily always greeted with joy." The situation in Cologne was made easier by the fact that "Entrepreneurs for the Cologne Region," the association that commissioned the work, did not specify a particular brief for the study. The association was even prepared to accept that with this or that transport project AS&P had reached conclusions diametrically opposed to the prevailing opinion among the entrepreneurs, for example, AS&P's rejection of elaborate tunnel projects. "Personally, I would have been much faster as regards the big issues, but then I'm a typical Cologne inhabitant, full of verve and zest and thus not exactly circumspect," comments Ulrich Soénius. "The way we thought, we forgot all about money, but AS&P swiftly showed us that funding is something you need to be circumspect with – as there is often not enough of it."

Cologne's inhabitants love their city and identify strongly with it. People here love partying – the city is renowned in Germany for its KARNIVAL, which, while admittedly not on a par with Rio's, is one of the most colorful in Europe. Since the citizens are so proud of their city, they tend to think about it a great deal, and they are supported by a large number of critically-minded architects and designers from the local universities. "That is an ideal seedbed in which we then planted the project," explains Bauwens-Adenauer. While Speer simply likes to call Cologne that "lovable city of chaos."

In terms of how it originated, the master plan for Cologne is quite unique in Germany, but will no doubt set an example for other cities to follow. In doing so, they must remember that the decision-making process has to remain open, in line with the overall holistic methodology described in this book, and must not be precluded by the business world or by politicians taking preemptive decisions. Nevertheless, there is a growing recognition that it is crucial to poll the ideas of all the relevant stakeholders in a city, and many other German cities are already exploring whether they cannot follow Cologne in this regard.

↑
Skylines of cities worldwide are increasingly similar. Civic decision-making processes have yet to follow suit.

Albert Speer cautions here that it is important not to forget that "the City of Cologne itself would not have been able to commission us to do the work. Municipalities tend to have to put such studies out to tender, with all the swings and roundabouts this involves.

The red tape can smother the study before it gets going. Which is why it is so important not only to think outside the box, but also to find ways of getting paid outside it, too." To this end, Speer recommends a position that interfaces citizens, business, and politics – that is to say, as an intermediary agency in dialog with all the stakeholders. Yet neither architectural theory nor democratic systems foresee such a special go-between function for the planner as honest broker. This can be a real advantage, however, and be a factor that kindles imaginations locally. Today, many citizens have lost much of their past faith in politics and can safely assume, however, that the planners as citizens without a vested interest will be far more likely to heed what they say, especially if they are not being paid to do so by politicians. An association such as the one in Cologne, with its broad base in local commerce and industry, is not far removed from the composition of the city itself – so it is essentially interested citizens who commissioned the master plan, which lends greater credibility to the findings.

"As long as planners and architects do not morph into politicians then they should make certain they intervene more than ever before," demands Ulrich Soénius. It is specifically cities which have grown 'organically,' such as Cologne, that need people who are willing to think in the longer term, stand up, and make their voices heard. Cologne has shown how an urban society – the prototypical civil society – can, in a democratic system, develop a procedure that involves as many groups of citizens as possible in urban planning. This lays the foundations for holistic urban planning that can rely on acceptance among a broad section of the population. For any such master plan to be successful, care must be taken to make certain it does not become appropriated by the politicians and merely an item in party manifestos at local elections. Experience shows that only if a master plan is accepted by all the main parties will it have a chance of not being carved up later at political negotiating tables.

EMERGING DEMOCRACIES   Transferring the insights gained in Cologne onto projects in other countries may not be easy. After all, Cologne is a city with a 2,000-year history and thus, perhaps with the exception of India and China, not something often encountered in threshold and developing countries, and certainly not in Africa. Furthermore, the critical focus on the city's specific history was a key factor driving the creation of the master plan. Yet civic participation is a must elsewhere, even if the present is still a sobering sight: "We are often active in countries that can best be described as 'emerging democracies,'" Michael Denkel says. For example, Nigeria. "And the difficulty in such countries is that we as planners never come into significant contact with the actual inhabitants, and the same applies to China and Russia, too. We simply progress from one government or private office to the next, meet investors, developers, political decision-makers, etc., but only rarely do we officially meet the local citizens."

Yet this cannot be taken as a general rule, for as Albert Speer himself says, one of the prime examples of civic participation he has encountered during his career was in China of all places. "In China," Speer states, drawing on the experiences he has gained through collaboration with the company's office in Shanghai, "major projects are now also put out to tender and are thus subject to a degree of control by the broader general public, which is definitely very interested in them. And no one person can now decide on such contracts. Internally, the discussions are fairly fierce – at several levels of the hierarchy." This is probably also because in this ancient administrative state the mandarins have always played an important part and does not want to see its powers curtailed. In the course of time, the vast number of citizens who have achieved a certain standard of living invariably clamor for more say in the design of their built environment.

Even if China does not fit the West European brief for a democracy and for transparency, it is precisely the country's surging growth in recent years that has created new opportunities in this regard and increased the pressure on the political system, which is already feeling the strain of managing a scenario in which millions are flocking from the country to the cities. These population shifts and the related challenges are quite unprecedented in the history of urban society. One would assume that a single-party state, with its clear lines of command, would be able to handle such a situation best – and one would be wrong, for the powers that be have evidently elected to take into account what people on the ground feel. Johannes Dell says that "agriculture still has immense potential to boost productivity levels. But if the Chinese were to change things as fast as may be required, then of the 100 Chinese on their little farms, 90 would lose their jobs and, for want of any other opportunities, would also head for the cities. The Party leaders know this because the Party functions as a large consultative process, a kind of seismograph with its ear to the ground. They poll the responses down through the Party lines to the very grass roots, and so, by the time a resolution is put to the vote it can be unanimously passed. The downside may be that productivity levels are only gradually being raised. But there is also an upside: the cities have not burst at the seams."

It remains to be hoped that the ruling classes in the "emerging democracies" of Asia, Africa, and Latin America always bear in mind that the immense challenges inherent in migration to the cities can be mastered in the long run only if the respective population has participated in urban development. Because, given the impact of climate change and dwindling resources, in the medium term the informal networks in the megacities of threshold

BUILDING FOR TOMORROW?   *"Modern urban environments decay much more quickly than urban fabric inherited from the past. As uses change, buildings are now destroyed rather than adapted; indeed, the over-specification of form and function makes the modern urban environment peculiarly susceptible to decay, The average life span of new public housing in Britain is now 40 years; that of new skyscrapers in New York is 35 years."*[4]

www.masterplan-koeln.de

and developing countries and even autocracies are themselves both unable to cope. Even in as long-standing a democracy as India, the government has not succeeded in the course of 60 years of democracy in getting a real handle on the problem of urban poverty. Indeed, one commentator has written: "Almost all attempts to find solutions on a large scale have spawned new problems instead. Modernization projects therefore often lead to people being robbed of the economic basis for their lives, which can happen if they are driven out of the city and into anonymous residential high-rises, where they can no longer offer their services, or at least only under tougher conditions because the apartments assigned to them are too small or unsuitable for them to practice their craft and sell their wares."[3]

Urbanization in the 21st century seems to be occurring as a series of parallel occurrences that have little in common. What we see is the asymmetry of islands of absurd affluence and high-tech facilities on the one hand, and huge districts with marginalized people who live in abject poverty on the other – often in one and the same city. Yet economically and ecologically, the social groups who live like this, cut off from one another, are long since mutually dependent. Sustainable solutions for the problems of urban development are not possible without involving everyone concerned – and this is presumably an insight applicable to all cultures. Air or water pollution, paved surfaces, and gridlocks are phenomena for which humans are responsible. The negative impact they have on everyone, and in particular in poorly governed countries or in failed states, can be ameliorated only if individuals choose to act differently. This has nothing to do with the Western notion of the citoyen. The actual form taken by civic participation will therefore depend on the particular culturally-specific condition, but this does not detract from the compelling nature of such involvement. In some places, it would no doubt count as progress if inhabitants at least knew beforehand that their houses were going to be bulldozed and did not first find out only when the walls started to cave in.

Back in the 1990s Albert Speer called on all the major banks based in Frankfurt to close their canteens. His goal: to force the thousands of employees out onto the streets and thus into urban life in the city center.

1   *Aristotle,* Politics, *1280*

2   *Quoted from "Schönes , neues New Islington," in:* Frankfurter Rundschau, *supplement on Bundeskongress Nationale Stadtentwicklung, April 25, 2008, p. 5. See also http://www.newislington.co.uk for an impression of the paintings.*

3   *in:* Archplus, *185, "Indischer Inselurbanismus", 11/2007*

4   *Richard Sennett, in* The Endless City, *(Phaidon Press: London), 2007*

IX

GET THE FUNDAMENTALS RIGHT BEFORE YOU BUILD A CITY

"Sustainability without human controls and supplementary intervention can result only if you use existing resources so sparingly that they last for as long as possible. If a shortage prevails, this will accordingly limit the possible utilization of that resource." **Josef H. Reichholf**[1]

HOLISTIC, INCLUSIVE PLANNING SYSTEMS

All too often, people forget that a few measures carried out right can achieve a high degree of sustainability if integrated early enough into the planning process, which is surprising given how obvious such an integration may seem. The reason it does not happen regularly probably has to do with the innate complexity of modern cities (with their multilayered processes, open systems, and interacting zones). As a consequence, a push for sustainability in cities at the urban-planning level can best succeed if built around an overarching concept that consciously includes everyone involved and addresses the fundamentals.

It is precisely because cities as a whole have long since ceased to be entities subject to straight-line planning and control (indeed some of them are countries in their own right) that all planning needs to be embedded into a holistic system. And that system must impact on the overall conditions for land zoning and the overarching political guidelines. Given the overlap in jurisdiction, particularly in European cities, and the interlocking nature of the individual fields of action, decision-makers have to weigh up a plethora of different interests and needs when choosing priorities, which can all too easily spawn bad decision-making.

At the same time, planners face a new role in that they need to motivate and inform the populace, coordinate the numerous agencies involved, and ensure cooperation. The problems are compounded by it being virtually impossible to avoid a fuzzy definition of sustainability for urban planning, as facts and figures are open-ended because future-oriented, specific relevant criteria and responsibilities are often in a state of flux and constantly being redefined.

When concentrating on fundamentals it is worth bearing in mind that this sidesteps the problem that many of the criteria used in urban planning and the measures taken are not "quantitative but qualitative, as they are the strong expression of a cultural understanding or of personal need. Only if we remember the diversity here can we make certain planning does not nurture monotony. We all know that monocultures die out sooner or later and tend to 'mine' the soil, destroying resources. We urban planners must seek instead to foster what I would call cosmopolitan difference by stressing the fundamentals and building on them," suggests Albert Speer.

Sustainability therefore depends on persuading politicians that taking long-term decisions is to their benefit, even if they may not be in office to see the results. And it means,

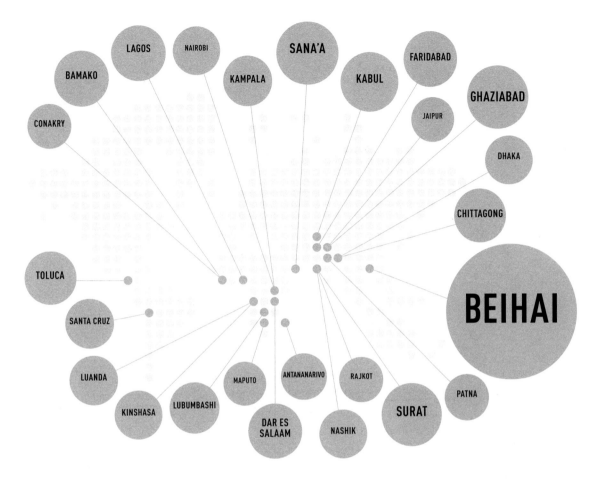

Fastest-growing cities and urban areas 2006–2020
(average annual growth in per cent).

if necessary, trying to deter them from bowing to the fashions of the day. Both insights revolve around a focus on who will use what further down the line. This in turn implies that defining firm and binding goals must dovetail closely with actual projects awaiting realization. In other words, the planner's role must be to assist politicians in getting the fundamentals right when combining the pragmatic and the visionary. An episode from Albert Speer's early days as an urban planner typifies this approach.

"Many years ago, the politicians in the marvelously old city of Worms were hell-bent on modernizing their town. Planning approval had already been forthcoming for an overpass that was to run parallel to the Rhine, separating it from the old town center. That was all the rage back then. And I was involved in the arduous task of melding modernization and restoration in precisely that historical heart. I knew that the overpass was a holy cow, but it simply ran contrary to everything I and the company believe in. What to do? I went to a public meeting of the City Council and asked innocently whether the overpass really fitted in. That sparked a debate. Fortunately, the debate went my way and the overpass was never built. Essentially, the lesson here is that planning is sometimes the opposite of proposing something: it may invol, ve opposing something, and this requires the courage of conviction."

GARNER THE SUPPORT OF POLITICAL DECISION-MAKERS

In today's day and age, sustainability hinges not on individual projects, specific eco-friendly buildings or sets of buildings, but on making certain there is sufficient political will to get the fundamentals right, and that is something increasingly given in a world where the main issue is climate change. After all, the real breakthrough in renewable energy sources in Germany was not a product of the market, but of political decision-makers insisting on feed-in tariffs that gave new energy sources a chance. The goalposts were set in this way, and a fledgling industry had the opportunity to evolve. The major energy utilities were henceforth bound by legislation to input all the electricity generated by wind and solar sources into the grid at a price set by central government and to pass those costs onto the electricity consumers, whether the latter liked it or not. This has prompted the major power corporations to invest heavily in renewables – and they have also been moved in this direction by the EU's 2007 resolution to boost to 20 per cent by the year 2020 the proportion of overall electricity generation accounted for by renewables. Political decisions have created a market, and the big players have swiftly moved into it, perhaps discovering a "green" conscience in the process. This is the pattern that needs to be put into practice in our cities, too.

Michael Denkel suggests in this context that "the key debates on social change tend to entail a linkage of private consumption, that is to say, the users, the inhabitants of a city, and institutionalized politics, markets and models. A corollary to this is that the results have to be financially feasible in the long term. Without financing there can be no sustainability." Put differently, urban planners must strive to forge sustainable foundations for a new city (thinking in cycles) or the right changes to a living city (due concentration) while ensuring these are embedded in the building and zoning plans. And they must do so while conscious of the fact that sustainable configurations are often the product of organic and highly diverse structures that are self-organized or self-organizing. Getting the sustainable fundamentals right therefore includes integrating the relevant criteria into the planning process at an early stage, involving the "private consumers," and fostering transparency in the ensuing debates. Only then will the results be accepted, as society has without doubt moved on since Worms in the 1960s (or in 1521, for that matter). The long-term success of the proposals will be decided by whether each step along the way is duly documented and controlled – and, of course, by long-term financial viability: the cost/benefit ratio of individual projects and/or master plans, something that could be measured by the economic benefit the master plan brings to a city or region in the long run. Not to mention the non-quantifiable enhanced image the city or region may derive from the changes.

FUNDAMENTAL 1 – REMEMBER MACRO-PLANNING

AS&P firmly believes that the supraordinated levels of planning, such as federal or state government, must set the scope for all activity and define what agencies are in charge of which areas. Supraordinated national or municipal concepts offer a wide-ranging overview of the relevant topics and create an awareness of sustainability by anchoring these principles in national political agendas and fleshing them out in planning instruments (e.g., land zoning). Is this why AS&P now finds itself acting as a think tank, churning out ideas for politicians and always keeping the big picture in mind? "Yes, I do feel that this is the case. Over the years we have constantly found ourselves creating our own briefs. In fact, we were the first consultants in Germany to compile supraordinated regional studies, rather than focus just on this or that city. And we started looking at such conglomerates from the viewpoint of economic and ecological well-being, and with a view to population growth trends. A prime example of this approach was our comparative study on Rhineland-Palatinate, completed back in 1973, Albert Speer recollects. It was the same mindset that led AS&P also to assume the role of pioneer when it came to modernizing cities. "We started out up north with Lübeck and then moved south to Speyer and Worms. And in the process of redefining land use we worked closely with sociologists. That was something quite unheard of back then."

Another field in which AS&P became a trailblazer was that of planning outside its home turf. Indeed, AS&P was one of the first German companies to engage in know-how transfer by accepting contracts in developing countries – the first such projects were tackled as long ago as 1980. "German urban planners or thinkers," Albert Speer judges, "are still too few and far between in the developing world. And far too few of the politicians in this country have understood how crucial it is, particularly in this Age of Global Warming, to engage in active planning abroad. One of the few honorable exceptions to the rule, so I would suggest, is former Federal German Minister of the Environment Klaus Töpfer, who in his function as Executive Director of the UNEP worked and lived abroad." This is especially puzzling if we bear in mind that the phenomenon of urbanization in the Third World is not new. Speer homed in on the attending problems as long ago as 1978 in an article for Germany's leading architectural journal, in which he wrote: "Overall population growth in the majority of developing countries is 3 to 4.5 per cent, but the increase in cities is as much as 6 to 10 per cent per annum. In Lagos or Lima, about half of the two million people live in slums. Urbanization in the Third World is taking place on an awful scale."[2] At the time, it was not a story that met with much resonance among (inter)national planners seeking to create new cities.

NATIONAL URBAN DEVELOPMENT POLICY

The teams at AS&P now face different tasks, however, the focus being on finding the appropriate role to be played by urban planning in the Age of Global Warming rather than the Age of Globalization? If one thing is certain, then it is that this has heralded the end of the urban planner working in isolation, and, so Albert Speer believes, likewise the end of the architect working away on his own. The scale of the issues now being faced implies that they can be meaningfully addressed only by interdisciplinary teams. In the process, attention has to be paid to finding the right way for the overall decision-makers to move projects forwards. After all, just leaving everything to politicians is to expose change to a four-year election and reelection cycle and leaving it to the quantified technological approach of the engineers is to keep quality out of the equation.

Speer comments in this context that "sustainable structures tend to be those that have grown organically, multifaceted, and multilayered configurations. Now, simply ordaining such by decree is always going to be a difficult if not impossible job. It hardly seems realistic. The more fruitful path here is to organize a project process that can draw on an extensive knowledge base. That is what we seek to provide." However, the standard alternatives to politicians are forums, standing committees, or working parties, and they can be as unwieldy as they are bureaucratic. Given just how pressing many of the issues are, such snail-paced deliberations can be frustrating if not to say disastrous: in Germany, for example, the board of trustees of the national urban development policy unit is proud to have 50 illustrious members, who convene once a year. One of the board members recollects, however, that at the first meeting of the board, the time allocated for the convention was completely taken up by the statements each of the various members had prepared, which meant that the convention did nothing more than affirm its own commitment to itself. "The problem is to find a medium that can convene far more often and also have the clout and knowledge to get things moving." One result of this commitment to interfacing between planning and politics is the work an AS&P team is performing on structuring the policy-making basis for the Federal German Ministry of Construction. Through to 2012 the team will propose the key issues the ministry should focus on, preparing the groundwork in each case.

FUNDAMENTAL 2: KNOW THE FUTURE – OR FUTUROLOGY

In light of the above, it seems obvious that any effort to get the fundamentals for new cities right must take its cue from futurology. Now, given the pragmatic mindset at AS&P it might seem surprising to associate its focus on sustainability with futurology, but the connection is sound. After all, futurology is classically defined as the "interdisciplinary study of the medium to long-term future, by extrapolating present technological, economic, or social trends, or by attempting to forecast future trends. It also includes normative or preferred futures, but the real contribution is to connect both extrapolated (exploratory) and normative research in order to explore better strategies." That means considering issues such as peak coal or oil, and endeavoring to explain what is likely to continue, what is likely to change, and what is novel. The term was coined by German political scientist Ossip K. Flechtheim, who explored ways to include the science of probability in forecasting. In this context, planners have to assume the importance of alternative and plural futures, while bearing in mind the limitations of prediction and probability, versus the

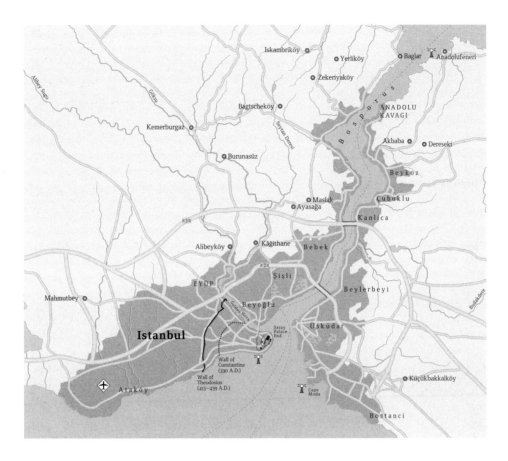

↑

Map of Istanbul, showing the two ancient town walls and the current reach of
the city. In 1975, on the European side, the main airport was still located next to
green villages and on the Asian side the city did not extend beyond Üsküdar.

creation of possible and preferable futures. In other words, there are three levels involved. Firstly, an attempt is made to postulate not only the probable, but also the preferable futures. Secondly, the interdisciplinary team generates its scenarios on the basis of a
holistic approach, "the fundamentals." Thirdly, prevailing and often ideological (or party
political) views of the future are challenged for the sake of exploring the possible.

In other words, AS&P is adamant that the complex task of anticipating the future is a
basic element to be addressed by interdisciplinary teams if they are to be able to think
outside the box and dream up new tasks for themselves that are traditionally not considered the domain of urban planning. This is doubly interesting, as such thinking has typically been the province of major corporations, like Shell, which has an entire division
devoted to studying the future,[3] of think tanks such as Rand Corporation or McKinsey,[4]
or even of such transnational institutions as the Euro Environmental Agency.[5]

The crucial moment comes when, after a discussion of the respective scenarios and proposed master plan, choices have to be consciously taken, with public participation. And this is the key to getting the fundamentals right if new or old cities are to be sustainable. To put it frivolously, this means interdisciplinary teams of specialists need to do what kids have been doing at their PC screens since the late 1990s, namely playing SimCity 2000 or SimCity 3000 – except it would not be a game and the focus would be on Sustainable City 2050. It involves taking a series of decisions on how we construe the credit units we have at our disposable – What trade-offs are there if I sacrifice my environmental credits for a better quality of life? Do I caution against SUVs and insist on compact cars? How do I strike the right balance between road and rail? Are there "organic" restrictions stemming from existing cities' histories?. Should I simply let some cities die? If I am a German regional planner do I "discontinue" Ludwigshafen, the focus of so much effort in the 1960s, because it has long since passed its zenith, or do the same to Kaiserslautern, where most of the AS&P partners studied under Albert Speer, because it is no longer an economic magnet? These are tough questions. The easier ones to answer are: Do I encourage short distances? Do I avoid new CBDs. Do I prioritize public transport? The answer any AS&P member would give to all three is "Yes." But that does not tell us how much electricity or water an average African, American, Chinese, European, or Indian urbanite will use or need in 2050. How to solve the problems of China urbanization? How to make megacities manageable? How to handle African city development?

THE KEY FUNDAMENTAL: POLYCENTRIC CONCENTRATION

In previous chapters we have at various points mentioned the notion of polycentric concentration as a critical factor for the sustainability of cities. It is AS&P's unwavering belief that this concept is quite simply the fundamental among fundamentals. Albert Speer himself describes the situation as follows: "The metropolis of the 21st century is definitely a regiopolis, a sustainable city with several sustainable cores arranged in a polycentric manner. Each of them must be on a scale that enables it to be experienced as a center, reached easily within the center, and not sprawl. Such regiopolises will thus be compact, concentrated cities offering a whole range of different functions and uses, all readily at hand." To put it differently, the ecotopia of tomorrow, a utopia perhaps if viewed from the vantage point of the early 20th century, is the multitopia, for that is what a regiopolis is.

The idea dramatically modifies the 1960s' idea of satellite cities, as these tended to be places populated at night by commuters who returned there to sleep after working during the day in a larger city. This meant the satellite city was an over-inflated suburb and a cause of traffic. Instead of moons orbiting a planet, or planets orbiting a sun, polycentric concentration entails a miniature galaxy: a system of suns, some bigger, some smaller, all connected in this case not by space travel but by rail. Smaller centers grouped as a cluster move gravitationally around larger centers that coexist by dint of mutual attraction. The space between them guarantees the presence of green belts and a fresh, clean airflow. The structure is one of independent interdependency. One of the centers may be predominant, but this need not be the case: the main centers may all be equals, like the cells in foam.[6] The structure brings to mind Holland, with its many mid-sized cities, all interlinked by fast and convenient rail systems that culminate in stations which boast a mass of parking space – for bicycles. (Holland nevertheless possesses countless interstates regularly gridlocked by single commuters in cars, prompting the simple question: why this unnecessary reliance on roads?)

A prime example of this thinking was the clear advice given to the mayor of Shanghai in 1994 as regards a strategy for the city's development. At the time, Albert Speer stated unequivocally that "growth must not be allocated in the core city alone. Given the target of 100 people per hectare, more than half of the additional growth should go into the region. The core city should be restricted to an absolute extension of 1,000 square kilometers, which is approximately the area of Greater London." He inferred from this that an agglomeration like the "future Shanghai with 20 million inhabitants or more must be seen as a metropolitan region and developed accordingly. Each different municipality should be developed into an independent city within the metropolitan region." The upshot of this was the "One City – Nine Towns" drive to expand Shanghai by creating new towns around it in line with the philosophy of the polycentric multitopia. The model the AS&P consultants had in mind was no doubt their home turf: the Rhine-Main region, which has enjoyed such success as a polycentric structure and which can offer tailor-made locations for commercial investors, inhabitants seeking recreation, and housing, too, with the various different municipal authorities benefiting from synergies in the process (see Conclusion).

A few years later, the idea of the One City – Nine Towns was being promulgated by the mayor of Shanghai and had trickled down to the subordinated municipal planning departments in the "new towns" to be. At this point, the Shanghai Nicheng Development Co. contacted AS&P with a view to a master plan for a branch of their new town – in terms of size, it would be more appropriate to speak of a city. They probably were not themselves thinking of polycentric concentration within their new city when the contact was made, but the multitopia was what they got when they commissioned AS&P to plan the Nicheng "branch" of Lingang New Town. The latter is located 75 kilometers south of downtown Shanghai and to the south of the Ningbo Bay. According to the master plan (commissioned by the Shanghai Urban Planning Administration Bureau), there will be 800,000 residents inhabiting this nearly 300-square-kilometer area; they will be engaged in, among other things, advanced manufacture, modern logistics, and R&D services. The pulse of this coastal town will beat in unison with that of Shanghai and become an extension of that city. Plans envisage the launch of an integrated solar-energy utilization project in Lingang provided by Shanghai Electric, thus solving the bottleneck problem of tense electric-energy supply in the economic development of coastal cities. Moreover, Lingang New Town is reported to have signed investment projects worth RMB 10 billion, and large enterprises like Siemens, Shanghai Automotive Industry Corporation, Maersk

Nicheng branch of Lingang New Town, Shanghai, China.
Courtyards and green areas combined with polycentric concentration.

Logistics, and Sulzer have settled in the New Town one after another. From the Nicheng branch, a bridge runs to the new deep-sea port.

What AS&P proposes is a branch of the city that was itself able to function as an independent city. The area of some seven square kilometers, destined to house about 120,000 people, has been densely configured, with around five million square meters in gross floor area, designated for a carefully balanced mixture of apartments, offices, service outlets, retailers, public facilities, as well as cultural institutions and manufacturing. The proposal hinges on the authorities' approval of the requisite land-use plan, which would then be followed by detailed project planning for the heart of the town and allowing work on residential buildings to get underway. The underlying idea is clear: by providing everything close at hand, be it jobs or shops, the city discourages extensive traffic, while nevertheless forming an integral part of a larger whole, Lingang New Town proper.

It seems obvious from the above that polycentricity depends on a raft of fundamental factors, primarily: mobility/transport connections/interconnectivity; possible redensification; combined heat and power plants that guarantee local energy provision and avoid unnecessary generation losses; a polycentric system of hospitals, schools, and, of course, markets. In other words, each of the centers must have the facilities equated with the classical Greek polis, the city-state – as defined by its members, not by its boundaries or territory – where people had all they needed.

PRIME EXAMPLE – ABUJA, NIGERIA

One prime example of such polycentric concentration on a far greater scale that outlines the sustainability the system is intended to deliver, and thus the benefits, is recent master planning for the metropolis of Abuja, Nigeria. In 1976, then President Murtala Muhammed initiated a search for a new capital city away from Lagos, where the population was subject to the unhealthy climate of the lagoon, conditions were cramped and congested, and only one of the four main tribes reigned supreme. In Lagos, moreover, the politicians came under excessive pressure from commercial interest groups and tribal considerations. A new site was identified in the very middle of the country, located in an ethnically neutral area in savannah countryside, and tenders were invited for a master plan for the new city, to be called Abuja. AS&P submitted a detailed bid that emphasized environmental and socio-political planning in addition to physical and infrastructure planning. The bid was contingent on the notion that "A city is never static. It is a living organism and the activities in a city are always dynamic and directed towards change. A city's structure should be responsive to social and economic innovation and its physical pattern should allow such changes to be made. It is the basic transportation and communication pattern of a city that more than any other system determines whether a city can cope with the element of change."[7] While AS&P today would most probably agree with this, they would no doubt beg to differ with the conclusions drawn back then: namely, that the city center was the most important feature of the planning and the space around it simply left open to allow it to grow. Back then, it was the US company IPA that was awarded the contract to compile the master plan for Abuja, destined to expand in four phases from a population of 230,000 through to a maximum of 3 million. The city center, the Central Area as it has been called ever since the first plans were completed, was designed in detail by Kenzo Tange and Urtec, and has encountered the opposite fate to the one originally anticipated by AS&P: it has grown, but not at the same speed as everything around it! The two wings either side devised by IPA, with a total of eight essentially self-contained "development sectors" stretched out like pearls on a double loop, have seen truly rampant growth, with the metropolitan area estimated recently to contain some 6 million inhabitants.

The growth has taken place primarily in the satellite cities that have sprung up outside the capital city proper. They include such names as, Anagada, Dobi, Gwagwalada, Bwari, Nyanya, and they stretch to the very boundaries of the Federal Capital Territory. The problem is that they are classical satellite cities, generating the traffic that then clogs the underdimensioned roads running into the capital city proper. AS&P was commissioned in 2000 to solve the attendant problems, and insisted that the only meaningful solution was polycentric concentration, a new system of mass transport links, and to ensure that each of the centers was provided with its own market, school, hospital, etc. – meaning that each center would have to have its own town, or rather city, center. The intention was to lock into two interdependent co-determinant benefits: first, to spare transportation resources (car traffic), and thus congestion; and secondly, to establish a coherent mix of residential housing and built work space, that is, of business and residential urban life.

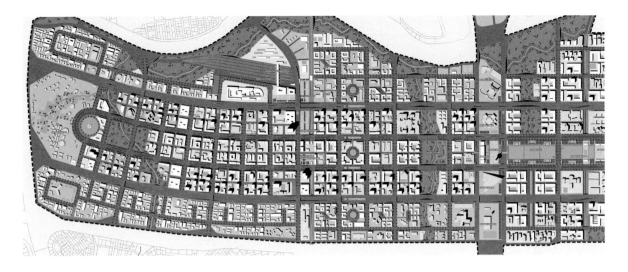

←
Abuja, Nigeria today: view of one of the residential
areas that flank the Central Area.

↑
The Central Area. The possible central boulevards the length of
downtown connecting the super-blocks are clearly marked.

Things are complicated by the fact that, to date, these shanty towns within the east/west wings spreading out from the Central Area are the product not of controlled development in line with land-zoning plans or land titles, but of spontaneous settlement or uncontrolled land allocation, and therefore may not even lie in zones designated for settlement, but perhaps plum in the middle of a drawing-board dual carriageway instead. Given the density of such inhabitation, these shanty towns also serve as potential health and fire hazards for the entire area. (A prior danger of such expansion is, of course, that all notions of fringe belt or green-belt get lost along the way.) If these decentralized "suburbs" are to be given a structured shape in the form of the requisite infrastructure, then the choices for planners will be tough and may entail deciding to tear things down and start again (see Chap. 7 on Lagos).

Needless to say, that could precipitate the need for low-cost substitute accommodation, and the alternatives would have to be codified by title deed. This ties in to the theory championed by Hernando de Soto, who suggests that clear land-ownership rights are a critical criterion that both decide growth and offer the administration a clear instrument with which to control growth.

Indeed, development control can in this regard be implemented more easily on a hard and fast legal basis, once title deeds make monitoring compliance with zoning easier. However, the gap between healthy, low-cost estates and squatter settlements is one that remains to be bridged.

Any businessman travelling into the Central Area in the morning from the direction of Bwari, Nyanya, or Gwagwalada will quite probably experience gridlocks similar to

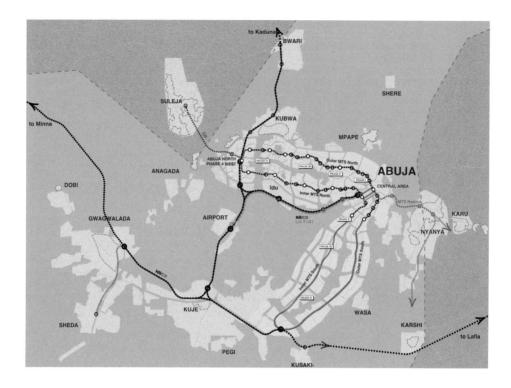

↑

Outline of growth in Abuja: the south and west wings would feature a light rail mass transit loop that link up to the main railway lines coming in from the outside. The only sensible way to provide transport for the 6 million-plus inhabitants.

those in Lagos and which prompted the move to Abuja in the first place. History has leapfrogged itself. Perhaps that businessman is thinking about doing interstate business in the now thriving border towns of Karu, Suleja, or Yanyan instead – towns that are already attracting commerce away from the metropolitan area. Alternatively, he may think it more sensible to do business closer to where he lives and thus spare himself the journeying.

This was one of the scenarios that probably passed through Michael Denkel's mind when he was plotting the shape that polycentric concentration should take and it no doubt confirmed his belief that the shanty towns within the metropolitan area needed to be a) formalized and b) instilled with a stronger independent identity. The first move taken was to block the end of the two wings by introducing two new, and therefore planned, satellite towns, named somewhat unexotically Abuja South and Abuja West. This would make it easier to control development in the rapidly urbanizing growth corridors, would take the sting out of the transportation issue, and help to create a structure to the whole. In order to bring about such polycentric concentration the focus had to be on establishing mass transit corridors between the district centers and assisting the gradual upgrading of the shanty towns into full-fledged district centers (containing the requisite educational and health institutions, not to mention commerce and administration), and thus generating jobs close to where the people actually live. And the Federal Capital Development Authority has been infected by his enthusiasm and is trying to find ways of putting the ideas into practice. Having initially, by no fault of their own, got the basics wrong (as the IPA planners could never have foreseen the speed at which the city has grown, or envisaged that the center would not be where the growth took place) the FCDA is now busy getting the fundamentals right.

Albert Speer summarizes the benefits of polycentric concentration, the multitopia, when he declares that "the key factors which indicate that regiopolises will become increasingly important are their sustainability. While the initial costs of switching a large city over to high-grade, resource-sparing, and partially recyclable infrastructure spread over a number of centers may be high, politicians should bear in mind that exceptional long-term savings beckon. The return on the city's investment will make such projects worthwhile." However, as stated at the outset, this stands or falls by the politicians' ability to agree. In Abuja, thankfully, this has been the case, and the legislative side to such concentration so pivotal for its implementation is being pushed through, namely, the appropriate organization of land use: zoning. Here, again, we can discern that the actual work of zoning itself needs to be undertaken in line with a policy of sustainability.

Another city is a prime example of how things have gone the other way over roughly the same period. Abuja was declared the capital in 1991. As we have seen (Chap. 5), three years earlier Brisbane used the opportunity afforded by a World Expo to upgrade itself. Yet it was not on board when the boat of polycentric concentration left the harbor. Today, it is by far the largest local government authority in terms of the area it governs, despite the fact that Sydney and Melbourne both have significantly larger populations. Brisbane demonstrates that an Expo alone, like any other single mega-event, does not suffice to create a viably structured city. The city's population has rocketed from some 700,000 about 30 years ago to an estimated 1.8 million today, and the city continues to grow at about 2.2 per cent annually – a growth rate not unlike Abuja's. However, only 54 per cent of the population lives in the city, and there are no satellite cities that could morph or be morphed into a polycentric structure. Instead, there is one massive sprawl of suburbs. This creates a highly visible, if not especially striking, high-rise city center, but not a

PROPERTY AND POVERTY   Hernando de Soto, Peruvian economist, in his pioneering book, THE MYSTERY OF CAPITAL (Black Swan, London, 2001), suggests that property is the only way to accumulate capital. The basis for evaluating property, and thus possible trading of it as an asset or its use as collateral, is a property system. And that is what is lacking in most developing countries, he claims. "If you don't have a property system, you don't have the representational device with which you can capture value, store it, make it liquid, and invest it." Without the accumulation of capital, the poor remain poor and the socially dysfunctional and potentially divisive side to urbanization persists.

←←
Simulations of the Central Area in Abuja, Nigeria, with
the heart of downtown structured in line with a boulevard
concept to breathe greater life into the business and
ministerial district.

functional city. Despite attempts to create dedicated bus lanes both downtown and on roads leading to suburbia, and a rigorous one-way system in the center, traffic regularly grinds to a standstill. Things are not helped by a lack of systematic traffic-light coordination. The tax revenues that growth has brought with it are quite manifestly being spent on upgrading and expanding infrastructure, but the latter has not, to date, kept pace with growth. The "City," the actual downtown area, may boast new high-rises apartment blocks, but as yet many are still empty and real mixed usage has still to happen. This is a missed opportunity, leaving the City home mainly to shopping malls and offices, despite offering a great residential basis in the form of the riverbank, the botanical gardens – as well as the culture the technological university brings with it. Maybe the politicians will at some point realize that the only way forward is to get the fundamentals right "after the fact," as it were. As Abuja shows, it can be done.

1   Josef Reichholf, Stabile Ungleichgewichte, (Suhrkamp: Frankfurt/Main, 2008), p. 117.1
2   Deutsche Bauzeitung, 9/1978, p. 283
3   Shell, with its focus on an oil value chain, inevitably sees a long-term take on business as exploring for new oil fields, unlocking the resource in them, and then bringing it to market involves many years. Therefore the company needs to know whether its massive upfront investments in developing a particular field is going to pay off – after all, society might have shifted out of oil and into an alternative energy source by the time only half the oil in the field has been tapped, rendering the investment worthless. Over the last 12 months, Shell has published a study on energy scenarios through to 2050 and sponsored a survey on how 18- to 24-year-olds view society in 2050.
4   McKinsey authored a seminal study in 2008 on urbanization trends in China.
5   Peter Sloterdijk recently suggested in a lecture at Harvard on the metaphor of foams: "Through the motif of the inhabited cell I can uphold the spherical imperative that applies to all forms of human life but does not presuppose cosmic totalization. The stacking of cells in an apartment block no longer generates the classical world/house entity, but an architectural foam, a multi-chambered system made of relatively stabilized personal worlds." That multi-chambered system is exactly what polycentric concentration seeks to achieve.
6   AS&P Bid Book, p. 18

X

PRIORITIZE THE THREE E'S:
ECOLOGY, ECONOMY
AND EQUALITY

"First of all, a group may fail to anticipate a problem before the problem actually arrives. Second, when the problem does arrive, the group may fail to perceive it. Then, after they perceive it, they may fail even to try to solve it. Finally, they may try to solve it but may not succeed. While all this discussion of reasons for failure and societal collapses may seem depressing, the flip side is a heartening subject: namely, successful decision-making." **Jared Diamond**[1]

In the introduction to the study on "Frankfurt for Everyone," published in February, 2009, and setting out a vision for the city in the year 2030, Albert Speer recounts that when compiling the study the authors assumed the first objective had to be to secure the city's long-term prosperity, i.e., its economic sustainability. They assumed that this could be achieved if the city succeeded in attracting a sufficiently large number of highly qualified "knowledge workers." However, he explains, they soon determined that this did not on its own ensure the desired result of a "prospering urban society in which people wanted to live." He goes on to conclude that: "Only a stable community with balanced, fair, and social structures, with actively committed citizens prepared to perform on behalf of the city, and a well-integrated immigrant population from all manner of different backgrounds, with educational and residential opportunities for everyone can form the foundations for the desired urban organism. The working title 'FRANKFURT FOR EVERYONE' stands for this comprehensive approach."

It is an approach that essentially runs like a central thread through the nine "commandments" of this manifesto discussed thus far. The holistic methodology advocated there can be summarized in our tenth commandment: Prioritize the three E's: a sustainable city is a city that is economic, ecological, and equitable. Only if we manage to get all three right can we achieve the cross-generational pact necessary to forge a future. In this regard, sustainability means a transcendent outlook, as is underscored by the fact that Albert Speer and many of the other authors of the above-mentioned study will be close to being centenarians by the time their vision of Frankfurt in the year 2030 becomes a reality – assuming it does. It means self-reduction now for that hopeful future in 2030. It means intervention in the structural order of the built environment in coming years with a view to the quality of life at least a generation later.

→

Albert Speer with the Lady Mayoress of Frankfurt presenting AS&P's vision for the city in 2030, "Frankfurt for Everyone," to the press in 2009.

And it is therefore logical that in its 16 recommendations for the city, FRANKFURT FOR EVERYONE advocates those three E's, calling for urgent improvements to the actual and the perceived quality of life, insisting that the city morph from office center into a "residential city" that encourages civic participation, championing a more differentiated education and academic system, demanding model sustainable districts that will fire the imagination and spark me-toos, reducing mobility to a level that the city can sustain, enhancing the amount of green in the cityscape, and expanding its main business hub: the airport.

In other words, in order to create sustainable cities in line with the three E's we will need to bring about change on a quite unprecedented scale, whereby, as Barack Obama never tires of saying, "We can!" We must build houses that are not driven only by electric appliances – whatever happened to hand-powered whisks? We must also dissuade home users from acquiring such vast numbers of appliances, and run campaigns urging that appliances be shut off when not in use and not simply left on power-guzzling standby. After all, 30 per cent of the energy consumed by private homes in London is gobbled up by those eager appliances. The functionalists' cry of "Less is more" certainly applies here. Less dependence on appliances, more future. If we take the Stern Report's call for an 80-per cent reduction in CO_2 emissions seriously, then we must significantly change the way we operate our homes – which means educating people for the change as well as planning it, that is to say, persuasion and innovation, driven by economics and ecology.

Some may immediately assume that change at the private level is not possible, but in doing so forget that change is often, if not exclusively, market-driven. For example, British supermarkets recently resolved to replace their open-door freezers with closed-door units in order to cut their electricity bills. The old argument was that the average customer would not bother to open the door of a freezer and would therefore not buy anything. Needless to say, there was initially a slight drop in sales, but the supermarkets in question were then able to rely on a "green" cachet in their marketing and soon made up the ground lost. This may just be a small step, albeit one taken in the right direction, given that a considerable portion of London's ecological footprint is the result of fast food

DEPLETING NATURAL RESOURCES *"We all agree that a lot more economic wealth is needed for six billion people, let alone the nine billion people we expect to have living on our planet by mid-century. I suggest that doubling wealth is the least we should aim for. On the other hand, we are already overexploiting the Earth's resources to such an extent that stabilizing carbon dioxide concentrations alone would require cutting carbon dioxide emissions by more than 50 per cent each year. Ocean fishing should also be cut in half – we apparently kill off about 50 species of flora and fauna every day. In order to halt this trend, we ought to radically reduce land conversion. It is fair to say that we should reduce the consumption of natural resources by roughly a factor of two." Ernst Ulrich von Weizsäcker[2]*

dumped in trash cans. Yet Albert Speer is firmly of the opinion that the market can help. "Once energy prices rise again above a certain level people will start thinking twice before wasting power. The wasteful use of oil today is merely a reflection of the fact that it is too cheap. After all, it is not users who have to foot the bill for the damage caused by the CO_2 emissions, which is why we need to foster a culture in which people abandon short-term gains for long-term benefits, and prioritize the Three E's along the way. Then all will benefit, and that includes future generations."

ECOLOGY

It would seem obvious to insist that the sustainable city should prioritize ecology. In its proposed vision for Frankfurt in the year 2030, AS&P emphasizes that in the world of tomorrow such a priority will be a way in which a city can market itself. Based on the fact that in Germany, Frankfurt is the city with the most houses built to the PASSIVHAUSSTANDARD, the study identified an important field of action, namely, that the city must master the major challenge of converting all existing residential and commercial properties into energy-efficient structures. In this context it is worth noting that since 2003, all tenders invited for new public buildings have been for energy-saving designs rather than for ones relying on conventional systems. At the same time, the city should seek to use only brownfield areas and, wherever possible, to increase the density of dwellings.

Given the progress made in eco-friendly construction techniques and the development of renewable energy sources, such as geothermal pumps, higher-yield solar energy systems, etc., the time has come to integrate their use into the main fabric of our built environment – be it by retrofitting or with regard to new projects. To this end, the insights need to be reflected in the work addressed by urban designers and planners. In 2008, a policy document pointed out that the issues addressed by planners all too often fall short of prioritizing ecologically sustainable developments, and pointed the finger at the development of land consumption and suburbanization. It concluded that it was high time to start fleshing out "an urban development policy which addresses the problem of the demise of the era of cheap energy." We can safely generalize and say that this shortcoming is not specific to Germany alone. The document went on to state that "incorporating environmental issues into construction and spatial targets has to be a priority on the agenda of national urban development policy. For instance, a national competition for an 'eco neighbourhood' could be run on the topic of energy and CO_2-neutral urban areas. In this way, a step-by-step implementation of integrated housing and mobility development, from local district to urban region should be pursued. International examples of green urbanism lead the way."[3]

In other words, it is overly apparent that the ecological factor must be heeded not only as regards buildings, but also as regards mobility. A sustainable city must rely on a sustainable system of mobility that is fit for the future. Thus, the disadvantageous impact of (road) traffic has to be minimized. To this end, the needs of inhabitants and pedestrians must be taken into account more strongly than is typically the case in cities today, whether in Europe, the United States, Asia, or Africa. To this end, a greater proportion of overall transportation must be handled by resource-sparing systems that are as silent as possible and foster a healthy environment.

In the case of Frankfurt, for example, AS&P advocates a stringent speed limit of 30 km/h throughout the city (see Chap. 7), the only exception to the rule being the trunk roads, where cars would be permitted to accelerate to 50 km/h. Moreover, it couples this policy recommendation with the remark that, in future, travel chains will tend to consist of links involving different means of transport. The future, they suggest, will hinge on long- and longer-distance rail travel, car-sharing, and cycling – the zero-emission form of transport par excellence (if one ignores the water given off as we perspire cycling uphill), but one that to date accounts for only 7 per cent of total traffic in Frankfurt, despite the city's compact footprint. AS&P therefore calls for extensive cycle-track infrastructures (see Chap. 7) in the cities of tomorrow, (perhaps borrowing on the Oxford example, where no student really owns a bike, but simply takes a cycle from the racks). And it also says cities should possess "multimodal transport nodes and mobility stations that offer all types of transport as equal opportunities and facilitates their combination, with, as the backbone, a high-performance and attractive mass transport system."

Taken together, these measures would reduce energy emissions, improve the energy efficiency of mobility, and bring more fresh air into the city. And if the sustainable city also makes certain it gets its green-belt policy right by ensuring its overall accessibility and links into the green regions that surround it, then it has a sporting chance of gaining a seal of approval as what Michael Denkel calls the "ecotropolis of tomorrow." Indeed, in tomorrow's world, cities will seek to obtain the certification we associate with, for example, fair-trade products today. The internationally recognized European Energy Award® is one such symbol of distinction for which cities are already competing, as is the title of European Green Capital bestowed by the EU Commission.[4] A future is quite conceivable where a mobile population bases its choice of residence on precisely such certificates.

Just how critical concentration becomes apparent if one considers what will happen if cities continue to sprawl into the countryside, eating into agricultural land and potential recreation "hinterlands" alike. At present, housing and transport in Europe tends to consume as much as 100 hectares a day. Reducing that figure by at least half would be a strong symbol of sustainable urban development and energy efficiency. It would also function as a yardstick for improved quality of life both in cities, with shortened dis-

URBANIZATION AND INEQUALITY *"The evidence shows quite clearly that India's economic growth was urban led, with the gaps in living standards between the cities and the countryside widening in recent years. My studies with Nirupam Bajpai had found that the rate of urbanization at the state level was the strongest predictor of the relative growth rates among the Indian states." Jeffrey D. Sachs[5]*

tances to be covered and more facilities close at hand, and outside, where greenery would await inhabitants at weekends or fields would be there for the tilling.

"Imagine that people only ever know single houses, each with its own little path leading up to it. Surely they would not survive more than three days. It is the large cities with their traffic axes and their economies of scale that provide the potential to protect both man and the environment at the same time. They provide the greatest leverage for emission mitigation. What good is a zero-energy house if it gobbles up the landscape?" Gerd Held[6]

ECONOMY

A fact all too often forgotten is that a city's economy plays just as much a role in its sustainability as do ecological criteria. This holds true at various levels. If a city fails to provide the requisite number of jobs then its population will contract. Moreover, the tax revenues it garners will likewise fall. It is all a matter of input/output ratios. The city has to be a value proposition, as the management theorist might put it. If a city does not have good governance in this regard then it will soon become what we earlier termed a failed city: bankrupt and with a sharply declining number of inhabitants, a downward spiral from which there may be no recovery. To avoid this, a city must foster corporate loyalty to it. After all, one of the most acute problems that a city could face would be a dwindling number of businesses tied or allied to it. At the more general level, frequent relocation by businesses tends to spark social problems, regularly tearing apart the urban fabric and the associated infrastructure (e.g., foreign-language schools that spring up to cater for their staff, or subway links specially provided for them). Moreover companies that are not tied to a specific location can rarely be persuaded to commit to playing a role in improving "their" city.

A city that succeeds in binding companies to it will eventually benefit from that bond, for the more types of jobs and levels of employment there are, the more likely it is that the city will attract skilled staff, and the greater the likelihood that the entrepreneurs will develop a sense of loyalty to the city and play their part in promoting it. Their bottom line profits, and the city benefits. It is worth remembering here for the European scenario that dynamic corporate service industries tend to prefer city locations. For some time now, a soft location factor such as urban ambience has been important – one need think only of the number of people flocking to Seattle. Often, such major corporations, Deutsche Bank being a prime example in Frankfurt, themselves become interested in the problems associated with urban living, help to promote public debate on the related issues, and get involved in local communities.[7]

Frankfurt is again a case in point. In terms of jobs, and given the city's reputation as a financial and IT center, the focus is on improving it as a magnet attracting the knowledge elite. Frankfurt is primarily perceived worldwide as a powerful banking center with a major international airport. Yet its achievements in education and R&D are less known, and the chances are that foreigners are unaware of the quality of life, the marvelous surrounding countryside, or the sports and leisure-time facilities that Frankfurt has to offer, and think in such terms of Heidelberg or Munich instead. To this end, so AS&P suggests, and to support that vibrant corporate sector, the city needs to do three things on the economic front, all of which could apply in different ways to other cities.

First of all, it must overcome its shortcomings in the image-and-identity field, by consistently marketing the advantages it offers as a business location. "The central message of the marketing concept 2030 must be the image of a future Frankfurt as the core of an internationally-linked Frankfurt Rhine/Main regiopolis." In Frankfurt, the speed of renewal is quite simply greater than in other cities, the study concludes, and therefore the city must seek to better market the strengths it currently has, which are a mixture of creative minds in the ad and media industries, on the one hand, and its academic and research facilities, on the other. "Frankfurt Rhine/Main is one of Germany's most innovative regions. Education, cutting-edge research, development, and business together constitute the solid foundations for a prospering region and enhance one another. The city should focus on ways to tap the latent synergies here."

To this end, the study devotes an entire section to highlighting Frankfurt's prowess as a seat of superlative scholarship, as a center of theoretical and practical excellence, as an interface between R&D and its application in business and society, as a cluster of science cities that are scaled such as to be family-friendly. It likewise attempts to elaborate on how the "creative sector" could be better supported and given a sharper profile through geographical concentration. The associated "elite staff" could, it proposes, be offered new downtown apartments in existing high-rises, thus killing two birds with one stone. The heart of the city would cease to be devoted mainly to office space, the skyscrapers would start to enjoy a new lease of life as mixed-use structures, and the city would polish its appeal to this mission-critical group of employees.

Secondly, it must emphasize the geographical advantages it offers. In this regard, it should, AS&P proposes, press ahead with formulating a master plan for its "airport city" and prioritizing ways to avoid congestion at its airport – thus potentially felling trees. (Making sure its prosperity continues may involve unpleasant and unpopular policy decisions, something not easy in a policy-making structure that hinges on re-election cycles.) The airport city aspect is easier to plug. After all, offices in an airport city will appeal to global players among the service corporations, who will choose to locate there thanks to the outstanding transport links provided, and also because of the enhanced image they will get. Frankfurt is already pursuing major projects such as the Airrail Center and Gateway Gardens, and is thus swiftly becoming an airport city. "The urban design and overall functional structure of the entire airport-city complex are still incredibly imprecise," the study notes. To make certain that the long-term networking potential such a complex affords is exploited, it recommends tailoring developments here to the role an airport city could play as a distinct new district of the city itself.

Thirdly, a city must always remember what critical factors are driving any economy. One key indicator that allows us to quantify the sustainable nature of a business hub is

its ability to reinvent itself through dynamic innovation. AS&P defines this as product innovation, process innovation, market expansion, social and institutional change within corporations, not to mention entrepreneurial R&D. Such innovation is often driven by start-ups. However, it is often precisely such companies that shy away from locations where rental and operating costs – along with the cost of living – are high. Frankfurt, the study advises, needs to foster a start-up culture that facilitates the experimental phase in which new business models prove their worth, one possible solution being centers destined specifically for such fledgling companies. Again, the analytical approach could be applied to any other city seeking to shore up its future. Identify the sources of innovation and support them.

EQUALITY – EQUITY

Robert Kennedy once remarked that "few will have the greatness to bend history itself; but each of us can work to change a small portion of events, and in the total of all those acts will be written the history of this generation..." For "each of us" to work towards a sustainable future there has to be a sense of common purpose, and such an outlook will arise only if we feel that we are all rightly involved as equals. The sustainable city of tomorrow must therefore rest on equality in the sense of equal opportunities and on equity in the sense that no one of us may be treated unfairly along the way. A city that is structured by social disparities, as recent history has shown only too often in France, for example, is a potential flashpoint rather than a place where families will wish to reside for any length of time. The sustainable city of tomorrow is therefore an "all-inclusive" city, whereby the "all" means the totality of inhabitants and not just one social stratum among them. This may seem like common sense, but a glance at cities worldwide shows that all too often this basic rule is simply ignored.

It follows from this that a sustainable city must be able both to provide good dwellings for all income brackets and ensure the quality of life of its residents. The greater the latter, the greater the potential identification with the city in question. To this end, cities must, for example, proactively integrate their immigrant populations. That means establishing, among other things, the facilities to enable the children of such groups of inhabitants to face equal opportunities in local schools.[8] After all, it is almost commonplace to say that a high-school leaver's certificate is a young person's meal ticket to a better fu-

---

DEMOGRAPHIC CHANGE

"Demographic change will shift the balance between growth and shrinkage in Germany. Quite aside from energy and climate issues, it will require new initiatives for shaping life in the city and country, for mobility and infrastructure, culture of heritage and integration policy." Volker Hauff

"The ThyssenKrupp Group is planning and building a new head office in Essen on an inner-city site. The Quarter will not be a closed-off area, but a vibrant urban space open to all citizens. Social tendencies such as demographic change, globalization, and sustainability at local level bear ever new challenges for urban development. The ThyssenKrupp company accepts these challenges by showing social responsibility." Ralph Labonte [9]

ture. It likewise means equal access for all to leisure-time facilities – public parks, plazas and spaces, public theater halls, and public museums form part of the very core of urban life and need to be nurtured. At the same time, demographic trends need to be carefully considered to ensure equal opportunities. While the baby-boomer generation in the West may currently be focusing on how to integrate an ever older population into the urban fabric, cities in developing countries are seeing an unprecedented influx of young people. Young people spell young families, and young families invariably have less disposable income. If cities are not to become almost-all-exclusive and therefore foster social unrest, they must find ways to provide an adequate quality of life for both the young and the old. This may lead to a focus on supporting new apartments tailored to small families, as well as to more apartments for smaller families, as the number of singles and of retirees living in cities rises. The solution must be to foster vibrant residential quarters and to promote mixed-use buildings, while keeping an open mind to unconventional and experimental forms of living.

In this context, AS&P emphasizes the function of "shared spaces," a concept that has not yet come into its own. They offer cities a useful tool to prevent all-inclusiveness as defined above from deteriorating into social leveling and instead deploy it as a tool that enables diversity. Shared spaces in this sense are densely used spaces where traffic and people can mingle. They serve to strengthen the quality of the lived and the built environment and thus to underpin the foundations for small retailers and hospitality outlets. In a shared space, there is no longer competition between the people using a road: all are treated as equals. The spatial and functional separation of individual areas into pedestrian zones and zones for cars gets elided. Points of orientation are provided in the form of local landmarks, public furniture, and lights. The street suddenly starts to be home to functions previously possible only in non-traffic spaces: fountains, benches, plants, and kiosks find their way back into the street. The hope being, of course, that this will return the street to the status it once enjoyed in our cities, and it is one whose virtues were espoused as long ago as the 1950s by the grand old lady of urban design, Jane Jacobs.

In all probability, inhabitants will identify more strongly with such an all-inclusive and thus sustainable city; and that, in turn, will no doubt be reflected in greater civil partici-

SAVING THE STREET   *"To think of city traffic problems in oversimplified terms of pedestrians versus cars, and to fix on the segregation of each as a principal goal, is to go at the problem from the wrong end. Consideration for pedestrians in cities is inseparable from consideration for city diversity, vitality and concentration of use. In the absence of city diversity, people in large settlements are probably better off in cars than on foot. Unmanageable city vacuums are by no means preferable to unmanageable city traffic. The problem that lies behind consideration for pedestrians, as it lies behind all other city traffic difficulties, is how to cut down absolute numbers of surface vehicles and enable those that remain to work harder and more efficiently." Jane Jacobs[10]*

pation. Visions will then not be provided only by planners, but will also be prompted by debate among citizens themselves. "Educating to assume civic responsibility," the AS&P study on Frankfurt 2030 diagnoses, is a "task in the interest of the entire urban community." It is to be hoped that the sustainable city of 2030 will so inspire its citizens that specific education will no longer be necessary in this regard, but will come naturally to the citizens, who will once again be citoyens, persons committed to a civil society based on liberty, equality, and fraternity. After all, as Confucius once said, "Virtue never stands alone. It is bound to have neighbors."[11]

1 *Jared Diamond,* Collapse. How Societies Choose to Fail or Survive, *(Penguin: Harmondsworth, 2006) p. 421*

2 *E. U. v. Weizsäcker describing his Factor Four proposal to the Club of Rome.*

3 Auf dem Weg zu einer nationalen Stadtentwicklungspolitik. Memorandum, *published by German Federal Ministry of Transport, Building and Urban Affairs, (Berlin, 2008), p. 33*

4 *AS&P recommends that Frankfurt seek to become the first city of over 500,000 citizens to win this award.*

5 *Jeffrey Sachs,* The End of Poverty, *(Penguin: Harmondsworth, 2005) p. 184*

6 Auf dem Weg zu einer nationalen Stadtentwicklungspolitik. Memorandum, *loc. cit.*

7 *In Frankfurt, Deutsche Bank's Alfred Herrhausen Foundation addresses the intellectual side to urbanization and its consequences while the non-profit organization Common Purpose seeks to ensure the constant exposure of management to local issues.*

8 *Cultural diversity is a factor that contributes to the success of a city. And cultural diversity is something fueled by an integrated local immigrant population.*

9 Auf dem Weg, *pp. 26-7*

10 *Jane Jacobs,* The Death and Life of Great American Cities, *(Random House: New York, 1993), p. 454*

11 *Confucius,* Analects, *Book IV, 25, (Penguin: Harmondsworth, 1979), p. 75*

APPLYING THE TEN COMMANDMENTS: CAIRO

Cairo is often forgotten when it comes to the trend list of megacities worldwide – possibly because Western minds associate the city more with the pyramids than with immense size. Rarely is it mentioned in the same breath as Shanghai, Tokyo, Lagos, or Mexico City, yet in population terms alone it certainly should be. Metropolitan Cairo is today home to an estimated 18 million people, close to a fourth of Egypt's total population, with the figure projected to rise to about 27 million by 2027. After the Revolution of 1952, Cairo saw a dramatic population explosion, with the influx taking the total to 9 million by 1976, only for it to double over the next three decades – and the core downtown area houses eight million of them, more than double the figure only 40 years ago. Since the 1960s, the city has spilled over onto the west bank of the Nile, a move that was swiftly followed by new suburbs. At the same time, construction also spread into the Western desert in the form of satellite cities (given that to the east the conurbation is constrained by the Muqattam mountains) one such new town being 6th of October City, which at present has a population of some 500,000 but is expected to house up to four million inhabitants before long. Others like it lie or were planned up to 100 kilometers from the city center. Greater Cairo, consisting of three zones (West, Central, East) and divided into four governorates at present (6th of October, Cairo, Giza, Qaliobeya), is a rough circle bisected by the Nile and likewise some 100 kilometers in diameter. New plans envision a ring road (400 km) being built around this admixture of dense urban settlement, partial desert, and farmland.

Like its fellow megacities, all of them essentially states within states, Cairo faces seemingly intractable problems. In this regard, the megacity is an impossible construct because it is dysfunctional. In Cairo's case, not only is the megacity the capital city and seat of a central government, it is also a conglomerate of old cities and new cities, cities that have come about through organic growth, new urban communities that are the product of planned growth, and cities in-between that were planned, but whose plot evidently got lost. It is a greater city in which the populations of the various constituent cities commute to other cities to reach their workplace. It is hardly surprising, then, that two million cars fight for road space into the city each morning, only to battle their way out again after the office buildings close – assuming, that is, the building in question is not one of those that has just collapsed. Given spatial constraints, Egypt's industry, which is concentrated in metropolitan Cairo, has completely inadequate waste-disposal opportunities – as does the city as a whole, which has to contend with continual problems in sewage and refuse disposal, not to mention with the level of air pollution. On top of this, property speculators have made a tight housing market even more difficult. Hardly conditions to attract new inhabitants, one might think, but Cairo as the capital of Egypt is growing at a good 2 per cent a year. So the urban planners here evidently have a tall order to fill. Given its almost random "planned" growth through the ages, Cairo is a planner's nightmare.

A glance back in history shows that Cairo has, since its foundation in 969 by the Fatimid Dynasty, been a commercial capital with a fortress. Not long after being established it was already bursting at the seams, spilling out over the city walls, merging to the west with the port of Bulaq and then in the south with the island of Rhoda (now downtown).

The first wave of modernization came in the second half of the 19th century when Ismail Pasha hired Belgian, French, and Italian engineers to dry the swamps that lay beneath what is now the modern downtown area (São Paulo and Shanghai both have to contend with similar topographical constraints). Ismail, who had studied in Paris, wanted a capital built to European standards. In an era of modernization driven by the Suez Canal, this was perhaps not surprising. The mid-19th-century "Haussmannization" of the swamps, to create the contemporary "old" downtown, was followed in the early 20th century by the creation of a Garden City on the English model on the outskirts of the city (which has needless to say long since become part of the metropolitan center). Since then, the city has seen plans for new districts in the 1970s, the foundation of extensive new settlements, such as 6th of October City, as satellite cities in the 1980s, through to the New Urban Communities currently being planned. A number of questions remained unanswered: Can the archetypally dysfunctional megacity be rescued? Is there any way it can be rendered functional? What would the alternative be? After all, the efforts to modernize the city have simply compounded the problem, and history has bequeathed the city center little more than perpetual gridlocks, regular power outages, and water cuts. Are these problems really that complicated, indeed impossible?

They most certainly are, or so US writer Maria Golia would probably say. She lived in Cairo for many years and for all her love/hate relationship with the city, comes to a very sobering conclusion: "Egypt is an advanced culture that has reached a very advanced state of decay, and is truly a showcase for all the challenges for which the other cities need to be prepared." All the more reason to choose Cairo as our litmus test, as the perfect occasion to put the ten commandments of sustainability to the test to see whether they can be applied to solving the city's problems – both those of the central area and of the now moribund satellite cities. To this end, we traveled to Cairo with two board members of AS&P, Albert Speer and Joachim Schares, and set out to explore the city's underlying structures together. And found out that solutions are not only conceivable, but decidedly possible.

1 COMBINE THEORY AND COMMON SENSE

To apply this maxim, in seeking sustainable solutions to Cairo's tangible problems we must endeavor not to rely solely on the rational tools of urban planning, but to combine these with the insights afforded by other disciplines. These must include a knowledge of the immediate history, local cultural specifics, property regulations, political constraints, weather, etc.

In Cairo, AS&P works closely with Professor Ayman Ashour, the founder of Archplan, one of the key urban planning offices in Cairo, and a professor of urban planning at the Al Shams University. He firmly believes that the key to sustainable urban planning is an approach that, from a Western perspective, seems all too obvious. Professor Ashour suggests: "Only a very few people in Cairo have an awareness of their own history, by which I do not mean the pyramids. And even fewer have ever thought about what the concept of 'quality of life' could or should mean." To put it harshly: anyone who has never experienced real changes in the structure in which they conduct their everyday lives, who has never known clean air or what it could mean to get to work on time day in, day out, using public transport is not likely to demand that his or her city provide quality of life, if only in those two areas.

As regards the ancient Chinese wisdom on the size of a city (see Chap. 4), or in this case a metropolitan region, Cairo has the good fortune to be located close to the fertile Nile Delta. As a consequence, it is close to the farmlands that can sadly source only a small portion of its food, whereby that proximity shortens time-to-market and transportation costs. (In this respect Cairo fails at the first hurdle of sustainability, as Egypt is now the world's largest importer of wheat, for example.) Tilled fields also exist scattered in bands between the center of the city and the new suburbs and satellites. To this extent it is sustainable in terms of being able to feed itself and will remain so until its population exceeds agricultural output (whereby this, in turn, hinges on agricultural productivity). Unless a holistic, interdisciplinary approach is taken, there can be no planned attempt to free the city from the stranglehold of population growth coupled with income deterioration and transport nightmare.

The problems may be immense, the difficulties manifest, but the solutions must start at the local level, for example, by changing car-parking patterns and negating the notion that "I have a divine right to park outside my home for free." At the same time, the issues must be tackled at an abstract, open-ended level to take into account that the city will not stop evolving while its planners are thinking about solutions. Stand at the large round-about outside the former Cairo American University – a building not dissimilar in proportions and airs to Moscow University – and you will see that by mid-morning "modern" traffic has come to a standstill. But in between the buses spitting diesel fumes, the trucks belching soot, and the ubiquitous Peugeot taxis (in which it is the passengers who insisted on the meter being switched on that are to be pitied), a goatherd drives his animals. The modern city cannot stop this medieval mode of transportation to the butcher. If it were not for the fumes, one could but recommend that Cairo's inhabitants take their cue from the China of yore and ride bikes, for with the exception of Saturdays and holidays. the traffic, so we compute, moves at a rate of about ten kilometers an hour, when it moves at all. After we elect to walk round downtown and abandon our taxi in favor of sidewalks (themselves all too often half taken over by shop shelving on one side or wrongly parked cars on the other), Albert Speer comments on Cairo as a whole: "You don't have to be an urban planner to figure out where to start changing things. What immediately strikes the eye is the traffic, the environmental pollution, and the uncoordinated growth. In this context, 'one size fits all' will definitely not function. There is no obvious solution, given the scale of the problems, and they require intensive study and discussion by all the disciplines. A holistic brace of solutions needs to be devised that combines those insights with common sense – make car-parking exorbitantly expensive – and there's a double benefit: in the time it takes for owners to elect not to use their cars, the city will profit from an injection of additional tax revenue."

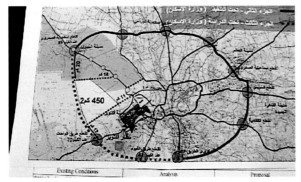

2 GO BROWNFIELD, NOT GREENFIELD

The bouts of planned growth, interspersed with "organic" or random growth, have left the city with countless spaces that have long since ceased to possess a meaningful function. This land is an unidentified asset crying out for reutilization and thus for the rejuvenation of urban value. Straightforward examples are freight rail stations and sidings that are no longer used, but which first need to be "unearthed" and catalogued. This offers space that could be put to a new purpose in the new fabric of the city. Such land offers great potential for downtown development, be it as residential or as commercial property, and provides a means of limiting the otherwise unlimited spread outwards by enhancing the efficiency of land use. However, to date work has not yet started on charting the total number of such spaces, in itself a gargantuan task.

The "modern" city center offers massive potential for building recycling. Here, it is more the historical residential structures built in the late 19th and early 20th centuries that are best suited to adaptation, whereby their ground floors have in many instances long since given way to retail outlets, ensuring their mixed use, and their cellars have been refunctioned to serve as ad hoc underground car parks. There are clear reasons why such a mass of buildings are so run-down. First, ever since President Gamal Abdel Nasser froze rents as part of his Revolution, there has been little or no incentive to acquire property in the city: it was simply cheaper to rent. Secondly, and as a result, there is likewise no incentive for house owners to maintain the buildings if the rents they are receiving are so low. Thirdly, and again as a product of the first reason, there is little established mortgage market. By contrast, many of the office buildings erected in the 1970s or later should be destined for a straightforward fate: demolition. Not only are the storey heights inadequate to allow for modern suspended ceilings or raised floors containing the requisite facilities, but, structurally speaking, they are also often unsound, a fact sadly borne out by the number of buildings that have collapsed in recent times. Yet the older buildings offer a prime example of the density "that a sustainable city requires," Speer comments.

In Cairo, we come across a marvelous example of assigning new functions in keeping with our second commandment. Disused or rather abused space west of the old souks has been given a new lease of life. The oldest garbage dump in the Middle East used to be located here, just below Saladin's citadel and outside what was presumed to be the perimeter of the old city wall; along with an eight-lane road, it essentially separated the Islamic Old Town from the City of the Dead, the huge cemetery that now serves as home to countless poor. A brave decision was taken to eliminate the dump and replace it with a park, perched on the mound that was the remainder of the dump. The mound itself was hollowed out, most organic waste removed, and replaced with three massive underground water reservoirs serving downtown. Based on plans devised by the Historic Cities Support Programme and under the auspices of the Aga Khan Trust, and financed by US foreign aid in the course of a decade of effort, a green hill-top park with a museum and restaurant has emerged, as have parts of the old city walls. The site offers schoolchildren and adults alike a welcome expanse of green in an otherwise dusty beige location.

3 DECREASE ENERGY, MINIMIZE TECHNOLOGY

The importance of this commandment is quite obvious in Cairo. The city is an energy-guzzler, and not just in terms of fuel consumption by cars, all of them hell-bent on getting somewhere, but most of them getting nowhere and thus burning more fuel on costly air-conditioning systems than actually on forward momentum. They are not alone: Cairo's buildings themselves consume far too much energy. The buildings almost invariably have antiquated cooling systems that rely on split-unit air-conditioners, and their facades often feature more glass than common sense would advise in a climate with so much sun. There are easy and obvious solutions for both: better internal planning of ventilation patterns, centralized cooling units, cooling ceilings, and double-skin facades would all contribute to lowering the energy inputs required.

4 KEEP SPACE OPEN

One of the new satellite cities created in the 1980s to ease congestion in terms of traffic and population in central Cairo, namely, 6th of October City, is a good example of how space needs to be kept open, rather than abused. It is a city bereft of people during the day, with wide streets and run-down properties. The people here work elsewhere, and the city's industry is manned by outsiders (yet another source of traffic in Greater Cairo). AS&P is busy formulating a new master plan for it that hinges on two key concepts. If the city is to be viable, so planners argue, then it needs to be given a clear central backbone, a spine that serves both as a main traffic artery and also as a structural and civic structuring device. The current "high street" may be great in length – it runs well over 10 kilometers – but it is decidedly off-center, does not bisect the city, and bends acutely. It therefore functions neither in terms of a central location nor as a visual connector. By contrast, the new spine orders urban space, connects the new ring road envisaged at both ends, and helps to position a series of green belts that run at right angles to it. These green spaces are configured in such a way that they provide parks at regular intervals, interrupting the run of office, industrial, and residential properties. Yet they are nevertheless clearly urban spaces, and in that capacity offer opportunities for people to meet and mingle in their leisure time. Likewise, where the existing streets are wide areas of lost space, destined only for use by cars, in the new master plan they have been greened, pedestrianized to create the internal spaces so typical of old Arab marketplaces, where people could mingle, or narrowed to include cycle paths and green central reservations. In this way, space is taken away from cars and returned to the inhabitants, and the roads become places for life again, in keeping with the call made by Jane Jacobs in the late 1950s for a return to the notion of street life associated with an era before motorized transport.

In other words, the emphasis on keeping spaces open and reconfiguring them is meant to ensure that "dead" space is given a new lease of life. As a result, so the hope, the hierarchy of public spaces (parks, large plazas, smaller squares, neighborhood squares) will help to nurture a sense of neighborhood at all levels of the city, and thus contribute to giving it an identity of its own that will encourage people to want to live there. In this regard, urban management of spaces potentially helps the city more in the long run than do iconic buildings intended to catch the eye, fire the imagination of investors, and provide an emblem with which the city is associated. After all, as Albert Speer himself comments on the effort that has gone into the new master plan: "To date, our brief has been to transform a disastrous state of affairs, whereby some 500,000 persons live in a city without a heart or even a well-formed body, into a vibrant living entity that will house eight times that number. That is no small task, to put it mildly. In the master plan we have proposed, we have focused on giving the city a fundamental and clear structure consisting of public spaces and infrastructure that will, of this I am convinced, function far better than those in place today. If you drive through 6th of October City today you simply do not know where you are." His local partner on the project, Professor Ayman Ashour, comments: "We have no interaction at present between working areas and recreation areas, let alone between working areas and homes. We believe that the revised master plan for 6th of October City will, for the first time since the new city first came off the drawing board, succeed in combining not just the latter two, but all three. And it does so, among other things, by creating the right urban spaces, an aspect that has been completely neglected to date."

5 CREATE A CLEAR IDENTITY

What are the pyramids of Gizeh other than one of the first urban icons? Albeit ones that today all too swiftly disappear from view in the smog, and really only re-emerge at the weekends when there is less traffic. There is perhaps therefore no more fitting place for architecture to act to forge a new identity – under the shadow of a history that dates back well over three millennia. If we assume that the men behind the pyramids wished to leave their mark on the world, then we can only congratulate them for having succeeded and having created a sustained 'icon'. Yet today perhaps that historical beacon no longer suffices. After all, would not a restructured 6th of October City by its very appearance signal change. And were Cairo to make a bid for the Olympic Games, this, too, would forge an unmistakable identity for the city. Both identities would go well beyond the city's current identity – which is a mixture of ancient history and traffic chaos.

6 THINK IN OVERALL CYCLES, NOT IN SECTORS – AVOID SHORT-TERM BENEFITS FOR LONG-TERM GAINS

In Greater Cairo, outside the city core proper, we find another example of planning that fits one of our commandments for sustainability and combines the right urban management to create private homes for the lower middle classes. It is a new "housing estate" called Haram City, located on the outer edge of 6th of October City and it illustrates that the city's difficulties – the morning/evening movement of inhabitants, the provisioning of new concentrated accommodation in keeping with the principle of polycentric concentration, and situating the clusters or centers in a framework that takes into account the history of the city as a whole – can be rectified only if thought of in the context of Greater Cairo as a whole, of which Haram City forms less than one third.

Haram City is being built (it is almost complete) by Orascom Housing Communities (OHC), a company strategically focused on offering affordable housing across Egypt. The company OHC is 58-per cent-owned by the Orascom Group, which has a strong tradition in waste management, construction, and, most recently, telecoms. OHC is a joint venture with an interesting partner, namely Homex, a vertically integrated home development company focused on affordable housing, headquartered in Mexico and listed on the New York Stock Exchange that has locked into the Mexican government's mortgage plan for lower-income families, the INFONAVIT.

Here, we have an example of thinking elsewhere in the globe being reflected on and put to use in a new local context. The INFONAVIT system states that in Mexico if someone is in gainful employment, then the employer shall be obliged to pay social-security contributions not only to the IMSS Mexican Social Insurance Institute but also to the INFONAVIT Institute for Social Residential Construction. The size of these contributions depends on the salary and risk category of the employment. The contributions are paid for salaries up to 25 times the minimum salary. Prospective home owners can, after a number of years, apply to INFONAVIT for a mortgage loan. Thanks to this system, 3 million families are already living in houses part-financed by INFONAVIT. The sizes of the homes on offer are carefully trimmed to both what such families are accustomed to and what they can afford. And this is the model Haram City has adopted and adapted – albeit in the absence of such a mortgage assistance program.

To this end it has prioritized sustainable development, going so far as to carefully compute overall water requirements to ensure that sufficient water can be provided and that the city has its own sewage plant and water treatment plant. As a consequence, all treated water can be used to water the green spaces: each little square between the houses boasts grass, bushes, and flowers, inviting the inhabitants of the neighboring houses to use them. Energy is sourced from the grid because calculations showed that, given the subsidized price of state electricity, solar power was simply not an option.

The estate features its own shopping clusters, schools, cinemas, and hospitals to make certain that its inhabitants (and its 8.4 million square meters will in due course boast 50,000 houses destined to be home to 400,000 persons) need not rely on public transportation to reach these fundamental facilities. At the same time, the estate is designed to be zero waste, with its own waste separation plant. The houses themselves are designed according to the example set by Egypt's Hassan Fathy, a sustainable architect long before the term was first coined and first winner of the Alternative Nobel Prize: local materials are used, in this case brick rather than clay, the smaller houses are designed in such a way that enables them to be expanded later, and generous use is made of barrel ceilings to ensure natural cooling. In terms of appearance, the houses resemble those in Fathy's watercolor drawings, bringing to bear the insights of countless decades of traditional domed

houses in the region. The footprints of the houses have, moreover, been optimized to provide all the requisite rooms and facilities without any loss of space.

The estate also seeks to be sustainable in a social sense, encouraging a social mix in its population, and avoiding the pitfall of its high-end counterparts, namely, the afflictions associated with gated communities. Albert Speer took up this point when he commented that the estate is "a successful example of low-cost planning. However, it would be great if such estates were not built on such an immense scale in such a place, but as city quarters, spread across the entire space specified for the city." In other words, the ideal would be for many far smaller Haram Cities scattered around 6th of October City, mingling with higher-end areas in such a way that the combination would itself improve the quality of life.

7 MOBILITY, NOT IMMOBILITY

Cairo is an outstanding example of the fact that the thirst for personal mobility in the guise of automobiles can, if not planned and controlled, swiftly become a reality characterized by continual immobility. After an hour spent walking round the modern commercial center, a form of ballet between sidewalks too narrow to accommodate the pedestrians and the street vendors, and streets too narrow to house the two or even three ranks of cars parked in them (a fact that at times turns four-lane roads into one-way, single-lane streets), Albert Speer comments on the traffic congestion: "The problem of traffic is at the heart of all Cairo's difficulties. There is no organization of personal transportation discernible here, no traffic management in any meaningful sense." As in many other metropolises in the developing world, countless hours of each working week are spent not working, but waiting – in traffic jams. Property developers tells us quite cheerfully that if anyone foolhardy enough to live in the west of the city, in one of the pleasant suburbs lined with villas, but with a job on the eastern side of town, would need so long getting to work in the morning that it would make more sense simply to move house to the Red Sea coast and drive the 100-odd kilometers on the highway to work each morning. It is a sad commentary on an absurd state of affairs. There is, after all, a vicious circle underlying this side to life in Cairo. If you lose your job, you may – if you are fortunate to find a new job – also have to give up your home if it is no longer close enough to your new workplace. Or you may have to turn down jobs that are, for example, located more than an hour's drive from the kind of residential properties that would offer you the quality of life you expect (namely, the right home, access to schools and hospitals, cultural facilities, etc.).

Small wonder that the city dissolves into micro-centers such as the Islamic Old Town, and that some people never leave them. They would, given the traffic, have a tough time leaving easily. The old districts are typified by traditional mixed usage – and perhaps this is the example to follow: to insist on new mixed usages.

Yet the obvious solution would be to revolutionize Cairo's transportation. Joachim Schares of AS&P suggests that "while a subway system, and as we have seen there is one on a small scale, is one possible option, I am not sure that in a city like this everything can be placed underground. And I am not even thinking of the possible subsidence. After all, efficient tram lines would cost only a tenth of the price." Albert Speer interjects that the main lever to start changing things must be the one that creates the requisite parking spaces, away from the streets. Then at least two or four lanes would free up and some sort of traffic flow would ensue. But how to bring about such a major change?

8 ENCOURAGE CIVIC PARTICIPATION

Some time soon, the Olympic Games are bound to come to Africa, the continent the IOC has for so long passed over. And why should it not come to Cairo, the second largest city in Africa and one with a strong sporting tradition, be it in football, or in disciplines one would not necessarily associate with Egypt, such as rowing and fencing. Yet given the travails the country faces, why should it seek to attract the Olympics? Would it not be far better off doing its homework and improving the population's quality of life? However, we have just witnessed how the Beijing Olympics helped to change not only the international perception of China but also conditions in that country, with the city's inhabitants insisting after the Games that the measures introduced to lower air-pollution levels, for example, during the Olympic marathon should be retained as they very much liked the result. Could not a similar effect be triggered in Cairo, albeit with far stronger civic participation, not just as volunteers (as was the case in Beijing), but as persons included in the policy-making that decides the changes to the face and fabric of the megapolis.

Friedbert Greif, a partner at AS&P with in-depth experience of preparing Olympic bids and the reasoning behind them, reports: "If a candidate city is nominated to host the Olympic Games, then the Olympic rings start to do their bit for the city. Any number of things that would otherwise not be possible then start to move into the realm of the possible, and from there onto the planners' drawing boards." He continues: "The perception of a city changes completely. And red tape dissolves in thin air. The Beijing example was truly a case in point. There, normal people found pride and joy in volunteering for their city and in being part of the wave of changes that swept through it. The Olympic Games, and not just the National Stadium in Beijing, functioned as a form of icon for identification, for changes in mindset. When we helped Baku's bid by conducting a feasibility study for the city fathers, what we were essentially doing was paving the way for urban change. While Baku did not emerge as a candidate, the city has benefited from the insights gained in the study and has been able to start urban redevelopment in a manner that was previously hidden from sight."

For Cairo, the potential for change would begin with the application phase itself, when the city would start to consider in detail what and how it needed to change. So in a sense, the decision to apply, to prove that it is a worthy candidate for the short list, would in itself be a decision in favor of massive change. If it then overcame all the hurdles it would have seven years in which to galvanize the initial cohesion and thrust into infrastructure change. The inhabitants of the city, and with them civil society, ever aware, as the past has shown, of the potential embarrassment of failure, would then act as the constant corrective ensuring things move forwards. Sustainability overall, the application of the appropriate technologies, the right choices in terms of land zoning and usage, the right solutions to energy and waste issues would all come to the fore. In its World Governance Indicators, the World Bank has something similar in mind when it lists as one of the six indicators "government effectiveness." It defines this as the quality of public services, the quality of the civil service and the degree of its independence from political pressures, the quality of policy formulation and implementation, and the credibility of the government's commitment to such policies. What better acid test for the effectiveness of Greater Cairo's government than for it to adopt these categories as key performance indicators that the people judge it on.

In the long run, you cannot change a city without the backing of the people – and CAIRO 2020 offers a perfect fit in this regard, as it would be an emblem of metropolitan pride with which everyone would be able to identify. In this sense, the Olympic Summer Games could become the spark that ignites the real changes outlined above as necessary. Only in this way can the population be persuaded to accept changes that will possibly eat into their pockets and also cause (initial) inconvenience. CAIRO 2020 would significantly push infrastructure development in the city, could drive extensive transportation reforms and fuel an anti-congestion revolution, and could give the city mayor the political leverage to solve pollution problems – with the full support of all tiers of government, enabling fast-track, straight-line policymaking. The added benefit would be that it would gift a sports-mad city with new, extensive, and first-rate sports and residential facilities into the bargain, while forging a new sense of identity and, to quote Professor Ashour, combining a new quality of life with a sense of history.

9   GET THE FUNDAMENTALS RIGHT

6th of October City is not only an example of the need to keep spaces open, rather than abandoning them to motor vehicles, but also a case study in what happens when you get the fundamentals wrong and, by extension, in what has gone wrong in Cairo as whole as a result of organic rather than controlled growth. The new city, as we have seen, has a population of 500,000 but that figure is destined on the virtual drawing boards to reach 3.5 to 4 million over the next 20 years. A large area, namely, 2.5 million square meters, has been purchased by developers for transformation into a gated community providing luxury homes as well as a golf course for about 8,000 people. The ecological aspects, such as water consumption, and the questionable sustainability of such gated communities bereft of meaningful infrastructure are two sides to a problem that illustrate how crucial it is to get fundamentals such as land use patterns right from the very start. According to Albert Speer: "It is a lot easier for civil servants simply to assign large sections of ground than it is to reassign them further down the line. In fact, in many cases, changing things after the event is well nigh impossible as built facts have a weight of their own."

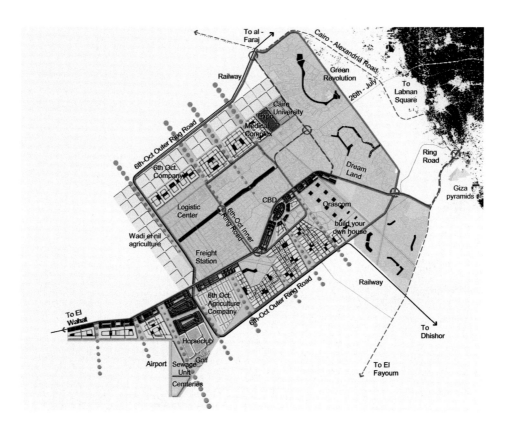

The map contains the following labels:

To al - Faraj · Cairo - Alexandria Road · Railway · Green Revolution · 26th - July · To Labnan Square · Cairo University · Expo · Medical Complex · 6th Oct Outer Ring Road · 6th Oct Company · Dream Land · Ring Road · Giza pyramids · CBD · 6th Oct Inner Ring Road · Logistic Center · Orascom · build your own house · Wadi el nil agriculture · Freight Station · 6th Oct Agriculture Company · 6th Oct Outer Ring Road · Railway · To El Wahat · Horseclub · To Dhishor · Airport · Golf · Sewage Unit · Cemeteries · To El Fayoum

If only to establish the new spine and the segment-ing with green spaces, the planners are having to persuade the men from the ministries that the local cemetery (unfortunately located close to downtown) must be relocated (a costly exercise), as must gas and fuel pipelines, power lines, and the railway. At the same time, a coherent ring road must be introduced to alleviate cross-town congestion, and areas of the city allocated dedicated bus lines that are integrated into an overall system. Water sourcing also has to be got right, as green spaces need to be kept green and houses provided with an adequate supply. At the same time, if the city is to be filled with life, then its inhabitants must be convinced that it is worth their while staying there – in other words, local jobs in newly designated industrial zones must be filled by locals. This will create greater vibrancy during the day, ensure that more people identify with the city, and slash commuter traffic while increasing the potential for people to walk or cycle to work. The greater vibrancy will trickle through into the informal economy and retailing, whose productivity levels would then rise, bringing better and more shops into 6th of October City, which could be restored to its proper state and provide a living

↑
The AS&P plan to revitalize 6th of October City: green belts, a new central backbone, and clear zoning. It will mean relocating power lines and pipelines.

→
6th of October City in late 2007.

testimony to the efficacy and efficiency of polycentric concentration. To this end, land use and zoning need to be redefined in order to establish the coherent mix between residential housing and built work space, and thus between business and residential urban life, and the consumption/waste cycle needs to be considered. While some of these elements may seem overly minor, Johannes Dell of AS&P China suggests that "the philosophy has to be right, be it in Shanghai or in Cairo. You must get the smallest detail all the way through to the largest master plan right – the interaction between parts must make them more than the whole. Even the houses need to be designed correctly. Otherwise only lip service will be paid to energy efficiency."

10 PRIORITIZE THE THREE E'S: ECOLOGY, ECONOMY AND EQUALITY

During our visit, Albert Speer and Joachim Schares propose that Haram City is a successful example of more than just holistic architecture and urban planning: the way the housing and the space it encloses have been designed, the referencing of local building traditions is, as stated, reminiscent of the approach championed 30 years earlier by Hassan Fathy. In retrospect it is fair to say that his methodology was consistent with our three E's, namely, a concept of architecture that integrated economic, ecological, and social aspects – yet Fathy was only ever able to try to put this into practice on a village scale, but never on the scale of a city.

In Cairo, ecology manifestly needs to be a "best practice": if you can't breath the air, there is something wrong with the city planning. If you waste a third of every day in traffic jams, then here, too, something is wrong, and your city is not economically viable in the long term as it will quite simply not be able to compete with cities whose human resources are used efficiently. Cairo will thus move forward only if these twin problems are solved. Without traffic jams, human resources would be freed up to drive the economy. Without excessive reliance on cars, the air would be cleaner, saving costs and saving energy, again driving growth. But how to do it without a trigger, such as the Olympics?

Equality, on the other hand, would mean a well-functioning public transport system affordable for all, greater equality in land use and thus less reliance on informal settlement, and, in the long term, an end to the need for gated communities such as those sprouting up around 6th of October City, communities that are cut off from "life" and where the children have to be bused to school and the parents rely on a car to commute to work or to get to the shops.

Here, Haram City provides a tale of how equality can be applied, as its developers have shown that even a settlement for 400,000 members of the lower middle class is possible in a manner that offers decent accommodation – and can be opened "downwards." In early September 2008 a terrible rock slide precipitated by human-induced erosion at the foot of the Muqattam mountains, that front-line to the desert, killed hundreds in a slum below. The Sawiris, the Coptic family that owns the majority stake in the development company, decided spontaneously to offer the victims new homes – in Haram City. Yet many of the survivors were frightened by the idea of formal residence and left the Manshiet Nasser slum only reluctantly, clinging to their arbitrary Egyptian favela or gecekondu, the ashvaiyata. After all, their lives hitherto had truly been arbitrary in structure, be it their homes or their incomes. For them, the very notion of "low-cost" was still far above what they could afford. This brought the next difficulty with it: accustomed as they were to selling their wares in the street, they set up shop outside the homes allotted them in Haram City, trading in whatever they felt might find a buyer. This ran counter to Orascom's underlying plans for a clear shopping zone in Haram City, deliberately positioned so as to be equally accessible and to function as a focal point. A bitter dispute followed, one that was solved by common sense. A second, far smaller shopping zone was built in between the new homes. Simple, square, whitewashed shops with an open area between, a Greek market as the locals call it, the fundamental unit of a souk, we might suggest. In this new market hall, Haram's latest inhabitants can now earn a dignified living by selling food and goods to the 5,000-odd construction workers. In doing so, they unintentionally contribute to the holistic notion of sustainability and are returning Orascom's favor – provisioning this small army of men had previously been an unsolved problem. And after the workers leave, there will soon be a large captive market in the form of the 400,000 inhabitants.

THINK LOCAL, ACT GLOBAL

The old Islamic town souk of Khan el-Khalili is a place where the density is right, if not perhaps too great. It is an admirable mixture of commerce at the ground-floor level and residential utilization upstairs – even if the building is only 3 to 4 storeys high, and therefore not high enough. Issues still to be tackled in this bustling thrive of activity are water supplies, a proper sewage system, and refuse disposal. This is hardly surprising given that the structure of the old Islamic town is essentially medieval; and none of the three elements was high on the list of planning criteria back then. However, this is the point where the thinking should not be global, but local. Speaking of the Khan el-Khalili, Albert Speer fondly suggests that "While this is a delightful place, it is not one that is sustainable as it hinges on a monoculture, namely, tourism, and we do not know how that mainstay of commercial activity will develop. I firmly believe this is a case where local academics and their students should devote themselves to finding ways of modernizing the area. In that way, it can potentially continue to serve a (tourist) purpose for many years to come, but offer the quality of life that my friend Professor Ashour so rightly says is missing. We have seen in other cities around the globe how such cramped, ill-lit quarters will at some point give way to a new form of life or be condemned to the dead status of museums, and that would be a real shame here."

In summary, it is fair to say that the currently dysfunctional megacity of Cairo will only ever become sustainable if it becomes functional. Until now, there have been only small attempts to rectify its problems in this respect. As we have seen, the commandments for a sustainable city of tomorrow can all be applied, if to differing degrees – again reflecting the fact that thinking must be local even when the action has global implications and is the product of insights gained elsewhere. In Cairo, the key to sustainability lies in property rights and mobility. And these two crunch factors will come to bear unless there is a sufficiently strong driver to change existing conditions. We suggest that a serious, well-prepared bid for the Olympics could, in the absence of political will or feasibility for such a return to getting the fundamentals right, act as such a driver. Otherwise the Greater Cairo of tomorrow, irrespective of a new, 400-kilometer ring road, will be characterized by piecemeal engineering that constantly seeks only to alleviate the symptoms without ever tackling the causes.

ALBERT SPEER & PARTNER   Albert Speer & Partner combines innovative methods in architecture, urban design and transportation planning to provide clients with holistic solutions. In the process, it can draw on many decades of experience in designing and managing international planning and construction projects. The company's portfolio includes multi-storey dwellings and high-rises, urban planning, urban design and regional development, planning for tourism and leisure-time facilities, conceptual transportation planning and project management through to the planning for major international events and expert consultancy for politicians.

The office is headed by Albert Speer, Friedbert Greif, Gerhard Brand and six other senior partners who wholly own the company. AS&P prioritizes lean structures, with a core payroll of some 120, and alongside the head office in Frankfurt/Main, Germany, and the large representative office in Shanghai otherwise opts for temporary project offices, staffed by highly qualified, highly motivated and highly specialized experts. Each project is handled by teams assembled specifically for the purpose. Given the growing complexity and diversity of the tasks AS&P tackle, it also draws on a broad and proven network of outside specialists from a variety of fields as additional consultants.

From their head office in Germany, AS&P brings creativity and knowledge to bear in many countries world-wide. And, conversely, the team consciously seeks to utilize the raft of cultural, technological and human insights gained globally and apply them locally in each and every assignment. As a matter of corporate policy, all the office's projects combine high-quality planning and common sense, and rest on a backbone of a comprehensive notion of 3E sustainability, delivering ecological, economic and equitable solutions that aspire to improve the quality of life in general.

PICTURE CREDITS

Book cover and 178, 179 *Urban design for Central Area, Abuja, Nigeria* AS&P–Albert Speer & Partner GmbH/Peter Tjie empty-form, Darmstadt, Germany

6, 7 *Lagos, Nigeria* Photo: Dieter Blum

14, 15 *Longleat's Hedge Maze, Wiltshire, England* Corbis/Photo: Richard Baker

21 (left) *Side, tourist center in southern Turkey* Speerplan

21 (right) *Ruins of Roman Amphitheater, Side, Turkey* Bilderberg/Photo: Milan Horacek

26 *International Automobile City, Shanghai, PR China* AS&P–Albert Speer & Partner GmbH/Uwe Dettmar, Frankfurt, Germany

32, 33 *Europa quarter, Frankfurt/Main, Germany* aurelis Real Estate GmbH & Co. KG, Eschborn

40 *Pfingstweide district, Ludwigshafen, Germany* Speerplan

43 (above) *Central railway zone (Central Station-Laim-Pasing), Munich, Germany* aurelis Real Estate GmbH & Co. KG, München/Mediaprojekt GmbH, Verl, Germany

43 (below) *Central railway zone (Central Station-Laim-Pasing), Munich, Germany* AS&P–Albert Speer & Partner GmbH

44 *Europa quarter, Frankfurt/Main, Germany* AS&P–Albert Speer & Partner GmbH

45 *Europa quarter, Frankfurt/Main, Germany* AS&P–Albert Speer & Partner GmbH/Photo: Uwe Dettmar, Frankfurt, Germany

46, 47 *Europa quarter, 'In den Stadtgärten', Frankfurt/Main, Germany* AS&P/aurelis Real Estate GmbH & Co. KG/Peter Tjie emptyform, Darmstadt, Germany

48 *Holbein quarter, Frankfurt/Main, Germany* AS&P–Albert Speer & Partner GmbH/Peter Tjie emptyform, Darmstadt, Germany

51 *Corniche & boulevard road, Baku, Azerbaijan* Photo: AS&P–Albert Speer & Partner GmbH

52 *Corniche & boulevard road, Baku, Azerbaijan* AS&P–Albert Speer & Partner GmbH

53 *Corniche & boulevard road, Baku, Azerbaijan* Photo: AS&P–Albert Speer & Partner GmbH

54 *Corniche & boulevard road, Baku, Azerbaijan* AS&P–Albert Speer & Partner GmbH

55 *Corniche & boulevard road, Baku, Azerbaijan* AS&P–Albert Speer & Partner GmbH/Gärtner Christ, Hamburg

58, 59 *TÜV Rheinland, test laboratory, Cologne, Germany* Bilderberg/Photo: Thomas Ernsting

64 *Concept for low-energy buildings* AS&P–Albert Speer & Partner GmbH

68 *Campo at Bornheimer Depot, Frankfurt/Main, Germany* AS&P–Albert Speer & Partner GmbH/UPG Urbane Projekte GmbH

69 *Campo at Bornheimer Depot, Frankfurt/Main, Germany* AS&P–Albert Speer & Partner GmbH/UPG Urbane Projekte GmbH

72 *VICTORIA Skyrise, Mannheim, Germany* AS&P–Albert Speer & Partner GmbH/Prof. Dieter Leistner, Mainz

76, 77 *High rise public housing estate, Hong Kong, China* Bilderberg/Photo: Marcus Koppen

79 *Urban design for the Central Area, Abuja, Nigeria* AS&P–Albert Speer & Partner GmbH/Peter Tjie emptyform, Darmstadt, Germany

80 *Urban design for the Central Area, Abuja, Nigeria* AS&P–Albert Speer & Partner GmbH

81 *Shanghai City, model, Urban Planning Museum Shanghai, PR China* Photo: AS&P–Albert Speer & Partner GmbH

82 *Appartment buildings and informal clothes market, New Delhi, India* Laif/Photo: Bialobrzeski

83 (above) *Ministry of Foreign Affairs, Riyadh, Saudi Arabia* AS&P–Albert Speer & Partner GmbH/Photo: Richard Bödeker, Mettmann, Germany

83 (below) *Ministry of Foreign Affairs, Riyadh, Saudi Arabia* AS&P–Albert Speer & Partner GmbH

87 *"Frankfurt for All" – Presentation of the vision for Frankfurt/Main, Germany, as an international city* AS&P–Albert Speer & Partner GmbH

89 *Master plan for the city centre-storyboard for midtown Cologne* AS&P–Albert Speer & Partner GmbH

92 *Oval mixed-use building at Baseler Platz, Frankfurt/Main, Germany* AS&P–Albert Speer & Partner GmbH/Photo: Uwe Dettmar, Frankfurt, Germany

96, 97 *Cologne Cathedral, Cologne, Germany* F1-online/Photo: Alberto Paredes/AGE

101 *Beijing National Stadium - PR China* Photo: AS&P–Albert Speer & Partner GmbH

105 (left) *Crystal Palace, Water Tower, c. 1861, London, England* Masterfile/Photo: Francis Frith

105 (right) *Eiffel tower, Paris, France* Fotolia/Photo: Felix Horstmann

106 *Master Plan EXPO 2000, Hannover, Germany* AS&P–Albert Speer & Partner GmbH/Photo: Lindner-Luftbild, Hannover, Germany

112, 113 *Mariposa Grove, Yosemite National Park, California, USA* F1-online/Photo: José Fuste/AGE

115 *Master Plan for Road Network and Transportation in Akwa Ibom State, Nigeria* AS&P–Albert Speer & Partner GmbH "Main features per local government area (LGA); agricultural products per LGA; entire transportation infrastructure in the year 2030; agricultural land resource potentials; key industrial and transportation facilities"

122, 123 *Changchun JingYue, Ecological City, Changchun, PR China* AS&P–Albert Speer & Partner GmbH

127 *Akwa Ibom State, Nigeria* Photo: AS&P–Albert Speer & Partner GmbH

130, 131 *Traffic on Street, Shanghai, China* Masterfile/Photo: Wei Yan

135 (left) *"Frankfurt for All" – Presentation of the vision for Frankfurt/Main, Germany, as an international city* Photo: AS&P–Albert Speer & Partner GmbH

135 (right) *Parking guidance system – Frankfurt/Main, Germany* Photo: AS&P–Albert Speer & Partner GmbH

138 *Masterplan for an Integrated Transportation Infrastructure – Nigeria* AS&P–Albert Speer & Partner GmbH

141 (above and below) *People waiting for the bus, April 2007, Parana Curitiba Passeio Publico Park, Brazil* Laif/Photo: Lalo De Almeida/Contrasto

143 *Bangkok 21 Urban & Transport Study – Bangkok Mass Transit System (BTS)* Photo: AS&P–Albert Speer & Partner GmbH

146, 147 *By raising their hands participants of the provincial assembly in Appenzell, Switzerland, vote on the provincial assembly square* Bilderberg/Photo: Keystone-CH

152 *Master plan for the city center-storyboard for midtown Cologne – intervention areas, Germany* AS&P–Albert Speer & Partner GmbH Inner green belt; riverside urban zone; rings; core zone & east bank of the Rhine; North/South approach; East/West approach

155 *Master plan for the city centre-storyboard for midtown Cologne – civic participation, Germany* Photo: Freischlad+Holz, Planung und Architektur, Darmstadt, Germany

157 *"Frankfurt for All" – Presentation of the vision for Frankfurt/Main, Germany, as an international city* Tourismus+Congress GmbH Frankfurt am Main, Photographer: Goesta A. C. Ruehl

162, 163 *Residents of Ballito look at remains of a beach front restaurant after the worst storm in 80 years lashed the coast of Kwa Zulu Natal, Tuesday 20 March 2007, Kwa Zulu Natal, South Africa* picture-alliance/dpa

169 *How Istanbul has grown over time* Map: Peter Palm/Berlin

172 *Nicheng Branch of Lingang New Town – Shanghai, PR China* AS&P–Albert Speer & Partner GmbH

174 *Wuse Market – Abuja, Nigeria* Photo: Julius Berger Nigeria PLC

175 *Urban design of the Central Area, Abuja, Nigeria* AS&P–Albert Speer & Partner GmbH

176 *Metropolitan public transport concept for Abuja, Nigeria* AS&P–Albert Speer & Partner GmbH

182, 183 *Floating houses on the river Maas rise and fall with the water, Netherlands* Laif/Photo: Swart/Hollandse Hootge

185 *"Frankfurt for All" – Presentation of the vision for Frankfurt/Main, Germany, as an international city* AS&P–Albert Speer & Partner GmbH/Photo: Jens Braune, Frankfurt, Germany

191 *"Frankfurt for All" – Presentation of the vision for Frankfurt/Main, Germany, as an international city* Photo: AS&P–Albert Speer & Partner GmbH

196, 197 *Giza Necropolis* picture-alliance/ akg-images/Photo: Gilles Mermet

201 *General Strategic Plan 6th October Sheikh Zayed Cities – Cairo, Egypt* Photo: Stefan Jaeger

206 *General Strategic Plan 6th October Sheikh Zayed Cities – Cairo, Egypt* Photo: Stefan Jaeger

210 *General Strategic Plan 6th October Sheikh Zayed Cities – Cairo, Egypt – illustrative master plan* AS&P–Albert Speer & Partner GmbH/ARCHPLAN Architects & Planners, Cairo Egypt

211 *General Strategic Plan 6th October Sheikh Zayed Cities – Cairo, Egypt* Photo: AS&P–Albert Speer & Partner GmbH

215 *Photo of partners and managing partners of AS&P–Albert Speer und Partner GmbH* AS&P–Albert Speer & Partner GmbH/Photo: Jens Braune, Frankfurt, Germany

Charts: 23, 37, 38, 62, 64, 118, 120, 165 Fine German

BIBLIOGRAPHY

Beck, Ulrich: *Cosmopolitan Vision*, tr. C. Cronin, (Polity, Camb., 2006)

Benevolo, Leonardo: *History of The City*, (MIT, Cambridge, Mass. 1980)

Bertelsmann Foundation (ed.): *Wegweiser Demographischer Wandel 2020. Analysen und Handlungskonzepte für Städte und Gemeinden*, (Verlag Bertelsmann Stiftung, Gütersloh, 2006)

Bodenschatz, Harald & Laible, Ulrike (eds.): *Großstädte von morgen – Internationale Strategien des Stadtumbaus*, (Verlagshaus Braun, Berlin, 2008)

Burdett, Ricky & Sudjic, Deyan: *The Urban Age Project. The Endless City*, (Phaidon, London, 2008)

Capra, Fritjof: *The Turning Point*, (Harper-Collins, London, 1982)

Diamond, Jared: *Collapse. How Societies Choose to Fail or Survive*, (Penguin, Harmondsworth, 2006)

Florida, Richard: *Who's Your City?*, (Basic Books, Boston, 2008)

Girard, Luigi Fusco et al, eds.: *The Human Sustainable City. Challenges and Perspectives from the Habitat Agenda*, (Ashgate, Aldershot, 2003)

Girardet, Herbert: *Cities People Planet. Urban Development and Climate Change*, 2nd. ed., (John Wiley, Chicester, 2008)

Hall, Peter & Pfeiffer, Ulrich: *Urban Future 21.* (Taylor & Francis, 2000)

Held, David: *Global Convenant. The Social Democratic Alternative to the Washington Consensus*, (Polity, Camb., 2004)

Jacobs, Jane: *The Death and Life of Great American Cities*, (Modern Library, New York, 1993)

Koolhaas, Rem et al.: *Mutations*, (Actar, Bordeaux, 2000)

Kostof, Spiro: *The City Assembled*, (Thames & Hudson, London, 1992)

Landry, Charles: *The Creative City – A toolkit for Urban Innovators*, (Earthscan, London, 2000)

Lindner, Rolf: *Die Entdeckung der Stadtkultur*, (Campus, Frankfurt/M., 2007)

Lovelock, James: *Gaia. A New Look at Life on Earth*, (Oxford Univ. Press, Oxford, 1979)

Mau, Bruce, Leonard, Jennifer & Institute without Boundaries: *Massive Change*, (Phaidon, London, 2004)

McKinsey & Company: *Preparing for China´s Urban Billion.* (McKinsey Global Institute, 2008)

Pearce, Neil & Johnson, Curtis: *Century of the City*, (The Rockefeller Foundation, New York, 2008)

Rogers, Richard: *Cities for a small planet.* (Faber & Faber Ltd., London, 1997)

Sachs, Jeffrey: *Common Wealth. Economics for a Crowded Planet*, (Allen Lane, London, 2008)

Sassen, Saskia: *The Global City. New York. London. Tokyo*, (Princeton Univ. Press, Princeton, 2001)

Schumacher, E. F.: *Small is Beautiful*, (Vintage, London, 1993) first published 1970

Sloterdijk, Peter: *Der Weltinnenraum des Kapitalismus*, (Suhrkamp, Frankfurt, 2005)

Toffler, Alvin: *Future Shock*, (Bantam, New York, 1970)

Van Susteren, Arjen: *Metropolitan World Atlas.* (010 Publishers, Rotterdam, 2005)

Von Weizsäcker, Ernst, Lovins, Amory & Lovins, L. Hunter: *Factor Four: Doubling Wealth, Halving Resource Use – The New Report to the Club of Rome* (Earthscan, London, 1998)

Cover image: Rendering, Abuja, Nigeria, see Chap. 9, pp. 178-179

© Prestel Verlag, Munich · Berlin · London · New York, 2009

Prestel Verlag
Königinstrasse 9
80539 Munich
Tel. +49 (0)89 24 29 08-300
Fax +49 (0)89 24 29 08-335

Prestel Publishing Ltd.
4 Bloomsbury Place
London WC1A 2QA
Tel. +44 (0)20 7323-5004
Fax +44 (0)20 7636-8004

Prestel Publishing
900 Broadway, Suite 603
New York, N.Y. 10003
Tel. +1 (212) 995-2720
Fax +1 (212) 995-2733

www.prestel.com

Prestel books are available worldwide. Please contact your nearest
bookseller or one of the above addresses for information concerning
your local distributor.

Library of Congress Control Number: 2009927198

British Library Cataloguing-in-Publication Data: a catalogue record
for this book is available from the British Library.
The Deutsche Bibliothek holds a record of this publication in the
Deutsche Nationalbibliografie; detailed bibliographical data can be
found under: http://dnb.ddb.de

Editorial direction by Curt Holtz
Copy-editing by Danko Szabo, Munich
Design and layout by FINE GERMAN,
  (Carsten Wolff, Nicole Lange, Thomas Rott), Frankfurt/Main
Production by Cilly Klotz, Nele Krüger
Origination by Reproline Mediateam, Munich
Printed and bound by Firmengruppe APPL, aprinta druck, Wemding

FSC

Mix

Produktgruppe aus vorbildlich
bewirtschafteten Wäldern und
anderen kontrollierten Herkünften
Product group from well-managed
forests and other controlled sources
Zert.-Nr. SGS-COC-004238
www.fsc.org
© 1996 Forest Stewardship Council

Printed in Germany on acid-free paper

ISBN 978-3-7913-4207